Don't Worry About A Thing

Growing Up in Maine

Katherine Yotides Sullivan

Green Reed Press

Published by Green Reed Press

The incidents in this book appear essentially as I remember them; however the names and certain identifying features of some people portrayed were changed to protect their privacy.

ISBN: 979-8-9871801-0-5

Editor: Francie King, TheMemoirNetwork.com
Cover & interior design: Sally Lunt, TheMemoirNetwork.com

Dedication

To Sophia and Tara

Table of Contents

Adulthood

Don't Worry About A Thing

Prologue

I have written in journals most of my life, so it was natural that I would one day put them together to create my life story. All my memories, at the basic level, are emotions tied to time and place. I've discovered that some memories are always at the surface, while others were hidden or buried deep within. Like a steam shovel digging deep into the ground, I've unearthed those buried memories. I remember old black and white movies where the passage of time was often depicted by the windblown pages of a calendar, with stops at various dates in the far past. Writing this book was like that. I could choose the date and time and travel back to one event or another—a teacher who embarrassed me, or an aunt who did something special for me when I felt sad or alone. I would land in that time and place because in some way, I had never left, and once back there, all of the life surrounding that event would reveal itself in sharp focus. I discovered that the more I delved into my past, the more I remembered, as if having unlocked one door, all the other doors opened too. It has been both a labor of love and a labor of pain to discover who I was, and in the process, I was better able to understand who I have become. Writing will do that. All the journals and the memories they elicited have led to this: my story.

Even though I shared many of the same experiences as my other family members, how we remember those experiences is often different. Just as no two people experience life in the same way, no two stories will be exactly the same. In writing my story, I have tried to depict my life honestly and truthfully, without causing harm to others or myself; this means I've tried to leave out events that, though they related to my life, would be telling another's story. I fear in some cases I may have failed at this; if I have offended anyone, I apologize, for that was never my intent.

Several names have been changed in these pages to protect the identities of people who have come and gone throughout my life.

Beginnings

"The Place where you are right now, God
circled on a map for you."
Hafiz

In the spring of 1911 in Libohovë, at the foot of Bureto Mountain in Epirus, Northern Greece, my father George was born, the eldest son of James and Olga Yotides. Like all the children in the village, George entered the world in his family's home, a slate-roofed, gray stone cottage hewn from the nearby mountains. Situated on the northwestern border of Greece, the area had a long history of border disputes. Libohovë, similar to other villages in the area, had fallen under the rule of different countries over the centuries, including ancient Rome and the Ottoman Turks, and when George was born in 1911, it was no different. While Greece claimed the territory, it was a contested zone.

In 1914, when George was three, Epiros was declared autonomous; however, with the advent of World War I, there was fighting in the border zone and autonomy was never formally established. It

11

would not be long before the village fell under the rule of the new communist country of Albania.

Despite the country's instability, James Yotides worked hard to provide for his family. Hoping for a bright future for his son, he sent George to the American Farm School, a boarding school 350 miles into the interior of Greece at Salonica, modern day Thessaloniki, where he would learn a trade. While George was learning English at boarding school, James, with his brother John, traveled to America to work in the textile mills in New England. James became a fixer of looms in the woolen mills, working in both Massachusetts and Maine. The two men worked for six months at a time, saving all their earnings before returning to Greece where they bought land, planted tobacco, and expanded their estate.

After making the trip back and forth for a number of years, the Yotides brothers found themselves, in 1927, in a politically unstable Greece where tensions were growing. Olga, sensing the winds of change, insisted that the next time her husband left for America, he would take his entire family along. James agreed. He took George out of school and with Olga, his brother John, and George's four- year-old brother Thomas, left their land and village for the last time. They traveled to America just in time before Libohovë was closed to the world behind the iron curtain of communist Albania.

The family traveled first to Cherbourg, France, and on August 15, 1927, boarded the ship *Leviathan*, and sailed to America where they settled in the factory town of Winslow, Maine.

In America, George, a young impressionable teenager, loved city life, so different from his mountain village. Although he grew up in a family with a strong work ethic—and contrary to his father's wishes—he showed no desire to learn a trade or continue his education. Instead, he spent much of his time pitching pennies on the sidewalk, playing cards, and thinking up get-rich-quick schemes.

During World War II in the army, George trained as a cook and was sent to the Aleutian Islands in Alaska where he saw little action. To erase the boredom after work, George set up card games in the mess hall. When he returned from WWII, he continued life as a short-order cook, working in diners and restaurants. Not afraid of hard work, he worked long hours, but played just as hard, spending his earnings on all-night poker games and horse races. By the time he met his future wife, Betty, when he was thirty-six, George was already firmly entrenched in bachelorhood and the gambling life.

While George was a teenager at boarding school in Greece, on the other side of the world, my mother, Lula, was born in the north woods of Maine on June 3, 1925, in a weathered clapboard house, the fifth child of Laura and Clarence Wheeler. Unlike George, who had had educational opportunities, Lula had joined a family and community of poor subsistence farmers who struggled to put food on the table and shoes on the feet of their children. Lula and her siblings often missed school because they lacked warm enough clothing to survive the long walk to school and back in the harsh Maine winters.

While still a baby bouncing on her papa's knee, Lula was nicknamed "little Betty," and that became her name for the rest of her life. When Betty was just four, her father was hit by a car, and not long after—

despite attempts by doctors to save his life (by inserting a steel plate in his head)—he succumbed to his injuries.

Life became even more difficult for Laura, who, now left with six kids, had to take in laundry to feed them. She eventually married Roy McCready who owned a logging business where he put his stepsons to work.

When she was twelve, Betty left school in eighth grade to work in the blueberry fields. At sixteen she gave birth to a daughter, Joyce Ann. Because there were so few opportunities in the country for a young single mother, she left Joyce Ann with her own mother and moved to Belfast, Maine. There, she found work as a waitress, moved into a boarding house with other young women, and sent money home.

Belfast, in the 1940s, was a shipping town, and it wasn't long before Betty met and married a man from the South. Soon after, they left for Maryland, leaving Joyce Ann with Laura in Maine, promising that they would return for her after they settled into their new home.

It didn't take long for Betty to realize she had made a mistake, and although she was unhappy in her new life, she and her husband returned as promised to Maine to get Joyce Ann.

The marriage lasted only a few months in Maryland before Betty wrote to her mother asking for money for the train fare back to Maine. Laura and Roy, who had raised Joyce Ann from a baby, were only too happy to have her back home. They agreed to send the money on one condition: that Betty would never take her away again. Joyce Ann belonged to them. Not in any position to argue, Betty agreed.

Back in Maine, Betty once again had to leave home to work. This time she went to Waterville, again leaving Joyce Ann, who would stay with her grandmother until she was a senior in high school. Joyce Ann then moved to Waterville (in 1959) to live with her mother, stepfather, and half siblings.

Waterville, Maine, situated across the Kennebec River from Winslow where James Yotides had settled with his family, was booming with paper and woolen factories. With the end of the war, a spirit of optimism prevailed there, and the town entered a new age where, with hard work and perseverance, anything was possible. Shops, restaurants, and banks lined Main Street to accommodate the emerging middle class.

And this was where George, the short order cook, met Betty, the waitress. On January 12, 1948, they were married.

Don't Worry About A Thing

Early Years

And all the monkeys aren't in the zoo
Every day you meet quite a few
So you see it's all up to you
You can be better than you are
You could be swingin' on a star

Songwriters: Johnny Burke /
Jimmy Van Heusen

Don't Worry About A Thing

Chapter One
Silver Linings on Silver Street

The heavy snow-bloated sky darkened the day even though it was only four in the afternoon. "Slow down, George, I don't want to have this baby in a snow drift!" Betty begged, gripping the door handle as they inched their way along the highway through the February blizzard to Sister's Hospital. The headlights glaring into the snow made visibility tricky on that wintery day in 1950. "It figures this kid would decide to come during a blizzard," she groaned, as another contraction gripped her.

George slipped a pack of Camels out of his shirt pocket, rapping it against the steering wheel and knocking one out of the pack. "Here, give me a light," he said, his hands trembling with the anticipation of the birth as he tried to keep the car from sliding into a ditch. "Not far now. You ok?"

"I'm fine. I've done this before. I can do it again."

"Everything will be fine this time; don't you worry about a thing." His dark brows were knitted in concern, as he tried to reassure himself as well as his wife.

"Dr. Guite said everything was fine. Now keep

19

your eyes on the road before I have this baby in your father's cab."

Eight hours later, at 11:58 p.m., on February 26, 1950, I appeared, Mumma's second daughter. As soon as they checked me for all the right parts, they wheeled Mumma into her room on the maternity ward, where she changed into her new bed jacket covered with blue roses and lace-trimmed neck and sleeves. Propped up on pillows, still groggy from the gas, she celebrated with a cigarette and coffee. The nurse brought me to Mumma with a bottle of formula made of Karo syrup and Carnation milk. The next day, aunts and uncles appeared to check me out, staying until visiting hours ended, when they left with Daddy who celebrated by getting drunk.

Mumma could relax now, relieved at my good health. Just a little over a year earlier, she had lost her baby boy, my older brother Christopher, at four months. There were no pictures to show that he had come into the world and had just as quickly left it. Although I was tiny, my wailing reassured her I was fine.

After a week's hospital stay, Mumma placed me in a small crib next to her maple bed in our two-room apartment. The bedroom was just big enough for the crib, a maple double bed, a dresser, and a pedestal ashtray on Daddy's side. On the dresser were piles of baby clothes—gifts from aunts, uncles, and grandparents.

My first home, at ten and a half Silver Street, was hidden upstairs above my grandfather's tiny eatery, Olga's Little Diner (after my grandmother), a taxi stand, and a poolroom. After leaving the mill, my grandfather's dream of establishing a business he could leave to his children had become a reality. The family all worked downstairs, cooking in the diner, driving the cabs, and late at night, managing the poolroom, along with a man named Foxie, one of the few employees who wasn't family. Dark stairs alongside the taxi stand led to three small apartments. Two elderly French-Canadian sisters, the two Miss Bs, occupied the two in the front, facing Silver Street; they lived in one and the other they converted into a beauty salon that saw a steady stream of clients throughout the day.

We had the apartment in the back. Looking out of our windows, we could see the fire escapes and roofs of the other buildings around us. Although our place was small, only a bedroom and a kitchen, Mumma was proud of her home that had been freshly painted and papered before we moved in.

My grandparents lived in a large two-story duplex in the neighboring town of Winslow. They lived on one side of the building and converted the other side into two apartments, which gave the family rental income. In his spare time, my grandfather tended to his garden and planted fruit and berry trees. Like most immigrants, he was driven to succeed and make a better life for his children. If life didn't work out as he'd hoped, it wasn't for lack of trying.

A growing extended family

By the time I came along in 1950, I had a good-sized extended family. Daddy and Uncle Tommy had been born in Greece and my *yiayia* (grandmother) had given birth to three additional children in America—

two other sons and a daughter who grew up in Winslow—so I had three uncles and an aunt. Uncle Tommy and Uncle Spike both married when I was very young, giving me two more aunts by marriage and eventually cousins to play with. Uncle Tony was a person with special needs and would always live as a child. Aunt Maria, the only daughter, never married but showered her love on her nieces and nephews.

On Mumma's side there were lots of kids. Her brothers and one sister all had large broods. She came from a line of hardworking lumbermen and subsistence farmers who struggled for generations to tame the rocky Maine soil, never managing to make it out of the woods and off the hard-scrabble farms. Because jobs were scarce in the country, Mumma had to leave in order to support her first daughter, Joyce Ann. She was twenty-four when she met Daddy.

It was easy to see why she had fallen in love with Daddy. Looking like a short Clark Gable, with black, wavy hair and large dark eyes, Daddy learned as a young man that he could get by with his looks and charm. When he smiled, we melted under his gaze, and when he laughed, doubling over, his entire body shook, making everyone around him laugh too. When Mumma married him, she knew he was a gambler, but if it bothered her, she never complained, even when he lost his paycheck at the races or the card table.

Early years on Silver Street

Those first years in our small Silver Street apartment were happy, routine-filled days and I looked forward to exploring the city with Mumma.

Rolling her nylons with both hands, Mumma would cross her legs and carefully place her toe into the end of the rolled-up stocking, then unwind the stocking all the way up to her garter belt where she snapped it in place. Checking to make sure the brown seam on the back of her leg was perfectly straight, she would then cross the other leg and do the same. I would watch, impatient to go outside.

"Ah, ah, ahh! Don't touch!" Mumma would warn, as I tried to feel the silky smoothness. "They'll get a run, and I'll have to throw them away. Now get your yellow dress and slip, and the yellow anklets." Mumma loved nice clothes and enjoyed dressing us up for our daily walk. "We'll stop at Woolworth's to buy bobby pins so I can put pin curls in your hair tonight." Mumma's pin-curled brown hair was already brushed out and fell in waves around her shoulders.

"I want penny candy."

"We'll see. If you're a good girl." I knew that meant no tantrums.

This day was like many others of my first three years. Mumma always put me in cotton dresses smocked with embroidered ducks or kittens on the bodice, all the wrinkles of the skirt meticulously ironed out, slightly stiffened with starch. I liked to watch when she ironed, and I pretended to do the same with my dolls' clothes. When my dollies got dirty, I spanked them, scolding because now I'd have to wash and iron their clothes all over again. If I became untidy with a bit of food or dirt on my dress, off it would come, quickly replaced by a spotless one.

Once a day, rain or shine, spring, summer, and fall, after cleaning the house and putting on her favorite shopping dress, hat, and nylons, Mumma would place me in the carriage in my seasonal coat and matching hat for our daily walk. I was always excited to leave the apartment for the sights and sounds of the city streets. Winter was a different story. Fearful of catching a cold and the dreaded pneumonia, we only left the house when the sun was shining and the snow was cleared from the downtown streets. On those cold days, I would wear my furry muff to warm my hands.

But in summer, we would stroll up and down Main Street, stopping at Castonguay Square, the park in town center, where I loved to somersault on the grass and climb on cannons from wars past. In the distance I could see smoke billowing from the factory stacks, and if the wind was blowing from the direction of the yellow churning water of the Kennebec River, the sulfurous odor of rotten eggs from the nearby factories would catch in our throats. But we were used to it. Just one street over from where I played, beyond Front Street, the river fell over the Ticonic Falls, not far from the bridge that connected us to Yiayia and Grampie in Winslow.

After our walk, we often stopped for lunch at Woolworth's. Mumma always had coffee and a cigarette, while I made bubbles in my chocolate milk and nibbled on a grilled cheese sandwich. Mumma had come a long way from her childhood in the north woods of Maine, when she had to wear dresses made of grain bags and in winter, newspaper boots wrapped around hand-me-down shoes with holey socks she inherited from her older sister, Doris.

Waterville's Main Street bustled with a cheerful atmosphere as shoppers checked out the newest fashions. Mumma, not in any hurry, stopped on the sidewalk to talk to a friend while I stared into the shop windows. Sometimes we went into Montgomery Wards to buy new nylons or underwear or a dress for me. If she caught me rubbing against a window, she'd take my hand, pulling me away for fear I would get dirty, and someone would think she was a bad mother for not keeping her child clean.

My favorite store was Bea's Candy Kitchen, smelling of chocolate and sugar, and filled with so many sweet choices. I always asked for chocolates, but, afraid I'd stain my dress, Mumma always bought me the same cherry-flavored lollipop. Sucking on my lollipop, I was satisfied to stroll down Main Street, one hand in hers and the other holding my treat.

Back on Silver Street, I could see Aunt Maria behind the glass picture window with the sign: City Cab Service 2-9402. She was the receptionist. As soon as she spied us coming down the sidewalk, she came out to greet us with a broad grin. "How is my *koukla* today?" she would say, grabbing my cheeks with her first two fingers, pinching until they turned red. With smarting cheeks, I would wiggle away, but the truth was, I enjoyed the unabashed love and warmth directed at me. She and Daddy had that same wide smile that made me feel as if everything in my world was good. Aunt Maria had no children, and I was her only niece at the time, so she lavished her love on me, spoiling me in the process.

After checking in to talk to Daddy in the diner, we went back upstairs to our apartment. Mumma would rather have stayed in the diner, helping Daddy. I think she would have liked to work with him there or even return to waitressing herself because

25

she always laughed when she was around Daddy and her waitress friends. But here I was and she had to take care of me, so when I got restless, we went back upstairs.

A Greek Christmas

Although we didn't spend as much time outside in the winter, I looked forward to the festive atmosphere downtown during the Christmas season. I loved the store decorations and the music coming from the shops as we hurried in and out of the cold. Because I was the only grandchild for four years on Daddy's side, at Christmas, aunts and uncles bought enough toys to cover the linoleum floor under the cut spruce we had decorated with glass ornaments and silver tinsel. The scent of pine filled the small kitchen. I knew that Mumma hid the toys in the attic when I awoke and caught her moving them from the attic to the tree. She made up an elaborate tale that those toys were bought by her for other little girls and Santa would take them, leaving different ones for me. How strange that on Christmas morning, the same toys were under the tree, but I didn't challenge her, excited to be the recipient of so many presents, no matter who brought them. So, I played along every year, sitting on Santa's lap with his fake beard and black hair under his white wig.

As soon as we got ready on Christmas, dressed in our new clothes, we went to Yiayia and Grampie's for a mid-day feast. Entering their kitchen, aunts and uncles hugged and kissed us amid cries of "Merry Christmas!" in Greek, which made Mumma uncomfortable. "Why do they have to hug and kiss us?" she always commented before we left the house. Besides hugging her own mother and Joyce Ann after not seeing them for months, I never saw her hugging, let alone kissing, anyone else in her own extended family.

Then the party would get under way. The adults toasted each other with shots of Metaxa and Ouzo as we feasted on lamb, spanakopita, Greek salad, potatoes and Greek green beans. The air of celebration was enhanced by Greek music playing in the background. After dinner, presents were passed around, and I received more toys than I could ever play with. As soon as the food was put away and the dishes were washed, the table would be pushed up against the wall and chairs were moved out of the way to prepare for dancing. With Northern Greek village dance music playing loudly, Grampie held up his white handkerchief and began the line dance. Daddy was next and then came all the men in order of age. With the line forming a circle, I watched as Daddy jumped into the middle, balancing on one leg as he flipped around and squatted down, kicking one leg and then the other in front of him while everyone clapped and cheered him on. Mumma didn't know how to do the Greek dance, but no one was exempt from the dance line. We all pranced around the kitchen, through the den with its large blue flower-papered walls—where we were forced to sit quietly and watch *The Lawrence Welk Show* when we spent the night—then through the living room with violet flowers covering the walls and where, for this special day, the plastic linings were taken off the couch and chairs, and finally, back into a circle in the kitchen. The adults only rested to replenish their drinks and change the 78 RPM records on the Victrola. Pies and cakes and baklava, coffee, and more drinks for the adults ended the day.

These parties repeated every Christmas and Easter. Eventually, when Yiayia and Grampie had eight grandchildren, we had our own kids' table in the kitchen.

Mumma usually didn't drink anything but coffee, unlike Daddy who always partied more than anyone else. "George is feeling good already," she would laugh, watching him dance. His happiness was infectious. Then Daddy would take out his wallet. "Here you go, Katura," he offered, handing me twenty-dollar bills. "Merry Christmas!" he cheered, playing Santa by handing twenties all around to the cousins.

At the end of the evening, the party over, both Uncle Tommy and Uncle Spike drove us home, carried Daddy upstairs, and dumped him on the bed where his loud snoring reverberated through the apartment. The next day, nursing a hangover, Daddy would discover his empty wallet and pretend not to know what happened to his money. We had to hand over the twenties.

Mumma and I spent the rest of the winter confined to the apartment longing for spring and warmth to return. I played with my toys while she cleaned and cooked and tried to keep me from catching cold. One of my favorite toys was a slate with chalk on which Mumma taught me my ABC's. I played with all the usual girl toys, a doll bed and highchair, a ringer washing machine that really worked with water and a clothesline to hang up my doll clothes, and tea sets to wash and dry. But I wasn't enthusiastic about doing all the same chores I watched Mumma do every week.

Once a week Mumma wrote to her mother, Little

Grammie, telling her about her life in Waterville and asking about Joyce Ann, while I pretended to write letters too. I loved it when Mumma read to me from my book of nursery rhymes, and we listened to songs on my small record player, *Lucy Locket* and *How Much is that Doggie in the Window*? I sang along, baby dolls in my arms, while Mumma sat quietly and watched, cigarettes smoldering in the ashtray and instant coffee steaming from her cup.

Watching me play, Mumma would get quiet, with a sad, faraway look in her hazel eyes. I sensed her distance. Feeling invisible, I wanted to bring her back. But most of all, I wanted to erase the feeling of being alone, there, in the apartment with her. So, to get her attention, I sang louder, hoping she wouldn't get up and make me take a nap. To an outsider, it would seem that I had an idyllic childhood those first few years. And compared to what was to come, it was.

Unlike Daddy, whose brown eyes lit up when he saw me, who pinched me on my cheek like Aunt Maria, and who danced with me on his feet to Greek music, Mumma didn't outwardly show her affection. She showed me how to clean house and taught me my ABC's, but she wasn't a hugger or a kisser, and the few times she showed affection in that way seemed stilted, like she wasn't sure how to love me. I know I wasn't an easy child to raise; in fact, I was naughty quite often. I had temper tantrums, complete with stamping feet, and if those didn't work, I tried to get her attention by lying on the floor, kicking and screaming. According to Mumma's mother, I was a spoiled brat. We didn't see Little Grammie very often because she lived up north, but when we did, she was free with her opinion of me. "That little imp needs to be taught a lesson. Show her who's boss," she warned Mumma, "or she's going to be a handful." Daddy dealt with my tantrums by giving in, but Mumma, although she wasn't mean like Little Grammie, didn't fall for my nonsense either, warning me I'd better stop acting up or she'd give me something to fuss about.

Mumma did take her job of mothering seriously, showing her love by the way she cared for me, by not only making sure I was clean and fed, but by doing her best to teach me how to be safe in the house and on the street, warning me not to run with scissors, and on our walks, teaching me to look both ways before crossing the street. Cars were a danger, she cautioned, and I learned early on how to cross the street by myself. I don't remember getting lectured about strangers; a lesson that might well have prepared me for what was to come.

I was small-boned and skinny, and everyone said I didn't eat enough to keep a bird alive, so when I refused to eat supper, Mumma made me rice pudding or opened a can of Campbell's Chicken Noodle Soup. To her mind, fat babies equaled healthy babies. Maybe something was wrong with me. Maybe I had a tapeworm, or maybe I was coming down with something. My big plastic Mickey Mouse bib covered my dress as I perched on my knees at the table while she tried, without much success, to convince me to eat.

On cleaning day, I watched as she scrubbed the floors with a vengeance on her hands and knees, coaxing every speck of dirt out of the corners. On washday, she put clothes through the wringer of the fat-bellied washer, but not before removing her dresses and wringing them out by hand so the buttons wouldn't pop off. Then she hung them on the clothesline on the flat roof behind our apartment. I stood in the doorway, forbidden to step onto the roof that had no railing. She taught me how to clean because a dirty home was intolerable. She believed "cleanliness is next to Godliness" even though she never went to church unless she had to. This cleaning paranoia created a life-long dread in me that someone would walk into my home and find dirt in a corner or dust on the shelves.

We didn't see much of Mumma's family except during the summer when we visited them. Once in a while, Mumma's sister, my Aunt Doris, would stop by with my cousin Pat, and while they had coffee, we'd play with my toys. But usually it was just the two of us, Mumma and me, in our little apartment, and I think I tried her patience. It took a lot to get Mumma angry, but when she could take it no longer, she would blow up. She rarely spanked me, but I knew I had gone too far when I saw her reach for the paddle on top of the icebox, which was a toy paddle-ball paddle with the ball taken off. "If you keep up the whining, I'll give you something to whine about," she threatened. It worked most of the time because I usually got what I wanted, but when I got a bit older, after my sister was born, my temper got worse, and I felt the sting of that paddle.

I remember one licking that occurred when my curiosity got the better of me. One early morning, with both parents still sleeping, I climbed up on the counter to rummage in Mumma's junk cabinet over the sink. It was an area that was supposed to be out of reach, but I knew there were treasures up there: hard candies, rubber bands, old letters, safety pins, birthday cards, hair rollers, pennies, nickels, and dimes in an old jar, and the occasional stale piece of chocolate from an old Whitman's Sampler. There was even a silver tea service with numerous dents in one corner of the teapot, a testament to the time when Mumma had had enough and her temper had gotten the best of her during a fight with Daddy.

That morning while exploring the cupboard, I thought I heard footsteps on the bedroom floor. Turning to climb down, I leaned against the ice box. In doing so, I accidentally pulled the embroidered cloth that was draped along the sides, sending Mumma's rose-covered China dish crashing to the floor, exploding into a garden of pink roses. Footsteps raced into the kitchen where I was sitting on the counter, cowering beside the icebox.

"Jesus H. Christ!" Mumma exclaimed, fear in her eyes. I screamed as loud as I thought necessary to get me out of trouble. "Let me see! Are you cut?" she asked, eyes wide.

Seeing the top cupboard open, Daddy yelled, "What were you doing up there? How did you climb all the way up there?" And then to Mumma, "How can you let her climb up there?" Because whenever I got hurt or sick, it was Mumma's fault.

Relieved I wasn't bleeding, Mumma carried me over the China chards, put me down in the bedroom, and whacked my behind. "Don't you ever get up there again!" My dignity affronted, I wailed louder.

Mumma taught me other lessons in the early years, including superstitions she had learned growing up in the woods of northern Maine, such as, "If you sing at the table, you'll cry before bed," or, "If you drop a fork, company's coming, but if you drop a knife, you'll get in a fight." And, "If a spider appears over your head, it's good luck." And finally, "Never rock an empty chair; very bad luck!" She told me God watched over me and everything I did, and if I lied or took something that wasn't mine, He would punish me. And He did watch over me. In the bedroom there hung a wooden cross on which Jesus was nailed by his hands and feet. Under the cross, a wooden carving depicted Jesus's Last Supper. When I was naughty, all I had to do was glance up at Jesus staring down at me. I half-expected him to come and get me, so my conscience became strong and my sense of guilt even stronger knowing God was witness to my many indiscretions. I wasn't happy about God and not a little fearful of this man on the wall. At night, we said our prayers: "Now I lay me down to sleep. I pray the Lord my soul to keep. If I should die before I wake, I pray the Lord my soul to take."

"Am I going to die?" I asked on more than one occasion. "I don't want the Lord to take my soul." Where did he take it? What was my soul?

"It just means you'll go to heaven," Mumma tried to explain.

"Are you going too? And Daddy? I don't want to go to heaven. I want to stay here."

"One day we'll all go. But that's a long time from now when you are very old."

Then one day Mumma told me about baby Christopher. She said I had a baby brother who was born before me and had died when he was four months old. Mumma said he was very sick and went to live in heaven with God. I wondered why Christopher went to heaven so soon. He wasn't old. I worried about death for a long time until I heard Auntie Dee say one day, "When God decides it's your time to go to heaven, you will go. Until then, don't worry about it." Auntie Dee, Uncle Tommy's young pretty wife, spoke with an authority that made me believe she knew everything. So, relieved, I took her advice, glad I didn't have to think about dying.

One afternoon, Daddy surprised me with a baby gray tiger kitten. "We need a cat to keep the mice out of the attic. You can take care of him. What would you like to name him?" "Tippy," I answered immediately, not sure where that name came from. And Tippy became my unwilling baby, allowing me to dress him in doll clothes until he'd had enough and meowed to go out. Tippy stayed with us for awhile, bringing us mice every now and then, and curling up with me when I was forced to nap. Then one day he disappeared. We asked all the shopkeepers if they had seen him, but no one had, and I assumed that God decided it was time for him to go to heaven.

Kathy, age two with Mumma, 1952

Kathy, age two
with Daddy, 1952

Chapter Two
Two New Sisters

"Kathy, wake up," said Mumma in the middle of the night. Her voice was filled with excitement as she got me dressed for our trip up north to Little Grammie's house where we would stay for a week. Daddy had just gotten home from work, and we were going to drive for most of the night.

Lying in the back of the car with my blanket and pillow, I was too excited to sleep, so I watched the trees pass by as we drove along the country roads.

The sun was not yet up when we arrived at Little Grammie's tiny bungalow, set back from the road and nearly surrounded by thick woods. A light shone from the kitchen window, silhouetting Little Grammie and a little girl standing beside her. Doors flew open, and I stared groggily as a flurry of arms came rushing toward us. "Mummy!" Joyce Ann cried as Mumma wrapped her arms around her. Blinking away tears, Mumma's face, lit up with smiles, looked the way Aunt Maria and Daddy looked when they saw me. I knew about Joyce Ann from pictures, but she wasn't real until that moment. I was three and a half that year and didn't understand why Joyce Ann didn't live with Mumma, but it never occurred to me to question it. I just knew she was a part of our family even though she didn't live with us. Daddy never stayed with us on our yearly visits up north, so as soon as we were settled, he kissed us good-by and left for home. I looked up to Joyce Ann, wanting to have long yellow braids just like her. She was kind and patient with me as I followed her around the house until our week was over and Daddy returned to take us home.

The new baby

Just a month before I turned four, on a cold January evening, with suitcase packed, Mumma and Daddy dropped me off at Yiayia's house to stay while Mumma went to the hospital to get a new baby. This was the first time I had spent the night there. I imagined the hospital was like the stores where we shopped. She'd pick a baby and come home. When she didn't come to get me the next day or the next, I wasn't sure if she was ever coming back. Will she leave me with Yiayia like my half- sister Joyce was left with Grammie? I cried every day until Yiayia told Daddy to come and get me.

Back at home, I would no longer be sleeping in the crib in my parents' room. While I was at Yiayia's, Grampy and Daddy hired someone to convert our attic space off the kitchen into a new bedroom with newly painted white walls and linoleum flooring. I had one dormer window overlooking the backside of tenements down the street and a new bed big enough for two people. My toys were in a box at the foot of the bed. At home finally with Daddy, I waited for Mumma to come home with the new baby.

My new baby sister, Georgeanna, was a novelty at first, but when I told Mumma I wanted her to take her back and she refused, I had to accept that the change was permanent. Georgeanna was small and round with rolls on her arms and legs that Mumma and Little Grammie loved. "Ain't she a cunnin' little thing. I could just eat her up," Grammie cooed when she saw Georgeanna for the first time. Mumma always tried to make sure Georgeanna didn't cry hard because her face would turn purple; she'd lose her breath and have a convulsion. It was scary when Mumma had to breath on her face or sometimes even throw water on her to shock her out of it.

I liked my baby sister, but I didn't like sharing the attention I had had before she was born. Overnight I was now the big girl. But I didn't feel like a big girl. Instead I felt like I was not in the right place—wishing I could be where I was supposed to be, but not knowing where that was.

Cabin fever

Georgeanna was a year old on my fifth birthday at the end of February of 1955. Mumma and I had been suffering from a bad case of cabin fever. Waking up repeatedly to blizzards and Nor'easters, it seemed the entire world was contained inside that small apartment. Looking out of the windows, if I peered closely, I could detect miniature snowflakes floating in every direction. But I couldn't see beyond the thickness to the streets below. Everything was a wall of swirling snow. While I often felt safe in that cocoon of white, by the end of February we were all feeling claustrophobic.

Stuck inside for days at a time with Mumma and my baby sister, I missed our daily walks that had been put on hold as snow continued to pile up in drifts on the streets below. And my excitement over getting a red tricycle for my birthday in February was tempered by the fact I couldn't leave the apartment to ride it.

At first the new tricycle was parked under the kitchen table, waiting for another month or two before we could get out of our winter cage. But I soon began riding it around the kitchen. I went in circles, avoiding the stove, up and down the rectangular room to the front door, back down the hallway, circling the kitchen and back to the door, over and over, imagining I was out on the street, playing at shopping, driving a car.

Then one day Mumma opened the front door, and my world expanded as she let me ride around the upstairs hallway, with the warning not to bother our neighbors. The hallway smelled of hair dye and permanent waves as the two Miss B's had a steady stream of customers. The Miss B's were always kind to me, even making their French hamburger soup for us because they knew I was a finicky eater. I could play in the hallway as long as I didn't bother the customers, mostly elderly women, who came for a permanent wave or a weekly set. I also had to steer clear of the top of the stairs so I wouldn't go tumbling down. I enjoyed the added space to play and the attention I got from ladies who came for their hair appointments and who, sometimes, gave me lollipops and penny candy.

Spring in Maine comes in fits and starts. On warmer sun-drenched days, melting snow drips off the eaves, sounding like rain. And just when you think spring is finally here, you wake up to another blizzardy, white-out day. So I had to content myself with riding my tricycle indoors until we could escape down the stairs and back out into the world. One day when the sun sparkled through the frost on the window and the kitchen door was open, I had just finished racing down the hallway and back into the kitchen, when we heard a loud thud, followed by running feet and someone screaming.

Mumma froze and stopped feeding my sister. "Stay right here," she ordered. "Don't move." She looked scared.

Curious, I waited until she had left the kitchen before following her. At the opened door, I peeked around the corner to find a gaggle of ladies, some with heads covered in curlers, some with wet towel-wrapped hair, and the two Miss B's leaning over the top of the stairs, hands covering mouths in shock, staring at something below. I managed to squeeze between nyloned legs until I could see. At the bottom of the stairs lay a woman, flat on her stomach, face crushed into the floor, and shattered glasses alongside her body. Her hair, in a new undamaged permanent wave, was still perfectly coiffed. Her body lay unmoving, deathly silent. Then Mumma noticed me squeezed between the shocked ladies' legs, grabbed me by my arm and yanked me away.

"I told you to stay inside!" she scolded, dragging me into the kitchen. "Why don't you ever listen to me?"

Dropped at the kitchen table, I sat with the vision of the still body as the sirens sounded outside.

I couldn't play in the hallway anymore after that. Grampie had to replace the railing and the plastic mat that covered the stairs. Mumma said the lady's heel got caught in the mat at the top of the stairs, which sent her tumbling down to her death below.

Chapter Three
Fears and Night Terrors

I think that incident was the beginning of my nightmares. I had night terrors about the boogeyman under my bed and woke up screaming. Mumma would put the covers back over me, saying it was just a dream and to go back to sleep. I didn't believe her. I wanted her to sit by my bed until I went to sleep, but she always left to sit in the kitchen with Daddy to listen to the radio or watch our new Zenith television. Wide awake, I curled into a ball, arms and legs close to my body so they wouldn't be grabbed by the monster under the bed. I tried to stay awake to avoid the nightmares, watching the flashing lights across the ceiling from cars below as the late-night drivers cruised the streets. Even the intermittent sirens racing past the apartment were comforting compared to my nightmares. But relief only came with the first rays of daylight through the window.

During those frightening nights, I was overwhelmed by a feeling of loneliness. Lying in bed, I longed for something that I could not articulate, or someplace where I wanted to go. Not only to go, but to go back to, as if I had left a home from the past and wanted desperately to return to it. But I had no idea where that place was. I was lonely for what I didn't know I was missing. Later when I was older and had my first sleepover, I identified that feeling as homesickness. For many years, I felt homesick, but this was the only home I had ever known. Where had that feeling in the pit of my stomach come from? That feeling of separation, of belonging somewhere else? Where was that somewhere else? I learned later in life there was a word for this feeling: hiraeth, a homesickness for a home to which you cannot return, a home which maybe never was; the nostalgia, the yearning, the grief for the lost places of your past. That's what I felt. But when I was very young, I didn't understand those feelings of fear and homesickness.

After Mumma put us to bed, she'd sit in the kitchen with the only light coming from the TV, waiting for Daddy to come home. Sometimes Daddy didn't come home until way after the TV was over for the night. When the National Anthem came on, the TV would get all fuzzy and Mumma would turn it off. Then it was quiet until I heard the sound of Daddy's familiar footsteps on the creaking stairs. When Daddy came home that late, it was because he was playing cards, sometimes just downstairs in the pool-room. But when he came home earlier right after the diner closed, he often brought a steak or a couple of lamb chops home, and the smell of onions and meat frying made my stomach growl.

"Mumma, I can't sleep," I called from the bed-room.

"What now? Shh, go back to sleep. You're okay. It's the middle of the night."

"My tummy hurts."

"Let her get up. Come here, Kathy, are you

hungry?" Daddy, like my Greek Yiayia, thought every problem could be solved with something to eat. Sitting in his lap, I took a small bite of the meat, but the smell was always better than the taste, and I would chew and chew until I forced myself to swallow the gristly mass.

Nighttime was both frightening and mysterious. Under cover of darkness, with smoke curling up from cigarettes in the kitchen, my parents sat at the table watching television, bringing strange voices into our apartment. The light from the TV cast gray shadows on the walls, and the music from the late-night shows gave me the shivers. I was both attracted to and repelled by the sounds and eerie darkness of the kitchen.

Sometimes late at night when Daddy had had too much to drink, arguments would erupt. At first, their voices were low and one or the other would laugh about something, but then they got louder and angry and I knew what was coming next. Usually, it was because Mumma did something Daddy thought was wrong. The angry words would soon flare into full-fledged physical attacks. Mumma let it go at first, but when he wouldn't stop, she attacked with force, knocking Daddy to the floor. She was taller than he was and stronger. Frightened by the angry noises, I watched them rolling on the floor, hitting and screaming. Mumma did the hitting, and Daddy did the screaming as she pulled handfuls of his dark, curly hair from his head. "Betty, Betty, stop! I'm sorry! Stop! For Christ's sake!" he would cry.

I would jump off the bed pleading, "Stop Mumma! You're hurting Daddy! Stop!" When

Mumma saw me sobbing, her anger evaporated, and they stopped fighting.

With the late-night battle over, I'd again climb on Daddy's lap as if the explosion had never happened except for his rubbing his sore head. Finally, back to bed, curled into a ball, the feeling of being alone ached in the pit of my stomach. Only when I could hear laughter coming from the bedroom could I finally go to sleep, silently whispering the prayer Mumma taught me, "Now I lay me down to sleep, I pray the Lord..."

The new oil stove ... and another nightmare

I am running as fast as I can. My heart is racing, but The Monster is getting closer. Even though my feet are moving, I'm not getting anywhere. It's grabbing my leg!

"Help!" I howl in terror.

"Kathy, wake up it's just a bad dream," Mumma said, untangling my trembling body from the sheets and re-arranging the covers as she tried to soothe me, but I was too frightened.

"It lives behind the stove. It's coming after me," I hiccupped through tears.

"It's just a dream. We won't let anyone in."

"No, it's already in here. It lives here. It got you and Daddy. The Monster came and ate your heads. Bones stuck out of your neck, like chicken bones. The Monster ate you and Daddy!"

"Nonsense. Now go back to sleep."

Golump, balump, blub, blub, blub came the noise from the kitchen.

"Can you hear it?"

"Hear what?"

"That noise. The Monster noise. Galump, balump, blub, blub, blub."

"It's just house noises and the stove heating up the house. It's not anything bad. We are right here."

"Where's Tippy? Did The Monster get her?"

"Tippy is gone, remember? You're going to wake your sister with all this noise. Now go back to sleep."

Finally, making sure my arms and legs were not dangling over the side, I curled up in a tight ball in the center of my bed, flipped the sheet over my head and fell asleep from exhaustion.

My five-year-old imagination, filled with monsters that lived under my bed, and real death on the stairs outside the apartment, now had another nightmare to deal with: the oil stove.

From the day Mumma got her new stove, she made sure I didn't go near it. She spent a good portion of her day in front of the big beige and silver iron giant, but if I got too close when I was riding my tricycle up and down from the front door through the kitchen, I was quickly steered away.

Every so often a man would come upstairs carrying a tin drum. He took the old tin drum from behind the stove and replaced it with a new one. As long as the stove had oil, it made those strange noises—blubb, blubb, blubb—that were muffled during the day, but in the quiet of night, made the monster come alive for me. Nightmares of finding my parents dead behind the stove haunted me for years.

While nighttime evoked fear, I was always glad to see daylight seeping through my window. My favorite time of day being sunrise, I loved watching the light erase the darkness. Finally relieved of night terrors, and with the natural resilience of childhood, I looked forward to the new day.

The best mornings during those long winters were when I opened my eyes to sun streaming through the windows. With the sun shimmering on the new snow, the world was new and clean. In my snowsuit, hat, mittens, and boots, I was now old enough to go downstairs by myself with a warning to stay out of the way as Daddy and the other shop-keepers shoveled the front of their businesses. I watched as cars inched along the snow and ice-covered streets, and shoppers ventured out into the world again. My face red from cold, my feet wet, and my fingers like icicles, I stayed out in the cold until I couldn't stand it another minute and only then crept back up the stairs.

Chapter Four
Encounters with God

When I was very young, I didn't understand those feelings of fear and homesickness. I did, however, sense Mumma's feelings of isolation. She was the outsider in a Greek family that had never totally accepted her. Many times when visiting Yiayia and Grampie, they would speak in Greek and Albanian, despite the fact that we had no idea what they were saying, which rendered us invisible. They told me I was Greek too, but Mumma said I was only half Greek because she was not Greek.

"What are you?" I wanted to know. "English and Scotch/Irish," she told me. "Why is Daddy Greek and you're not?" I wondered. "We are from different families and even different countries," she tried to explain, but I didn't understand any of it. My Greek relatives did make it clear, though, that being Greek made us special in some way.

As their first grandchild, I was showered with love by Yiayia and Grampie who instilled in me pride about my Greek heritage. Despite their attempts, I was reluctant to place all my loyalties on my Greek side. I felt stuck in the middle of the two cultures, never quite sure which one to embrace. If I embraced one, was I rejecting the other? Sometimes it seemed that way, but over time the Greek side usually won, mostly because they cared so much. And because I was Greek, baptism in the Greek church was a given.

For the first five years of my life, my only experience with religion was the prayer Mumma taught me, an occasional visit to church on a holiday, and God staring down on me from the crucifix on my parents' bedroom wall. That would soon change.

St. George's Greek Orthodox Church, the nearest Greek church, was fifty miles away in Bangor, so we didn't go often enough for me to understand what church was all about. I knew we had to dress up and be quiet. I knew the church smelled of incense that made me dizzy, and I knew that the sounds of the priests' Greek chanting gave me goose bumps as they vibrated through my small body. Church, I thought, was for holidays or special occasions. Then one day, my two aunts decided Georgeanna and I had to be baptized.

When my grandfather settled in the Waterville area, he must have known there was no Greek church nearby. He could have gone to Worchester, Massachusetts, with his brother where there was an established Greek community. Instead, he chose the factory town where he had worked before bringing his family to America. I never saw my grandfather in church, so I don't think religion played a role in his decision to move to Waterville.

Daddy wasn't a churchgoer either. The only time Daddy spoke of God was when his hand, tight-fisted, rose toward the heavens, cursing in Greek and Albanian. That happened quite often, usually when the car broke down, or he got a flat tire on the way to the racetrack. Not mechanically inclined, he was sure God was out to get him, and he let Him know in no uncertain terms what he thought of Him as he kicked the damaged tire and let the curses fly.

And Mumma, growing up poor in the woods of Maine, only went to church with her siblings because they knew there would be "good eats" after the service. But that all stopped when they began attending a holy rollers church service where the congregants spoke in tongues. My mother, her sister, and three brothers laughed so hard that they were about to be thrown out. But when the snakes appeared, they dashed out on their own, never to return.

So it was no surprise that I was not baptized until I was five years old, and it was only thanks to the two Greek aunts, Maria and Dee, that my baby sister and I did not grow up to be heathens.

A Greek baptism

Once the aunts had convinced the rest of the family, they made an appointment with Father Pappas in Bangor for our family to have a private service on a Saturday morning. I was too old for the regular baptism service with the entire congregation.

"Kathy, would you like me to be your godmother?" Auntie Dee asked.

"Yes," I answered, not knowing what that meant.

And later, "Kathy, I'm going to be your godmother," said Aunt Maria.

I nodded, still in the dark.

An argument ensued between the aunts, each yelling back and forth in Greek until they both came to me. "Choose!" they ordered. Aunt Maria worked in the taxi stand office, and I saw her every day. So I said, "I want Aunt Maria." For what, I still didn't understand.

Ushered into a chilly side room in the church, we met Father Pappas, who led us to the font, a huge, gray granite basin that I soon discovered was filled with holy water and oil. The strong odor of incense floated in front of my face, making me dizzy. As the priest intoned the prayers in Greek, my clothes were removed, leaving me shivering in nothing but my birthday suit. Father Pappas then lifted me over the font.

Too shocked to cry out or make any noise, I closed my eyes and instinctively curled into a ball, my knees touching my chin. Before I realized what was coming next, I was submerged in the tepid water. Lifted up, I dangled above the water, sputtering as I tried to catch my breath. More prayers, repeated by Aunt Maria, and once again, another dunking. Coming up for the second time, I coughed, inhaling the strong incense smoking over my head as my body shivered with cold. And finally, for the third and last time, down I went again. Father Pappas then handed me to Aunt Maria, who was waiting with a towel to dry my quaking body. My new godmother then dressed me in new clothes from the inside out, new white panties trimmed with lace around the legs, new white slip, new white dress, new white anklets, and new black patent leather shoes.

Then it was Georgeanna's turn to suffer the same fate. But she wanted none of it, regaling the holy chapel with screams of terror that echoed through the empty church. Mumma looked scared and nervous, afraid that my sister would lose her breath and have a convulsion. But maybe being in a church would save her because she just cried like a normal baby. Auntie Dee was Georgeanna's god-mother. She dressed her, and the adults were given candles as they circled the font praying for us and welcoming us into the church of God.

Our baptisms didn't change our sporadic attendance in Bangor, however. Aunt Maria and Yiayia sometimes attended St. Mark's Episcopal Church, which was acceptable if for no other reason than, like the Greek Church, they broke with the Catholics. Despite my dramatic introduction to religion, I enjoyed attending the services at St. Mark's with them. I loved the hymns and the prayers that felt comforting. Kneeling in the back pew between Yiayia, who quietly prayed in Albanian during the Holy Eucharist, and Aunt Maria, who attended carefully to the latest fashions parading down the aisle, I waited patiently for the sermon to end and for the organ to begin again. When I got older, I attended Sunday school and sang in the children's choir.

Father Montgomery, a rotund man with a beaming smile and booming voice, gave me the weekly blessing, and I was convinced that if there was a god, it was embodied in that kind man. Or at least I preferred this version of God to the one Mumma talked about who would punish me for wrongdoing.

To further my religious training, one Saturday each month the Greek priest's wife, Mrs. Alexopoulos, drove from Lewiston to St. Mark's so that a small group of us kids, cousins and friends of two other Greek families, could attend Greek school. We were taught about Greek religion and culture and given a children's Greek language book. I looked forward to the lessons, but unfortunately, we didn't speak Greek at home, so when our teacher could no longer travel to Waterville, the Greek we had learned was lost. However, my dream of one day traveling to Greece was born during those lessons.

There were more Sundays than not when neither Aunt Maria nor Yiayia went to church, so Daddy would drop me off at the front door and speed off, glad not to have to go inside. Because they only attended church to hear me sing in the choir or when I had a part in a church play, I could tell Daddy and Mumma felt out of place in church. I watched as Daddy sat uncomfortably, fidgeting in his seat, looking around like a deer who accidentally gets into a building and desperately tries to find a way out. Mumma sat motionless, no doubt wishing she had a cigarette, not knowing when to sit or kneel or stand, but watching me. She probably wondered who this kid was, her daughter who liked being in church.

Caught between the faithful and the non-believers, I questioned God's existence during the day, but it was at night, in the throes of a nightmare, that I prayed to God to show himself, to let me know he was real and to banish the nightmares.

Chapter Five
Feast or Famine

Summertime arriving always filled me with a sense of relief. Gone were the days of being cooped up in the apartment as the snow piled up outside, and gone were the cold spring rains that also kept us from going to the park or walking downtown. We could look forward to playing in Yiayia's yard, across the bridge in Winslow, or on the sidewalk in front of the diner. On hot days we might go to Bang's Beach in the Belgrade Lakes or Old Orchard Beach at the ocean for the day. But, more often than not, when Daddy bounded up the stairs with a light spring in his step and announced, "Let's go!" we knew we were off to the horse races. Putting on her outside dress, and making sure Georgeanna and I were clean, Mumma hastily packed a picnic lunch, and we were out the door. Georgeanna sat in Mumma's lap, while I stood or sat in the front seat between my parents as we headed for Windsor Raceway, or wherever the races happened to be that day.

Off to the races!

Because we spent many days at the races, traveling around the state from track to track and following the horses, I knew what to expect. Bangor, Cumberland, Windsor, Skowhegan—it didn't matter where we went. The harness-racing grounds all looked the same. With a mile-long oblong racetrack, the jockeys sat on two-wheeled carts called sulkies and goaded their horses to go faster with their whips as they trotted around the track. Finally, near the end of August, the races became far more interesting because it was time for the county fairs. Then we could look forward to carnival rides, animal competitions, candy apples, and cotton candy.

Walking onto the Windsor fairgrounds early one July morning (the actual fair would not be there until the end of August), the familiar sweet scent of the horses and the clop, clop of their hooves greeted us as the sulky drivers warmed up on the packed dirt raceway. Shaking the blanket out on a grassy space near the fence, Mumma placed Georgeanna in the center with her baby doll and a bottle while I climbed onto the fence and waved as the jockeys trotted past.

I wanted to ask Daddy about the horses. Where did they sleep at night? What did they eat? But I knew not to bother him when he was reading the race program. This reading was far more serious than the books he read at night in bed—books with cowboys on the covers, the pages fluttering off his face as he fell asleep, snoring. Scrutinizing the odds in the racing form, he remained so focused that his unfiltered Camel dangled from his mouth, the ash longer than the cigarette. Only when he burned his hand or singed his pants did he stub the butt out with his foot; but even then, his eyes quickly returned to the form, unfazed by the hot embers. I watched as he scratched his head, marking his favorites with a pencil stub he had picked up at the ticket window. He studied those programs and the pros and cons of each horse with the same intensity as a lawyer studying his caseload or a doctor making a serious prognosis. Most of the time Daddy was always moving. Even when sitting in a chair, his leg would bounce up and down as if getting ready to make a run for it. The only time I ever observed him still was when he was staring at the race form with so much concentration I knew not to disturb him.

Suddenly he laughed, causing ashes from a new cigarette to fall in his lap. Brushing off his pants, he announced, "Well, well, Katura," using his pet name for me, "we have a winner here today!"

"I sure hope so," Mumma commented. When it came to Daddy and his "hobby," she never complained, even when we went home broke most of the time.

"Look at this; we have in race #1, horse #3, the lovely Bayside Betty!"

Mumma's name was Betty, and she said, "Oh God, better for us if it were Speedy Betty!" We laughed.

"Is that who we want to win?" I asked Daddy.

"That's the one," he answered, his head back in the program.

As the horses paraded around the paddock, he watched carefully to see which were skittish and which seemed calmer, but not too calm. A skittish horse might be too tired before the race started.

The ticket windows were near our blanket. "You stay here while we get our tickets, Kathy. Watch your sister, and make sure she stays on the blanket. We'll be right back." While they were gone, I pretended I was a sulky driver, racing around the track (blanket). Georgeanna laughed at my antics as she sat, pacifier in her mouth.

Before the race began, Mumma handed out bologna sandwiches with mustard and my favorite Humpty Dumpty potato chips, while Daddy went to get root beers for me and Mumma, and a beer for him. It wasn't long before the announcer ordered the jockeys to take their places. Mumma covered my sister's ears while I put my fingers in mine to muffle the shotgun signaling the start of the race.

"Aaaand, they're off!" the announcer bellowed.

Dad bounded toward the fence. "Come on, Betty, come on!" he shouted. Holding Georgeanna in her arms, Mumma watched as the horses raced past, clouds of dust flying into our faces. As Daddy's eyes followed the horses, he furiously dragged on his cigarette, eyebrows creased, and his mouth in a straight line, which signaled the race did not look good for "Betty."

The finish line was on the other side of the track, so I couldn't see who was ahead. As they sped around the final bend, it was neck and neck, Sagacity Sam and Bayside Betty! The crowd roared, and Sagacity won by a nose.

Dad's arms flew up in the air as he did his circling happy Greek dance. Mom's jumping up and down made my sister laugh at the new game.

"But Betty lost!" I knew what it meant when we lost.

"It's okay," Daddy said, "I got tickets for both win and place." It didn't make sense to me that he could win without really winning. Win, place, show, quinellas—they were all terms I didn't understand, but as long as Daddy was happy, we all celebrated.

After every race, I collected handfuls of losing tickets that littered the ground and pretended they were dollars for shopping. Daddy showed me where to look for the winning numbers on the tickets, just in case someone dropped a winner.

Four hours later, Mumma, carrying Georgeanna, who had fallen asleep, and me with eyes heavy, made our way slowly toward the car. Although we were tired, Daddy's buoyant steps assured me we were going home with some money, and that meant treats for us. We stopped at Hussey's General Store, famous in Maine for guns, wedding dresses, Italian sandwiches, socks, and everything else one could imagine. We celebrated with ice cream.

Baby Jimmy joins the racing outings

Those days at the races became routine every summer. Then when I was five and Georgeanna was not yet two, my baby brother Jimmy came along, so there were five of us at the racetrack. With Jimmy in the front seat on Mumma's lap, and Georgeanna and me in the back hanging out of the windows, feeling the warm summer air on our faces, we raced along the rural roads, inhaling the scent of fresh mown hay. Because we spent so much time in the car all summer riding from racetrack to racetrack, this was our family time. Speeding up and down the hills as

George and I bounced in the back seat, we urged Daddy to go faster. Giving in to our pleas, he pressed his foot on the accelerator going up the hills as we screamed in delight when our stomachs met our throats on the downward slopes.

The day always started out with excitement. Daddy was going to "win big" this time and we listened as Mumma and Daddy dreamed about what they'd do when their ship came in. Mostly it was about buying a big house in the country. Not too far in the country like where Mumma grew up, but out of the city. The house would be two stories with a porch wrapped around the front, with rocking chairs and swings for us kids. I'd have my own room and so would Georgeanna and Jimmy. As I got older, I'd add on other wishes, like a barn with my own horse and lots of other animals. By that time though, I knew it was only a dream. Daddy and Mumma continued to play the game, but I became more skeptical the older I got. I didn't believe we were ever going to win, and I began to hate the words, "when we win big."

Maybe they really did believe it would happen someday. Inevitably, Daddy would break into song in a deep baritone, pretending to be a conductor, one hand on the steering wheel holding his cigarette, and the other waving in the air. "Let's all sing like the birdies sing, tweet, tweet, tweet, tweet," and we'd all join in until we arrived for another day of playing the horses.

After a long day, we'd pile into the car for the ride home, exhausted and more often than not, completely broke. No songs or dreams of new homes with rooms of our own now. Hungry and tired, Jimmy would whine, while I complained, "When are we going to get home? I'm hungry. I want ice cream!" Georgeanna, sitting opposite me in the back seat, silently staring out of the window, seemed removed from all of it.

Finally, Daddy, fed up with my complaining would threaten, "Be quiet before I stop this car. Don't you make me stop this car!" he warned. "Why can't you be good like your sister? She doesn't say BOO!"

Then as usual, my temper flared as I poked my innocent sister. "Why don't you say Boo?" I asked, sticking out my tongue. I don't know why she never fussed, but I did know my complaints made me "not good." Even when I tried though, which was not that often, I never could be good like my sister, and no matter how hard Daddy tried, I didn't believe his dreams of "winning big" would ever become reality.

As we all finally quieted down, we would arrive in Waterville at dusk. I'd stare out of the car window into the lighted rooms of houses as we drove slowly through the city streets, wishing I lived in one of those houses where it looked like they had already won big.

Don't Worry About A Thing

Chapter Six
Adventures with Aunt Maria

I was lucky to grow up with three aunts who influenced my life. Aunt Maria was one of them. While I spent many days of my childhood playing at the racetrack, Aunt Maria, my Godmother, not having children of her own, often took me places and introduced me to other people and lifestyles. Like Daddy's plans, it was usually spur of the moment. Leaving the taxi stand office, she'd see me on the sidewalk and say, "Kathy, let's go for a ride." I would jump in the front seat of one of the cabs and off we'd go to a friend's house who had a new baby to show off, or shopping at her favorite dress shop, or to Winslow to see Yiayia, or maybe just to get an ice cream cone.

Aunt Maria's driving was erratic. She would stop at the very last minute at the light and rev up to proceed. It wasn't unusual for me to come home with a knot the size of an egg on my forehead when I went flying into the dashboard. Mumma always got so mad she threatened that that would be "the last damn time Maria was taking me anywhere." It never was.

The birthday party

"Maria is picking you up in a little while to go to a birthday party," Mumma told me one day.

"Whose birthday is it?"

"Her friend Sandra has a little girl your age, and it's her birthday. Let's put your pink dress on so you'll be ready."

"What are we going to do there?"

"I don't know, but there will be cake and ice cream." That was enough to convince me.

Soon, Aunt Maria arrived with a box containing a pair of shiny, black patent leather shoes and a new pair of white anklets with lace at the top. I hurriedly put them on and danced around the kitchen.

"What do you say?" Aunt Maria reminded me.

"Thank you!" As I twirled around, staring at the shiny black shoes.

When we arrived at the birthday party, I stared at the large green lawn in front of the two-story cape, surrounded by flowers and two large maple trees. Cars filled the driveway, and girls and boys emerged with present-filled arms. Betsy, the birthday girl, wore a fancy pink birthday dress with so many layers of petticoats her dress bounced up and down when she walked. As I handed her the present Aunt Maria had bought, I smiled shyly as she welcomed us into the house politely, like a grown-up, and herded us into the living room decorated with balloons. Her new puppy welcomed me by licking my face, and, disgusted, I grabbed onto Aunt Maria. Thankfully, the pup greeted the others as they arrived and left me alone to stare at the girls in their fancy party dresses. Before long, the house was overflowing. This place was a world away from my home on Silver Street, and my life felt lacking by comparison.

At my house, birthdays were celebrated with family. Mumma made us a cake and the cousins, aunts, and uncles came. After singing "Happy Birthday" and opening a few presents, the adults drank beer and talked while the kids ran through the house, playing hide and seek.

Not knowing anyone, I was bashful at first, but when it was my turn, I played Pin the Tail on the Donkey, which I thought was a stupid game (because I didn't win), and I took a whack at a large piñata, which was lots of fun when candy rained down on us. Just as I was beginning to enjoy the party, Betsy's mother herded us outside for the next game. Each of us was given a small brown paper bag and told to search for penny candy hidden in the yard. She blew her whistle, and off we scattered to fill our bags.

I found two root beer barrels, a piece of Double Bubble gum, and a red lollipop. Getting into the spirit of the game, I hurried around the yard looking behind the bushes and under the front porch.

When I couldn't find any more candy, I kicked the grass with my new black shoes and ambled off by myself, circled a large maple, and settled down on the soft grass. The red lollipop soon found its way into my mouth as I watched the other kids from a distance. Looking around me, I spied a branch a few inches away. I didn't see any candy next to the stick, but maybe underneath? As soon as I reached over and grabbed the brown branch, I realized my mistake.

A blob of dried dog caca covered my hand! Panicking, I rubbed my hands in the grass, hoping to wipe it off, but my hand was sticky from the candy, and I only succeeded in getting it on my dress. Attempting to wipe it off with my clean hand only made it worse. The whistle blew, ending the game, but I stood still, watching as the other kids rushed back to the house to count their loot. I remained frozen by the tree, wishing I could run home.

"Kathy!" I heard Aunt Maria call, as she noticed I was not moving, "come on back!" Slowly I made my way over to her. "Kathy? What is that on your dress?" A look of shock registered on her face as she realized what it was. "Skata! (caca)."

I burst into tears, sure I was going to get a yelling. But Aunt Maria, who could always be counted on to be unpredictable, laughed. "Come on," she said, chuckling, "come on, let's get you washed up."

She quickly rushed me past the other kids and into the laundry room, carefully removed my dress, washed it in the sink by hand, and hung it on the clothesline in the back yard. My embarrassment was mixed with sadness because I thought she would have to take me home, just when I was beginning to have fun. Maria scrubbed my hands, face, arms, and legs, and I stood in my white slip and black shoes, not knowing what would happen next. Drive home in my slip?

"It's cake and ice cream time," the mother announced. I looked up at Aunt Maria sadly. I didn't want to go into the other room, but I didn't like the idea of missing out on cake and ice cream either. Then Aunt Maria took my hand and led me into the dining room, where Betsy sat in a chair at the head of the table on a pile of phone books, wearing a tiara and surrounded by a mountain of birthday presents. I joined the others as we stood around the table and watched her open her gifts. No one seemed to notice I was missing a dress. I tried to hide behind some of the other little girls with their flouncy dresses and wished with all my might that we'd get our cake and ice cream soon so we could go home. Betsy took her good old time opening the gifts, and her mother made sure she politely thanked each of us. When she opened Aunt Maria's present, a Snow White coloring book and a box of crayons, and thanked us both, I said nothing, so she reached for another gift, ignoring me. By the time we were served the cake and ice cream, it tasted like dirt in my dry mouth, and I was afraid I was going to be sick. Finally, the party over, we retrieved my now wrinkled, still slightly damp but clean dress. It felt good to have all my clothes on again, but most of all, I was glad to be going home.

In the car, Aunt Maria asked, "Did you have fun today?" She chortled, remembering the incident.

"She got a lot of presents," I commented enviously, hoping my disaster would be forgotten. The bag of penny candy, given to us before we left, lay in my lap, and unusual for me, I had no desire to eat any of it. "She's not really a princess, is she?" I asked, remembering the tiara.

"Betsy? No, she's just a little girl, just like you, Koukla," she answered. "She just doesn't get dog caca all over her party dresses," she couldn't help adding while chuckling.

Don't Worry About A Thing

Chapter Seven
Out Into the World

In 1955, I started school at South Grammar in the south end of Waterville.

Excited but nervous, I awoke with the sun and put on my new red plaid dress with a large butterfly-shaped collar. Mumma parted my short blond hair on the side with a barrette that kept my bangs out of my face. I tied the new Buster Brown shoes, remembering the battle I had lost in the shoe store. Ugly brown shoes that laced up instead of the dressy ones Mumma refused to buy, which caused a temper tantrum on the floor of Barlow's Shoe Store. "When I was your age I would have been tickled pink to have those new shoes. And here you are, acting up," she said. And that was that.

After putting on my white cardigan, Mumma and I left the apartment, leaving Georgeanna with Daddy. Mumma told me school would be fun. They both told me to listen to the teacher and be a good girl. Though they were proud when I got good grades, they never pressured me to do well or paid much attention to my education, entrusting my teachers to the task.

Mumma and Daddy had never finished school. Mumma went through eighth grade, telling me her family was so poor she had to quit in order to work. Daddy attended a boarding school in Greece, but he didn't finish high school when he came to America. He told me a story about being a little boy in Greece, with a teacher who made him go to the board to do an arithmetic problem that he kept getting wrong. In a fit of anger, his teacher had picked Daddy up by the scruff of his shirt and threw him across the room. "I saw you riding your bicycle yesterday instead of working on your schoolwork," the teacher had yelled, "I had better not see you outside again until you have finished your work!" Bruised and embarrassed, Daddy had hated school from then on.

"Don't worry about a thing," Daddy said as Mumma and I left the apartment. "As long as you do what the teacher says you will be ok." As we walked down Silver Street, I felt both apprehensive and excited as she gave me instructions. "Now that you are in school, after today you'll be able to go by yourself. You know what to do. Make sure you stay on the sidewalks and stop and look both ways when you come to the cross walks."

Holding hands, we paraded down Silver Street, past the shops, until we turned the corner where the street now became residential with large, stately Victorian homes. Lined on both sides of the street with ancient elms, Waterville was known as the Elm City before Dutch elm disease would eventually kill them. But now in September, the sidewalks, covered with a blanket of gold leaves, made the day even brighter as the sun shone on the colors at our feet. I loved shuffling through the crackling leaves, covering my ugly brown shoes. The air smelled of rotting leaves and new beginnings.

We continued purposefully for a half-mile down Silver Street to Gold Street and turned left. Another block down Gold and there was South Grammar School on the right, a three -story looming brick edifice with tall windows on each floor.

"I'll pick you up when school is out today," said Mumma. "Then tomorrow you will be able to go by yourself since you are a big school girl now." She repeated the instructions once again about crossing the streets. So, after that first day, I ventured out alone, and although Mumma told me to always go the same way, when I made friends, I discovered new routes through the South End neighborhoods even though it took longer to get home.

"Are you coming in with me?" I asked Mumma as we arrived at the front steps on that first day.

"Do you want me to?"

"I don't know where to go."

"Good morning," Mrs. Daviou, our principal, greeted us at the door. The list of students is beside the classrooms, and the kindergarten classes are down the hall and to the left."

My name was on the list at Mrs. Winter's classroom. Mumma and I entered to find students playing in different areas of the classroom. Some were looking at books, some were coloring with large crayons, and some were stringing beads. I sat down and began playing with the beads. One of the boys began wailing as his mother was leaving. I stared at the others clinging to their parents as they tearfully said goodbye. Not knowing what to do, I looked at Mumma, and at the last minute, I rushed over to her and gave her a hug, which surprised us both. As I watched her turn to leave, I glimpsed tears in the corners of her eyes.

Back at the bead table, it wasn't long before Mrs. Winters called us all into a large circle, where everyone held hands. Everyone went but me. "No thank you," I said politely when she held out her hand for me to join the group. Ring Around the Rosy was a baby game. Mrs. Winters left me alone for a while, and then asked again. Finally, I put down the beads, and joined the circle next to another girl who I noticed for the first time. She had long, brown curls, and a red plaid dress exactly like mine. We smiled at each other and became instant friends.

I loved being in the kindergarten classroom, surrounded by letters and words, newsprint paper, and fat pencils. I inhaled the scent of crayons, and the clean wooden floors, and the blackboard with chalk dust creating motes in the air as the sun pierced the windows. I loved the sound of pencils sliding across paper as we practiced the alphabet in our best penmanship, of rain slashing against the panes, knowing we were safe inside, of Mrs. Winters playing the piano as we learned a Halloween song, "Tonight is the night when dead leaves fly/ like witches on switches across the sky/ When Jack the Sprite flits through the night on a moony sheen/ It's Halloween!" I loved the unusual melodies from other countries like Waltzing Matilda from Australia and Irish jingles.

I couldn't wait to learn to read. Mumma had already taught me my ABC's, so I quickly mastered the Dick and Jane readers and was placed in the high reading group. After the librarian from the public library came to school and signed us all up for library cards, reading became a fact of life.

Since I was in school all day and played outside after school, I didn't spend a lot of time with my sister and baby brother. As long as I was upstairs before dark, I could stay outside. I explored the neighborhoods around Silver Street where some of my schoolmates lived, playing outside until it was supper time.

And just as it became routine for me to play on their streets at six years old, it wasn't unusual for me to tread up and down Silver Street alone, and then cross over onto Main to stare into the shop windows. If I happened to be in front of the taxi stand, Grampie often approached me with a large bag of money. "Carry this in both hands and take it to the bank. Give it to the teller and wait for a receipt." I walked proudly to the end of Silver Street, waited for the light to change, and crossed over Main to The Federal Trust Bank. Once in the building, I was too short to reach the teller behind the big marble slab, so he got down off his stool and came around to take the money. With the receipt in hand, I hurried to bring it back to my grandfather. Sometimes Daddy gave me money and sent me on an errand to Joe's Smoke Shop to pick up the race form, or to the grocery to pick up some hamburger meat.

A wider sphere of exploration

By the time kindergarten was over and summer arrived, I had expanded my range over the city, continuing down the street to some of my favorite shops. Now I could go into Bea's Candy Kitchen by myself and choose my own candy. Turning back toward home, the smell of fried onions and popcorn lured me into Woolworth's; the shelves filled with toys and household products kept me occupied until I spent whatever change I had in my pockets. I always gravitated toward the comic book section to check out the newest Disney comics. Grampie always told me to put all my money in my piggy bank, but like Daddy, money burned a hole in my pocket until it was gone.

Most days though, there was enough going on right in front of the taxi stand. I met a number of people on the street in front of our apartment: visitors to Waterville taking taxis, Colby College students eating in the diner, and friends and clients of our upstairs neighbors, the two sisters who ran the hair salon. One day a little girl my age came to visit the two Miss B's. Lotti, their niece, was visiting from Quebec and could speak no English.

"How will we talk?" I asked them.

"You can teach her some English, and she can teach you some French."

I was proud of the fact that I knew one French phrase: Parlez vous Francais? Do you speak French? I had heard that many times when French Canadians visited Waterville.

Lottie arrived and her aunts introduced us. We sat on the steps. *"Parlez vous Francais?"* I asked proudly.

Of course she spoke French. That's all she spoke, and she let me know in rapid-fire French, with her intonation making it clear the question was a stupid one.

Not to be outdone by her tirade, I asked again, this time in English, "Do you speak French?"

She looked confused. So once again, *"Parlez vous Francais?"* And off she went, becoming increasingly frustrated with me. Finally, she stood up, stomped up the stairs, and turned around to let me have another final harangue in French that I'm sure was not very polite. That's the last I saw of Lottie. She learned no English, and I didn't add to my French.

Another stranger I met on the street was a man with a buzz cut fire-engine red head and freckles all over his face and arms. He hung out at the diner. I don't know for sure, but he might have been a Colby College student. The pool hall was behind the taxi stand, and it was not unusual for young men to eat at the diner and play pool.

He told me to call him Red. He bragged about how strong he was and said he was so strong he could lift me up with one arm. I took the challenge. Holding onto his red freckled arm with both hands, I was lifted into the air. I guess he was pretty strong. When I rode my tricycle, I pretended to run over him and he'd run away. One day I was at the end of the street, near Main Street looking in a shop window when Red sidled up beside me. "Kathy do you want to go for a walk?" he asked.

"Where?"

"Just around corner. Have you ever been to the ball field?"

"No."

"Come on. I want to show you something."

Curious, I followed.

We walked down Main Street until the shops ended at a hill covered in large bushes that went down toward the baseball field. Wooden steps led down to the parking lot in front of the baseball diamond, but instead of heading toward the ball field, he jumped off the steps into a wooded area with overgrown shrubs. "Come on. It's nice in here," he said, taking my hand as we pushed our way through the bushes. Then I began to sense his nervousness.

"I don't like it here; I want to go home now."

"We will, but first I want to ask you something. Will you take down your panties so I can see your peepee?"

"I need to go home now." Fear rose in my chest. Something was very wrong. Mumma didn't let us walk around the house without clothes. We weren't supposed to show our privates to anyone.

"Just for one minute. Will you just do it for a minute and we'll go home?"

"N-n-n-no, I want to go," I stuttered, barely breathing.

He paused, then giving up, he led the way out, "Ok, let's go, but you have to promise not to tell anyone we came to this secret place. Do you promise?"

I nodded.

Relieved to be back on the stairs and headed for home, I rushed up the street, no longer holding his hand. Before we reached the diner, he turned to leave, but not before reminding me once again.

"Remember, this is our secret. Don't tell anyone what I asked you to do, or we will both get in big trouble."

"I won't." Without looking back, I ran the rest of the way home, slowing down only when I approached the taxi stand. When I went upstairs, I immediately went to the bathroom to figure out what he wanted to see. I didn't understand what happened, only that it was wrong. I did something bad and had to keep it a secret.

I continued to explore my surroundings downtown, but now I was more wary, careful not to make friends with strangers, becoming suspicious if someone seemed too friendly. Mumma and Daddy never found out what happened that day because I kept my word and never told. I never saw Red again.

Don't Worry About A Thing

Chapter Eight
Elementary Anxieties

With summer almost over, we spent Labor Day weekend at the races as usual, but all I could think about was going to first grade after the weekend. No longer in baby grade, I would be going to school all day. I couldn't wait!

Instead of going home for lunch, like we did in kindergarten, we now ate in the cafeteria. The kitchen and lunchroom were in the school's basement, so the odors of lunch cooking floated up into the classrooms, and it wasn't pleasant. The day's menu turned my stomach before I even descended into the dungeon: chicken fricassee, American chop suey, tuna casserole, and other concoctions with unknown ingredients made my stomach recoil. The American chop suey wasn't too bad since Mumma made it at home, with macaroni and her own tomato sauce with onions, celery, and hamburger, but it didn't taste the same at school. One meal though, the absolute worst, was corned beef hash. The minute I entered the building on hash day, my stomach began flip-flopping, and I had to spend the day swallowing my spit for fear of heaving. Then at lunchtime I had to come face to face with the dish that looked and smelled like vomit.

The lunchroom monitor tried to get me to eat the horrible hash. She paced up and down alongside the tables, stopping when she noticed I hadn't touched my food. "Eat your lunch," she prodded. After a few attempts at goading me, I picked up a small forkful and put it in my mouth. I couldn't swallow it. My stomach lurched, and I glanced up at the monitor as my face went white. To her credit, she knew what was coming. "Go to the bathroom!" she ordered. I made it just in time.

That afternoon I raced home, not stopping to wave to Aunt Maria in the taxi stand as I stomped up the stairs and burst into the apartment. "I'm never going back to that school. It stinks! I quit!" I announced to Mumma.

"Why?"

"I told you. It stinks. I threw up today because it stinks. I couldn't eat the corned beef hash, and they tried to make me eat it."

"You're too young to quit. The truant officer will come to get you. You have to go."

"I don't care. I'm not going back."

"Daddy wanted you to have a hot lunch, but I'll talk to him tonight about taking your lunch."

That night when Daddy came home, I awoke to their laughter in the kitchen. "I thought she was going to say one of the other kids smelled, or the teacher's perfume stunk, but the food is making her sick," Mumma said. I brought my cheese or bologna sandwiches to school after that while many of my classmates not only ate the cafeteria food but enjoyed it.

Troubles in first grade

First grade wasn't turning out to be the best year. To make matters worse, Mrs. O, our teacher, was so strict she kept us in a constant state of dread. A matronly woman with an air of authority, she wore her gray hair in a tight bun, rarely smiled, and ran the class like a drill sergeant. Entering the classroom, we immediately were made to sit with our hands folded atop the wooden desks, feet flat on the floor. Talking or whispering was forbidden, but no one dared to make a peep anyway. Most of us, me included, were afraid to raise our hands to answer questions even when we were sure we knew the answer.

Then one day Caroline, a usually quiet student who sat in the front seat of my row, bravely dared to defy Mrs. O. She may have been tired or sick, so she put her head down on top of her arms on the desk. When Mrs. O noticed, she ordered her to sit up straight and fold her hands on the desk.

"NO!" Caroline boldly answered. Once again, she was ordered to sit up, and once again she blurted, "NO!" The room went deathly silent. All eyes followed Mrs. O as she marched from the chalkboard to her desk and picked up a ruler. Approaching Caroline's desk, she ordered, "Give me your hand." Slowly Caroline lifted her hand in front of the teacher. SMACK! Once, twice, three times, the noise of ruler hitting hand reverberated through the room making us jump with each whack. None of us dared to breathe as Caroline then put her head down on her desk and cried. Our fear of Mrs. O increased ten-fold that day.

She also spanked us. Before the year was over, most of us had had a turn as we were called up behind her desk. Standing beside her, she made us lie over her lap so she could give us a whack. Embarrassing as it was, those spankings didn't really hurt, and knowing we all got them for some small infraction, we accepted it as a fact of school. Another girl in my class was so fearful she never spoke in class. One day when the teacher singled her out by asking her a question, she threw up all over her desk. I think that girl moved away because she stopped coming to school and I knew she couldn't quit. First grade wasn't fun, but I tried to follow the rules, do my work, and stay out of trouble. I didn't bother to tell Mumma and Daddy what happened in the classroom. They never asked what we did in school. They believed the teacher was the boss, and I did too.

After school, I played with kids who lived in the neighborhoods on the route home from school. Some of them didn't go to South Grammar, but instead attended St. Francis, a Catholic school. Sometimes they couldn't come out to play because they had to study for a catechism class. I was curious about what they did there. "We say prayers and have to memorize answers to questions about God. We talk about the Ten Commandments and what happens when we die."

"What happens?" I wanted to know.

"Everybody knows that," my friend answered knowingly. "You either go to heaven, or purgatory, or to the other place, you know, H-E- double toothpicks."

"Oh." I knew about heaven and the other bad place, but I didn't understand purgatory. It didn't matter because what she told me next scared me.

"But you have to be Catholic to go to heaven, so I guess you know where you're going."

"My church doesn't say that," I replied, trying to defend myself but not knowing if that were true. Something else I needed to worry about. Since she went to a Catholic School, she was sure she would go to heaven.

Later on, when I went to Winslow with Daddy on his daily check-in with Yiayia, I walked over to Auntie Dee's apartment next door. I was still thinking about what my friend had told me and must have looked worried because Auntie Dee asked, "What's the matter?"

I was afraid to say anything, so I just shrugged, "Nothing."

"Why such a glum face then?"

"I'm going to H-E-L-L!" I spelled out.

Not expecting that response, she asked seriously, "What in the world did you do?"

I told her what my friend had said. Auntie Dee didn't only talk with her mouth and her hands, she also talked with her eyes, moving them back and forth as they flashed angrily. "That's people talking. Only God knows who goes to heaven. If you are good, that's all that matters." She pointed toward the sky, "If you're good, you go to heaven." Then her finger pointed toward the ground, "Bad, to the other place. And even if you are naughty, God forgives you." Shaking her finger back and forth in front of me, she stated. "Don't you let anyone tell you where you are going. God is the boss! Only He knows." Auntie Dee spoke with authority, and I believed her. And that was that.

Auntie Dee didn't have children right away after she married Uncle Tommy, but she loved her nieces and nephews and the feeling was mutual. But we didn't dare to misbehave. When we did something wrong, she'd raise her right hand and threaten, "Do you want the five brothers?" (and then raising her left hand) "Or the five sisters?" That's all it took. To my knowledge, none of us ever felt those "brothers" or "sisters". I half expected her to go after those kids and tell them what was what. I didn't worry so much about going to H-E-L-L after that.

But religion was confusing because everyone, even the grown-ups, seemed to have different ideas about God, which made me wonder who was right or whether God was even real at all, like Santa Claus. I knew Santa wasn't real because I pretended to be asleep when Mumma put our presents under the tree. It was all a mystery I couldn't figure out. The people at St. Mark's Episcopal Church never said bad things would happen to me, and neither did the priest's wife who came from St. George's Greek Orthodox Church. I took that as a good sign. At church I learned a new prayer, The Lord's Prayer, and liked it better than the one Mumma taught me. I used it as insurance just in case God decided he wanted to send me down below.

Chapter Nine
Up to the North Woods

Every June as soon as school let out for the year, we prepared for our annual visit to Little Grammie's in Aroostook County in northern Maine. Mumma was always excited to go. She didn't get to see her mother and other daughter very much, so she was excited to spend two whole weeks with them. Although I looked forward to playing with Joyce Ann and my cousins, when I was old enough to know what to expect, I wasn't as thrilled to be going.

We always left in the middle of the night, which created a sense of adventure. Mumma and Daddy packed us into the back of our old station wagon with blankets and pillows so we could sleep during the long drive up to Macwahoc. George and I tried to stay awake just in case we saw deer or a family of skunks or raccoons crossing the road, which inevitably happened as we drove deeper into the woods.

Grammie lived on the plantation of Macwahoc in the north woods of Maine. Maine is the only state with small populated areas called plantations. Macwahoc was originally Molunkus Plantation in the 1800s until it was later changed to Macwahoc. Smaller than a village, with only one country store, the plantation consisted of small farms and forests, and that was all.

Grammie's small frame house, set back from the road, was surrounded by woods on three sides. At night, thin metal screens on the windows were the only thing separating us from the nocturnal creatures. Situated near Molunkus stream, the area was a breeding ground for mosquitos. I dreaded the painful bites that would cover our bodies, making us look like we had the pox. Her house had a kitchen, two bedrooms, a living room, and an attic, and when we first started going to visit, the house wasn't finished. Her youngest son, my Uncle Harlan, had built the house for her. He came back from the army where he trained to be an airline mechanic and got a job working at Idlewild Airport in New York City. On vacations and holidays, he came home and worked on the house. At first the bedrooms didn't have walls, the floors were bare wood, and the outside didn't have siding. Every year when we returned something new had been added, but Grammie never did get running water or an inside bathroom.

Little Grammie, petite at five feet, looked like the typical grandmother, with gray hair pulled back in a bun and spectacles. Her benign appearance, in a flowered dress protected by clean aprons every morning, belied her cantankerous personality when she was crossed. And I was quite good at crossing her. It's not an exaggeration to say we didn't click. "Children should be seen and not heard," was her philosophy. That meant me.

I sometimes begged to go back home with Daddy, but my whining got me nowhere. "He has to work," Mumma would say. "Your cousins will be here in the morning to play with you." And that was that.

Daddy slept for a few hours until sunrise and then left us there in the woods. Georgeanna and I never heard him leave, as we were still asleep in Grammie's large white iron bed next to a window swarming with mosquitos. Macwahoc is Abnaki Indian for "wet ground" or "bog," so it was no wonder the mosquitos were carrying us off. Grammie pumped the spray tin filled with DDT ferociously around the window and bed in a futile attempt to protect us, but it did little good as they managed to get through the wire mesh to suck our blood. Inhaling the acrid smell of the DDT spray, which I got used to and kind of liked, I slept with my head under the covers to drown out the constant whining of those cussed bugs around my head.

In the morning I awoke to the stomach-grumbling aroma of bacon, eggs, and biscuits baking in her "spider", a black cast iron skillet. Those biscuits, cooked in the wood-burning oven, rose golden brown over the top of the skillet in circular rows like miniature chef's hats. But before we could eat, in the chill of early morning, Mumma hurried us down the dew-covered path to the outhouse, a two-seater with walls decorated from torn out pages of old Sears, Roebuck Catalogs. Mumma carried toilet paper from the house for us so that animals wouldn't get it when we weren't there; but sometimes when we ran out, we'd have to use the pages of the same old catalogs piled in a corner, which didn't feel too good on our behinds. We got used to it. Then we raced back to the house hoping to outrun the bears we imagined were following us. Back inside, we washed in cold water at the black kitchen sink after Mumma pumped the water from the pump outside the back door. Only then were we free to devour buttered biscuits with homemade wild strawberry jam. Breakfast was the highlight of the day.

The family gathers

It wasn't long before aunts and uncles arrived bringing our cousins to play. Uncle Vaughn, one of Mumma's brothers, always scared us, especially Georgeanna. A tall lumberman, he looked like the statue of Paul Bunyan we passed in Bangor with his overalls, flannel shirt, and huge boots. He would lumber into the house making the floors shake. Upon seeing us, he always roared out, "Well, look who's here! I'm going to throw you up in the air and let you come down alone!" Before he had a chance to grab us, George ran into the bedroom and disappeared under Grammie's bed where she stayed until he was gone. He never did throw us up in the air, but he thought scaring us was hysterical.

After breakfast, out the door we went until lunchtime. All the kids were condemned to the yard with the mosquitos, while the adults gathered around the kitchen table, drinking coffee and smoking until it was lunchtime. Even though we had been sprayed, the bugs competed for every inch of our bare skin. I could have created a dot-to-dot scene on my body, bite to bite. It wasn't long before I tired of scratching and begged to go inside. Being older, Joyce was allowed inside with the adults. Besides, she lived there. When I tried to open the screen door, it was locked. Pressing my face against the screen, I called to Mumma, "I'm tired. I'm itchy. Let me in!" Before she could answer, Grammie shouted, "Scat! Go play! You can come in at lunch time." Mumma didn't argue with her. Mumma never argued with her. Whatever Grammie said or did was law.

"No, let me in! I'm going to walk home if you won't let me in!"

"Ok, see you later. Now go on before I get the switch."

I kicked the screen, then turned around and yelled, "I'm leaving, and I'm never coming here again!" And then scooted away when I spied her coming toward me, black skillet in hand.

A while later I tried rattling the screen again. "Scat, go play!" Grammie warned.

"No, I want to come inside!" The next thing I knew, a stream of cold water came flying through the screen, covering my face and arms. She went back to get another dipperful from the water pail, but I was long gone, running down the driveway.

At lunchtime, the door was unlatched, and we dashed inside. Once again, Grammie used the spider for the homemade strawberry pie we had for dessert. I had a hard time reconciling her delicious food with her lack of kindness toward me, but I ate the sweet dessert with relish anyway. After lunch, the younger kids napped while the older ones were once again relegated to the yard.

Playing with my cousin Roberta was the best part of staying there for two weeks. We became close, and I looked forward to seeing her every summer. Since we usually went up north during strawberry season, we'd grab buckets and spend entire afternoons picking and eating wild strawberries. Sometimes we walked to her house not far down the road from Grammie's and spent the day playing in her yard, going in and out of the house anytime we wanted. We got as dirty as I've ever been while playing in the mud and making forts under the pine trees.

One hot day, when even the adults wanted to escape the summer heat, Aunt Ruby, (Roberta's mother who was married to Uncle Bob, Mumma's brother), and Mumma took all of us kids swimming in the river. We had a blast. Afterwards, back at Roberta's, Aunt Ruby gave us hot tea and chocolate cake. Like her name, she had ruby red hair, a face covered with freckles, and a roaring infectious laugh that made everyone around her join in. One day when Roberta and I were sitting inside, I asked her why Grammie was so mean. "She's not mean. Just set in her ways. She's had a hard life," she said, unconvincingly.

The trick

If it rained, we were allowed inside the house. For once I was minding my own business, quietly reading. Grammie had a bookcase in her living room filled with books that belonged to Joyce Ann and Uncle Harlan when they were younger. I read the children's books, like *Smiling Hill Farm*, and then graduated to more difficult ones. I discovered Nancy Drew in her bookcase and another book about the Dionne quintuplets that fascinated me. The quintuplets were from Canada, and they were quite a sensation when they were born, these five identical girls. The book was filled with pictures of their life that had been put on display for the world to see. I sat in Grammie's comfortable rocking chair, engrossed in the story of their lives, when she kindly asked, "Kathy, want to try something good? Here, have a bite. It tastes like candy."

Gullibly, I fell for her unaccustomed act of kindness toward me and took the small brown square that looked like a chocolate brownie, only lighter in color. I immediately realized I'd been tricked. "Uck!" I spit out the glob of yeast cake, coughing and gagging as my eyes welled with tears. I was furious, and when I get really angry, much to my dismay, I cry. Trying to keep the tears at bay, I yelled at her. "You are the meanest old lady in the whole world."

She was laughing too loud to hear me. Mumma didn't laugh, but she didn't try to help. In that moment I hated them both.

Although I liked my cousins and would miss playing with them, when my two-week forced vacation was over, I was happy to leave. Mumma always cried when she had to leave her mother and Joyce Ann, but I waited impatiently in the driveway, excited to see Daddy's car so we could go home.

Don't Worry About A Thing

Chapter Ten
Surviving Second Grade

As the long summer days turned cooler at the beginning of September, life revolved around home on Silver Street and school on Gold Street. I was excited to be going back to school, but nervous too. However, my worries of facing another mean teacher were unfounded; Mrs. M turned out to be kind and grandmotherly, or what I thought a grandmother should be. She sparkled with fancy brooches on her dresses every day, and her snow-white hair, impeccably styled, made me wonder if I had missed seeing her on a weekly visit to the Miss B's salon across the hall at home. She was a bit plump, and her make-up made her round cheeks look like soft pillows reminding me of Cinderella's fairy godmother. She was everything Mrs. O was not. Every morning as we entered the classroom, she greeted us with a welcoming smile. Second grade became stories and music and learning, all orchestrated by our loving teacher. And there was art, taught by Mrs. Ragsdale, who let us create with paints and paste and scissors.

After school activities

One afternoon, shortly after school began, Mumma asked, "Would you like to take tap and ballet lessons?" I was thrilled! I envisioned learning to dance like Annette Funicello on *The Mickey Mouse Club*. With my new leotard and tap and ballet shoes, Georgeanna and I headed down Main Street every Wednesday afternoon with our ballet bags to Miss Jeannette's Dance Studio on the second and third floors, over the shops in one of the large brick buildings. While I enjoyed ballet, I especially liked the sound of my black tap shoes on the hardwood floor as we did our shuffle ball-changes in unison, making me feel like Shirley Temple dancing with Mr. Bo Jangles.

I also became a Brownie along with some of my friends. So, on another afternoon, I walked down the residential section of Silver Street to the meetings held at Sarah's house—her mother was our leader. We had to earn different badges, some involving domestic skills, like how to make a hospital bed and how to bake. Mumma never let me help her cook because she was so afraid I'd burn myself, so my favorite was the cooking badge. Making cookies and muffins made it worthwhile putting up with some of the other more boring things we had to learn, like tying knots. What was so important about knot-tying anyway? We also learned songs, like the one that said, "Make new friends, but keep the old, one is silver and the other gold." With Mrs. M, dance lessons, and scouts, second grade was turning out to be a great year. Until it wasn't.

The pox strikes

One Monday upon arriving at school, I noticed some of my classmates were absent. On Tuesday there were more empty chairs, and by Wednesday, everyone there knew our classmates were home sick with chickenpox. On Thursday, feeling I was missing out, I lay my head on the desk, hoping Mrs. M would notice. "Are you feeling poorly?" she asked, concerned. "Yes," I replied, trying to sound sickly. Wrapping her finely manicured hands around my cheeks as she looked into my eyes, she asked again. "Are you really not feeling well?" I shamefully nodded, feeling guilty now. Taking my hand, we walked to the office where they called the diner to tell them I was on my way home. Outside in the sunshine, I skipped down Gold Street toward home. I wanted to be good, but it seemed like I couldn't help myself. God was probably watching too.

That night, I awoke scratching my itching belly and running a fever. The next day, Dr. Daviou came to the house and examined me as I lay in Mumma's big bed. I had brought chicken pox home with me, and it wasn't long before Georgeanna and Jimmy were scratching along with me.

No sooner had we all recovered then the measles made the rounds. The doctor appeared once again, and I was home for another ten days. Mumma was beside herself with all of us sick kids most of that winter, but it wasn't over yet. Mumps made the rounds as we all got swollen necks and fevers, making us cry every time we swallowed our soup.

"Jesus H Christ," Mumma cried. "What next?" It wasn't long before she got her answer.

Creepy crawlies

One cool spring morning on my way to school, I met my friend Linda in front of her house like I usually did, but this time her mother made me go inside. To my surprise, her mother said she wanted to check my head. Linda had come home with lice the previous Friday, and she wanted to see if she had gotten it from me. After picking through my head, she didn't find anything in my hair, so sent us on our way.

After school I told Mumma what happened, and after she checked my head and found nothing, she was furious. "She has a lot of nerve checking my kid's head," she fumed. "If she does anything like that again, you run home and tell me."

But I didn't escape the lice. After checking my hair every day for a week, she found some nits. Then began the daily nit-picking with me sitting in the chair crying and complaining while Mumma went through my hair with a fine tooth comb all the time warning me not to get close to the other kids.

I missed a lot of school that year, but everyone else did too, so I guess it all evened out. By May, we all looked forward to our big dance recital.

My debut

When I saw my costume for the first time, I was disappointed that I wouldn't get to wear a fancy tutu like some of the older girls, but I was somewhat mollified when I got to wear red lipstick and rouge on my cheeks. I was a tin soldier from the Nutcracker and my routine was tap. In our costumes of short red pants and jacket with tails and tall hats, we had to march on the stage, do our dance number and march back out.

Standing backstage at the Waterville Opera House, an imposing brick building constructed in the previous century, we had to wait for what seemed forever for the other acts to finish. Miss Jeannette's helpers kept us quiet. Standing still in a straight line, someone made sure our hair was under the hats, our make-up didn't get smudged, and our costumes didn't get wrinkled.

I raised my hand. A helper said, "What Kathy?"

"I have to go to the bathroom."

"Now?"

I nodded. "Can you hold it? You are about to go on soon."

I shook my head no. "Don't think about it. Just hold it. We can't take your costume all the way off and back on. You'll miss your act."

Bouncing up and down, I tried to hold it, but the next thing I knew, pee was trickling down my legs.

"That's your cue, you have to go on."

So, I did, and remembered every step of the tin soldier dance. When our backs were to the audience at the end and we bent forward at the waist, the audience erupted in laughter. The back of my red satin pants had a round dark pee stain.

If I had been a bit older, the embarrassment would probably have ended my dance career, but I went on to dance for two more years and loved every minute. I was a gypsy, a can-can dancer, and I sang *Ain't She Sweet* with my chorus line, among others, before my budding dance career was cut short.

Don't Worry About A Thing

Chapter Eleven
The Movies

Although I was sad when I had to bid goodbye to Mrs. M on the last day of second grade, I looked forward to the long summer days stretching before me. As a morning person, it wasn't unusual for me to wake up at 4:00 am when the new day broke. If the sun was shining through my dormer window, I knew I could leave the apartment early to watch the action on Silver Street and to find new ways to entertain myself.

Downtown was always a production. Delivery trucks doubled parked in the street as their drivers carried goods into the stores. Shopkeepers swept the street in front of their businesses, washed the glass windows until they sparkled, and when they placed the OPEN sign on the front door, the show began. Women appeared as if on cue, dressed in matching hats and dresses, their heels echoing on the sidewalk as they clutched their pocketbooks with an air of purpose. Inside the taxi's office, music blared from the radio as Aunt Maria answered the phone that never seemed to stop ringing. No one paid attention to me sitting on the stoop. I wondered where the shoppers came from and what they would buy today. Sometimes I felt lonely, wishing I had a playmate, but I had learned my lesson and no longer made friends with strangers. Georgeanna was still too young to come outside and play with me, and Jimmy was just a baby, so I sat and waited. What would the day bring?

Daddy might go to Yiayia's for the obligatory five-minute visit, or Aunt Maria might take me for a ride in the taxi, or maybe someone would show up to visit with Mumma upstairs. I had outgrown my tricycle, and when I didn't have chalk, I played imaginary hopscotch using the cracks in the sidewalk. Swinging my jump rope, I tried to be careful not to lasso a customer coming out of the taxi stand. At least once a day, I begged Daddy to let me play the pinball machine in the diner.

"What can I do?" I asked Aunt Maria when I was bored, hoping she'd suggest something fun.

"Go read some magazines," she said, waving me toward the small waiting room behind her with its stand filled with old battered magazines and newspapers, all grown-up ones, like *Photoplay*. Nothing interesting. But I sat and thumbed through the latest squabble between Elizabeth Taylor and Eddie Fisher anyway. I could hear the sound of pool balls smacking the corner pockets of the tables in the poolroom down the hall behind Aunt Maria's office.

The cash register ka-chinked as the manager, Foxie, a short man with a butch haircut, took money for the games. Someone was racking balls and getting ready for a new game of pool. I could picture two men in baggy pants, chalking their cue sticks while puffing on Pall Malls. The sign over the poolroom read, NO MINORS ALLOWED, which meant no kids, but I had been in there before. Sometimes Daddy gave me a hamburger or hotdog to deliver to someone playing pool. Sometimes, on a Sunday morning, when the pool hall was closed, Grampie took Tony, my special-needs uncle, to play pool and I played with him too. Tony was pretty good at pool, and I learned how to play.

Leaving the waiting room, I ambled back outside. Daddy knocked on the window and motioned me inside. "Here," he said, handing me money. "Go next door and buy five pounds of hamburg."

"Can I keep the change?" I always asked.

"Never mind about that. Hurry up and come right back."

I skipped to the grocery, opening the door to see Mr. Charles behind the counter in a large white apron that was covered in blood. As I watched him grind the beef, he looked like he'd been in a fight and lost. In spite of his dirty apron, the rest of the store looked clean and well organized, with boxes of Wheaties, jars of peanut butter and jelly, and cans of vegetables arranged neatly along the shelves. The cereals were on the top shelf. I stared as Mr. Charles lifted a long stick with a hook on the end that latched onto a cereal box, grabbing it as it flew off the shelf. He never missed.

"Hello, little one, you need to keep your fingers and face off my clean windows," he warned. Then in a softer voice, "What can I do for you?"

"Five pounds of hamburg please," I said, inhaling the scent of the pickles in the barrel in front of the counter and watching Mr.Charles grind the beef and wrap it up in white meat paper.

"Anything else I can do for you?"

"Do I have any change?" I asked as I handed him the dollars.

"Here you go," handing me thirty-five cents.

"Can I have two peanut butter cups please?"

Putting the candy bars and change in my pockets, I took the meat back to Daddy and went to sit in the doorway at the foot of the stairs to eat my candy bars. Unwrapping one of the peanut butter cups, I took bites of the chocolate in a circle until I had eaten a ring of chocolate. Then I ate the chocolate on top, leaving the peanut butter center on the chocolate base, which quickly disappeared all at once, a delicious mouthful of peanut butter and chocolate. Soon the other wrapper was slowly being shed and the ritual repeated.

When the diner wasn't busy, I could sit on one of the stools inside, twirling until I got dizzy. I watched Daddy work behind the grill, flipping burgers. When he let me, I played the pinball machine that stood against the back wall. But as soon as the diner filled with the lunch crowd, Daddy shooed me outside again. I walked toward the State Theatre, a tall brick building that stood beside the diner. Staring at the posters behind the glass cases that were changed frequently, I wondered what it would be like to go to the movies.

Always looking for new ways to make money, Grampie bought a popcorn machine, a huge blue metal boxlike container that he put in front of the diner so that moviegoers waiting in line could buy a bag of fresh popcorn. He bought a peanut roaster too, and the smells of peanut and popcorn permeated Silver Street.

When he cleaned the popcorn machine, he handed me the tray of un-popped kernels to feed the pigeons. I threw the kernels beside the curb between the parked cars and watched as the pigeons swooped down all at once from the tops of buildings and pecked at the corn until the street was clean again. I envied those birds, able to fly from the eaves, until one night I had dreams of flying. Fearful at first, I jumped from the tops of the buildings, just like the pigeons, and after the initial fear dissipated, I flew around the town, arms outstretched, looking down at the buildings and people, all going somewhere, just like the birds. Those were only dreams though, for in real life, my world was confined to the pavement of Silver Street.

Then I discovered the movies, which would take me places I could never even have imagined.

While Mumma helped in the diner, cutting vegetables for Daddy's homemade chicken, lentil, and bean soups, Georgeanna and Jimmy napped upstairs. One day, after getting underfoot one too many times, I got a handful of change from Daddy who told me to go to the movies. "Give the money to the ticket taker," he instructed. "Go in and find a seat and watch the movie." I have no idea if Daddy knew what was playing that day.

Following his instructions, I grasped the movie ticket in my hand, and made my way into the dimly lit theatre to an aisle seat not far from the exit door, just in case I wanted to make a quick exit. I waited, and before long the theatre went black. A light appeared on the stage as the red curtain parted and music began to play, sending shivers up my spine. I sat through the advertisements, short subjects, and cartoons, which were similar to TV only louder and bigger on the movie screen. Some of the kids in the audience laughed uproariously at the antics of Tom and Jerry and Popeye, but I was disappointed until I realized the cartoons were just what they called "short subjects" before the real movie began. Then the red curtains closed and instantly re-opened. Elvis Presley appeared on a large black and white screen in a movie called *Love Me Tender*.

I watched spellbound as the war story unfolds. The story is complicated. Elvis, a soldier, falls in love with his brother's girlfriend. But his brother is killed in the war, and even though his girlfriend does not love Elvis, she marries him. But his brother is not dead after all! He comes home from the war; they get in a fight and Elvis dies. Before he dies, he sings that sad song, *Love Me Tender*, and I can hear the audience sniffling in their hankies. Leaving the theatre with red eyes, crushed by the finality of death, I decided I wasn't ever going back.

But I was hooked. The movies became a welcome escape, both during the summer and after school when I had nothing else to do. With my bag of popcorn, I was set for at least two hours (or more if it was a double feature). This was before snacks were sold in the theatre, and when the owners realized how much money my grandfather was making, they opened up their own concession stand, which put a dent in the diner's earnings.

Spending time in the theatre, the hours evaporated as I identified with characters on the screen. I cried. A lot. I bawled more at the movies than I did in real life, and I sobbed even more profusely at some of the happy endings. Everything about them: the scenery, the characters, the music, the drama, seemed all more real in some ways than my own life on Silver Street.

Mumma and Daddy never paid attention to what was playing or considered whether the movie might not be appropriate for a child, so I saw whatever happened to be playing that week. I had definite preferences. Comedies were not my favorite. As the audience roared with laughter at Jerry Lewis, I thought he was silly. The Three Stooges were dumb, with Moe, Larry, and Curly constantly punching each other. Disney movies were fine, but I cried when Bambi's mother got killed, and when Cinderella got her dress torn off by the mean stepsisters, and then when she drove off in the coach with her prince to live happily ever after, I cried again. I was somewhat afraid of dogs, but the death of Old Yeller turned on the water works. And if I went into a Shirley Temple movie, I knew I'd be bawling at the beginning, middle, and end. I felt sorry for her because she was an orphan, but she always found a way to survive.

Best of all were the real-life movie dramas. I was transfixed by Patty Duke in *The Miracle Worker*, and I loved Debbie Reynolds in *Tammy* and Sandra Dee in *Gidget*, but my favorite actress was Hayley Mills. I saw *Pollyanna* and *The Parent Trap* so many times that Hayley Mills became my alter ego. I wanted to be her. I thought I was her. When I went to my friend's house to play, I insisted we act out the movies as I mimicked her English accent. Bossy by nature, no one else was allowed to play Hayley Mills. Knowing the songs and dialog by heart, I told my friends what to say. Secretly I longed to be a movie star one day.

And I wanted to travel to all the places I saw on the large screen, worlds I vowed I would visit someday. Even though Westerns were not my favorite, Roy Rogers and Dale Evans and The Lone Ranger transported me to the old West where I could pretend to ride horses. After watching *Rome Adventure* with Suzanne Pleshette and Troy Donahue, I decided I would go to Italy one day. I couldn't wait to grow up and go out into the world. Many years later in midlife, I did travel to Italy and threw coins in the Trevi Fountain, just like in the movie.

The following summer Georgeanna was only five, but Mumma and Daddy said she was old enough to go to the movies with me, so we spent many days at the State Theatre. Even though she was younger than I was when I started going, she loved the movies as much as I did. George even developed a love of horror movies, unlike me, whose horror show days ended after going to *Psycho* with a group of school friends when I was thirteen. Traumatized, I left the theatre that day and for years I never took a shower unless someone was in the house.

But before that frightening *Psycho* experience, other creatures kept us on the edge of our seats. I don't remember George, who shared a bedroom with me, ever waking up from bad dreams even though she was younger. But after trembling through *The Blob*, *The Night of the Living Dead* and other terrifying zombie movies, I would wake up screaming after being chased by the monsters in my dreams. Even though we knew we'd be scared silly, we couldn't stop ourselves from going.

The State Theatre was close to the diner, but it wasn't the only movie theatre in town. The Opera

House, a huge nineteenth century building in the center of town where my dance recitals were held every May, also had a movie theatre that played classic film noir horror shows with major actors and actresses, such as Susan Hayward, in *I Want to Live*. She died in the gas chamber at the end. That show stayed with me for months. I had no idea about the concept of capital punishment, but the idea that it was okay for the people in power to kill someone like that shocked me.

While I had outgrown my nightmares about my parents dying behind the stove, it was the low budget, B film noir genre where the fiendish monster made its second appearance in my life. The setting in these movies changed, but the theme was always the same. The women characters were punished for some wrongdoing. The main character, however, was not human, but a torture device, a large black, steam-and-smoke-emitting stove, the weapon of choice for the sadistic torturers. Whatever the scenario at the beginning of the movie, the outcome was always the same. It might be a housemother who punished the girls in the reform school for some minor infraction, or it might be a warden in a women's prison, or even the dean at a fancy girls' school. Watching the scene as wood was shoved under the burners, we could imagine the intense heat of the fire as the frightened women were forced toward its hissing frame. The evil housemother or warden or dean would then thrust the victim's hand on the burner, holding it down as she screamed in pain. The combination of evil humanity and crackling, spitting monster was enough to chase many moviegoers out of the theatre.

Not us. George and I sat through those horrors. We screamed in terror, hid our faces in our sweaters, and grabbed each other for dear life. At the end, we left the theatre, squinting in the bright sunlight, thankful for our tame and uneventful lives.

Chapter Twelve
Who Am I?

I was now eight years old and summer was coming to an end. I liked the dog days of August, the hot nights sleeping on sheets with only the heat for a blanket, and the occasional breeze from the open window. Going to the races in August meant rides and animals and cotton candy and candy apples because the fair was in town. Georgeanna and I left Mumma and Daddy by the track and disappeared for hours, spending most of the time looking at the animals and eating junk food until our money ran out, only going back to beg for more.

By the end of the month, my anticipation of the new school year was tinged with anxiety, because by now I understood that feast or famine was our normal way of life. If Daddy won at the races, everything was fine, but if he lost and there was no money left, we'd have to do without things. I hounded Mumma every day about when we would be getting new school clothes. Her answer was always the same, "We'll get them when we get them." No help for a worrier. If the timing was right, and Daddy won at the track, we went school-clothes shopping; other times I didn't know if I'd get anything new. Mumma didn't think it was a big deal because when she was young, her clothes were homemade hand-me-downs from her older sister. "We'll make do," she said, trying to console me while my whining fell on deaf ears.

Third grade

Back in school the day after Labor Day, with my new school dress and my worries abated for the time, I looked forward to third grade. I couldn't wait to be back in my dance classes. I missed Miss Jeannette, and this was the year I'd cross the bridge and become a Girl Scout.

I always tried to do my best because I enjoyed learning, but in third grade I experienced the thrill of winning for the first time. When Daddy won at the races, he would jump up and down and do the Greek dance with arms flying in the air like he was on top of the world. Now I understood why.

The contest

We had a penmanship contest in class, and the student with the best penmanship got a certificate. I wanted to win that certificate more than anything. We were given special newsprint penmanship paper and all the letters had to be placed meticulously on the page, curved at the same angle. If one was off, you could tell right away. I practiced at home and at school to make the best formed letters exactly the way the workbook showed us. F's, J's, and K's gave me a hard time even though my name began with K and I wrote it every day; but I kept trying, and after many erasures and torn paper, I was happy with the results.

On the day of the contest, we placed our numbers on the back of our papers so that no one could vote for his or her friend. We all took turns judging the class. Mrs. P announced the winner, and it was me! Walking to the front of the class to receive my certificate, I blushed with pride as the class clapped politely.

Back at my desk, my pride quickly turned to shame when Mrs. P glared at me over her glasses with an air of superiority and asked, "Kathy, is your family a part of the negroid race?" I was silent as all my classmates stared at me. I knew what a negro was of course, but living in central Maine, where there were only white people, we had no contact with children of other colors. I wasn't sure what a race was, but her manner and tone made it apparent it wasn't a good thing: "Members of the negroid race have noses like yours, so I thought maybe you were partly Negro."

I knew then that Mrs. P didn't like me, but I didn't understand why. I knew from the movies that black people were not bad. Shirley Temple had black friends in some of her movies. And I loved *The Little Rascals*. I also knew from watching the news on TV that people who lived far away turned their hoses on black people. One day, sitting on Daddy's lap, I watched as policemen hit black people with sticks. "Why are they doing that?" I asked. "Because they want to go to white schools and eat in white restaurants," he said. "Why can't they?" I asked. He shook his head, not wanting to explain. "I don't know,

Katura," he answered sadly. "I don't know." I felt bad.

Feeling I had to defend myself, I remembered what my Greek aunts always told me, and I don't know how I had the courage to speak up. But I stared back at Mrs. P and in a quiet but as clear a voice as I could muster, I proudly stated, "No, my family is Greek!" And that was that! But that incident was a defining moment for me. For the first time I understood that people might not like me, or others, because of the way we looked.

I wondered if other people I knew thought I looked different. At home, Auntie Dee always talked about how I should be proud to be Greek. She made me believe we were lucky to be born Greek. Now I wasn't so sure. Other people didn't think so. I knew already I wasn't pretty because Mumma's family always said I was too skinny, and now my teacher thought I looked different. That afternoon when I got home, I looked in the bathroom mirror to see what Mrs. P had seen, and for the first time I really noticed how I looked. My face, small and oval, was framed by wispy short dirty-blond hair, and two large brown eyes peered into the glass. Staring at my mouth, set in a straight line, I gazed upward and there it was: a nose I'd never paid attention to before, a nose that did seem large in proportion to my other features, even with my big brown eyes.

Feeling deflated, I later confided what happened to Auntie Dee, and when I finished, I stomped my foot angrily, saying, "I wish I was French like my friends at school." She looked at me in horror and once again made it clear that we were privileged to be Greek, as if our family was responsible for everything great in the world. "You don't know what you are talking about and neither does that teacher of yours," she said firmly. "You are Greek! You must be proud of your heritage. If it weren't for us Greeks, there would be no democracy all these French people are living in. Everything comes from the Greeks, science, mathematics, you name it, Greeks did it! And don't you ever forget it!" Her lectures on Greek pride always made me feel good. Maybe there was something special about us. "And there's nothing wrong with the way you look!" she added as an afterthought. After Auntie's lecture, whenever I felt less-than, I tried to remember to be proud of the fact I was Greek.

Mrs. P, on the other hand, never made it through the school year; she had a nervous breakdown.

Despite Auntie Dee's attempt to make things better, I couldn't help feeling I was different, that my family was different. I felt like an outsider who wanted to fit in. The incident upset me for another reason. I had placed teachers on a pedestal, right up there with God. They knew everything, didn't they? If my teacher didn't like me, what was wrong with me? I decided I had to prove myself, to show others I was just as good, and the only way I knew how to do that was by doing well in school. It was many years before I realized that teachers were human, like everyone else.

Longing to fit in

No matter how much I wanted to fit in, something always happened to expose me. Nothing made me feel more like an outsider than when the time came to get the polio vaccine. Daddy and Mumma rarely came to school, and secretly I was glad. The other fathers who came to our classroom were dressed in bankers' or doctors' clothes, looking stylish in their suits and bowties. I thought Daddy was handsome; his smile lit up his face and never failed to turn a bad day around, but unlike the other dads, the only time I saw Daddy dressed up was at a wedding or the few times he went to church for a special event. At five feet, he always wore baggy black pants that were too loose for his wiry frame, with the cuffs dragging on the ground, frayed and dirty from the floor of the diner. His white shirt was clean but covered with a grease-splattered apron. And although I was used to his Greek accent, I was afraid other people would see how different we were.

On that particular day, the entire class lined up in single file and marched to the nurse's office, where we would be getting the polio vaccine. I was nervous. When I brought the permission slip home for Daddy to sign, he had angrily crumpled it up and threw it in the trash. "You are NOT getting that poison!" he yelled as if it were my fault. "What is that school trying to do, kill you? Giving you the polio?" And then a tirade of swearing in Greek.

Standing nervously in line, I wondered what would happen when it was my turn. The girl in front of me opened her mouth and the nurse placed a sugar cube on her tongue. When my turn came the nurse couldn't find the paperwork. "Did you bring the permission form back?" she asked. "No," I answered shyly, not wanting to admit what happened. "Stand to the side," she ordered, and continued administering the cubes.

The secretary called Daddy, and to my dismay, he appeared in the doorway so fast he must have flown down Silver Street. He didn't even stop to take off his dirty apron. "What's going on?" he demanded. When he was told they had not received the form, he exploded. "Of course not! She's not getting that polio," in his Greek accent. The nurse tried to explain the importance of getting innoculated, but it was no use. He wouldn't listen. "Well, she's not; I don't want you to ever give her that poison!" And he left as quickly as he had arrived. I wanted to disappear. My teacher took me by the hand and walked me back to the classroom where I sat alone, waiting for the others to march back in single file.

Searching for answers

In Waterville, we were one of a handful of Greek families, and most of us were related. Unlike the French Canadians and smaller enclaves of Lebanese, Jewish, and Scotch-Irish families, I had no ethnic neighborhood that characterized an extension of the family. In fact, living downtown, I had no neighborhood at all.

Just like when I was small and had that feeling of homesickness in my own home, at school I didn't know where I belonged. Sometimes my fighting spirit kicked in, and I was good at defending my identity and proud of my Greek roots, but at other times, I tried to shrink until I was invisible. Because, in reality I wasn't completely Greek either, but only half Greek. So, who was I?

Still, I could escape by going to the movies and reading my small but growing pile of paperback books I bought through the school scholastic readers. One of my favorites was a book titled, *A Room for Cathy* where a little girl my age finally gets her own room. I could pretend that Cathy was me. My reading life expanded even further that year when our class had a visitor from the Waterville Public Library. The librarian gave us cards with our names on them and told us we could come to the library anytime it was open and take home a book. We could keep the book for two weeks and when we returned it, we could get others. The library was on Pleasant Street, which was not far from Silver, so I could walk there any time, and I did, often.

The library as refuge

The first time I went there was intimidating. The imposing three-story red brick building had a tower on one end, making it look like a castle. I climbed the steps and pulled the thick wooden door open. Now what would I do? Looking around, I saw only a reading room with magazines and newspapers. The tall ceiling and the silence almost made me turn around and run back out the door. Where were the kids' books? Before I could escape, the librarian noticed me and motioned me over to the desk. "The children's books are down those stairs," she said, pointing. "When you find a book, take it to the desk down there and show the lady your card so you can take it home." I did as I was told and was soon in possession of my first library book. I left the library, feeling proud and grown up. From then on, I was rarely without a book, or a place where I could go, like the movies, where I didn't have to worry about who I was or where I fit in the world.

Don't Worry About A Thing

Chapter Thirteen
Free-ranging Around Town

I had already been taking Georgeanna to the movies with me, when one day Mumma informed me, "Georgeanna is big enough to go out and play with you; you're old enough to watch her. Keep her with you and make sure she doesn't get hurt."

"Do I have to?" I whined. "She can't run as fast as the rest of us. I'll have to stay behind with her. What if she falls down and cries and can't breathe?"

"She's outgrown that now. And she's old enough to play outside with you if you watch her."

"No!" I insisted. "I'm not taking her."

"If you want to go out to play, you'll take her with you, or you can stay home."

I knew it was no use arguing. I'd have to make sure nothing happened to Georgie. The earlier incident in the woods taught me to be on my guard, to be wary of strange men, and to trust my instincts when I sensed something was not right. I now felt the responsibility of watching my sister because I knew there were people out there who might do bad things. I didn't tell Mumma the real reason I didn't want to take her.

After listening to strict instructions to always keep my eye on my sister, off we went. Leaving the pavement of Silver Street, we trudged down the steep hill into the South End where many of my school friends lived in this working-class neighborhood of three or four streets with small capes, duplex apartments, and tenements. The fathers were mostly mill workers, while the mothers stayed home with the kids. Because we didn't have a yard, George and I were the outsiders who came to the door to see if our friends wanted to come out to play, and then we'd spend hours in their yards playing house and creating plays based on the movies we had seen. At school we played with our hula hoops, jump rope, marbles, and hopscotch, and after school we continued with the same games.

Georgie was happy to tag along, and after I got over my initial reluctance about taking her with me, it wasn't so bad having her there after all. Being four years my junior, she was still in diapers when I was already in school, so we had lived mostly separate lives. Now we were together almost every day, and she turned out to be a good companion. She never fussed when I told her what to do, and no matter whether I was right or wrong when we got into arguments with friends, she always took my side. She looked up to me even when I knew I was not worthy of admiration. When I was a show-off and bragged that I was getting something I wanted—but knew it would never happen—she went along with whatever I said. When I got mad at my friends and told them I was never going to play with them again because they would not do what I told them to, she got angry too. She wasn't show-offish or bossy, and was never mean to anyone, but when I was all those things, she still stood by me.

Baby Jimmy

George was close to Jimmy too, more so than I was. He was a baby when I started school, so I don't remember a lot about his early years. I remember his early morning routine, when he would wake up and immediately jump up and down in his crib, singing, his soggy diaper falling down around his knees until he managed to jump out of the diaper altogether, making him naked from the waist down. That didn't bother him at all. Holding onto the railing, he jumped higher and higher as the singing got louder and louder. In the kitchen fixing breakfast, Mumma always had a smile on her face as we listened to his made-up songs. When Jimmy got a new toy, he played with it only as long as it took him to take it apart. Once it was broken, he never could put it back together, so it was ruined.

Some days George stayed home with Jimmy while I went out to play, but more often than not, she followed me outside. Every day was a new adventure. Leaving the house in the morning, we left the sidewalk at the end of our block and wandered down the steep hill to Kennebec Street to see if anyone wanted to come out. After spending hours losing our bags of marbles in the gravel driveways, jumping rope, building forts in the yard, and having pretend tea parties on the lawn, we'd hear Mumma at the top of the hill at noontime calling us to come home for dinner and later in the day she did the same at suppertime. One of Mumma's rules was to never go into our friends' houses because we would not hear her when she called us home. George was always more than ready to eat, but I was never hungry, and tried to ignore

Mumma's calls, lagging behind until the last minute when I knew I had to go.

One day we discovered a shortcut to the bottom of the hill. Next to the State Theatre was a beer joint with an alley separating the two buildings. When we walked through the narrow alley, we could touch both buildings with our outstretched arms. It was a place that smelled like stale alcohol, cigarettes, and urine. One day, taking a deep breath and holding it, we raced through the dark passageway, me leading the way until we were in back of the beer joint, only to stop short when I spied a drunk man with his back to us peeing in the bushes. He heard us and turned, weaving toward us. "Run!" I yelled to George as we bolted back through the alley, our hearts pumping. We took the long way around after that.

Laughter and tears

Not far from the house where my friend Nancy lived, a hill covered in long grass sloped down toward the little league field. This was the same area with bushes along one side of the hill where my "secret" had occurred. Avoiding the bushes, George and I were collecting rocks at the foot of the hill one afternoon when I spotted a cardboard box someone had discarded. It was empty. I thought, What if we got in the box and slid down the hill? The hill was steep enough and the grass long enough that this worked. Sliding on top of the slippery grass, we tumbled out at the bottom, screaming with laughter. Over and over again we went down the hill. It wasn't long before some other kids joined us, and we shared our box until it eventually fell apart. The next day we returned with another one that Daddy gave us, and more kids arrived. That continued for a number of days until the hill was filled with kids sliding on cardboard boxes. Sometimes we went so fast we slid off the cardboard and continued on our backsides. Eventually, the grass all but disappeared until mostly dirt and rocks remained, and sliding became more painful. Finally, our new game ended on the day I went home with holes in my pants and rocks stuck in my behind. I lay across Mumma's lap while she put Vaseline on my bottom and pulled out little rocks with tweezers, trying to keep me still as I screamed in pain. "Jesus H. Christ, didn't you feel the rocks scraping into you?" she asked. With Band-Aids covering my behind, I couldn't sit down for a few weeks without pain, and that was the end of our sliding game.

At the end of the summer there was a lobster festival in downtown Waterville, put on by a local service organization. Castonguay Square, in the center of town, was covered with tables and chairs, and giant pots of water boiled for the thousands of unsuspecting lobsters. The whole town smelled of cooking lobsters, corn on the cob, potatoes, and steamed clams. Butter was melted and rolls were heated and put on the tables. My parents and grandparents didn't attend, since they worked every day—someone always needed a taxi or a quick bite to eat. Curious to find out what was going on, George and I decided to hang around the square and watch the celebration.

We ambled through the crowd, gaping as people with lobster bibs around their necks cracked open their lobsters with nut crackers, juice squirting everywhere. The only time I had ever tasted lobster was one weekend when we all went to Belfast to the lobster pound with Yiayia and Grampie and had a picnic overlooking the ocean. I tasted a tiny piece of lobster meat but was happy to have my hotdog and potato chips. Even though we didn't normally eat lobster—they looked creepy, like giant bugs with all those legs—our mouths watered at the smells. Then we noticed a group of kids who, like us, were watching. They must have lived in a different part of town because I had never seen them at my school.

We watched as volunteers cleaned off the tables placing large trash bags of lobster shells and leftovers in the alley. Following the kids, Georgie and I stared as the kids opened the bags and rummaged for leftover rolls, pieces of lobster left in the shell, or potatoes. We sat with them, and they shared the leftover food with us. Up until this point, I didn't know what it was like to be hungry, so this seemed to be a game even though I knew we were being naughty. (A few years later, when I too experienced real hunger, I realized how those kids felt that day. It wasn't a game, but survival.) Back at home, we never told Mumma and Daddy what we had done, and if we smelled like lobster that night as we took our baths, they never questioned us.

Back to the fair

One day Grampie and Yiayia decided to take the grandchildren to the Windsor Fair. Since I was the oldest, I was responsible for watching over three of my cousins and my brother and sister while our grandparents bet on the races. The six of us explored the fairgrounds, spending most of our time at the animal exhibits.

We made our way to the cow barn just as a giant bull stormed out of his stall and came running around the corner right in the path of my little cousin Dino. Without thinking, I grabbed his shirt and pushed him out of the way just in time as the farmers chased down their wayward livestock. Jesus H. Christ! I thought to myself, shaking now that the danger was over. That was a close call. I didn't tell Yiayia and Grampie; little Dino was Yiayia's favorite and if anything happened to him, I would be in big trouble.

A confrontation

One of my best friends, Linda, had an older brother, Dan, who was a bully. Although Linda and I got along well, we argued a lot too. Sometimes I would stomp off home, and sometimes she'd run inside and slam the door.

One day, after a fight, Dan rushed up to me, grabbed me by my shirt like cowboys did in movie fights, and slammed me up against the garage door. He told me to go home and never come back to the neighborhood again. I was afraid, but I looked into his eyes and said, "You can't do anything to me." To my surprise, he let me go. As I left for home, I glanced back at Linda, and now that the encounter was over, my body shook. To cover my fear, I pretended to laugh. A few days later, Linda and I were playing again as if nothing had happened. While Dan often got into fights at school, that was the only time he bothered me. I learned a lesson that day: Bullies were just scaredy cats.

Fire danger

In the fall, Linda's neighborhood smelled of burning leaves, the smoke so strong our eyes stung. First the leaves were raked into huge piles on the side of the road and before the piles were lit, we jumped off the fence into the piles, covering ourselves with the multi-colored leaves. One kid swung a long rope around and around over his head like a lasso, pretending to be a cowboy. His rope slashed through the fire and caught the flame, but he didn't stop waving the fiery lasso. Staring in horror, I watched as the rope whacked George in the head and her hair started singeing. Before she even knew what happened, and without thinking, I took off my sweater and wrapped it around her head before her hair burst into flames. She didn't cry, but I was scared that I'd get a licking if we went home with burned hair. I think because her hair was in two tight braids, we escaped that potential disaster.

Big trouble for Kathy

Daddy and Mumma let us roam the neighborhoods freely to play with friends, but if we were invited to dinner or to play inside, Daddy always said no. We had to go home for dinner, and after dinner we could play until supper, but if we were hungry or had to go to the bathroom, we either had to run home or pee in the bushes behind the houses in the woods. And we always had to be within hearing distance if Mumma called us home.

I accepted Daddy's rule, but one autumn day, when Linda's mother asked if I'd like to go to Linda's grandparents' farm in the country for a harvest cookout, I didn't think twice about breaking that rule. I knew Daddy wouldn't let me go. George wasn't with me that day, or I wouldn't have been able to pull it off. I pretended to run home and ask Daddy if I could go. My conscience was strong when it came to stealing, but lying didn't seem to bother me all that much. I knew Dan would be there, but I really wanted to visit the farm. I raced back to Linda's and told her mother that Daddy said yes. I was excited to visit a real farm with animals.

The afternoon was everything I thought it would be. We rode on tractors and watched as the corn was harvested. We jumped in piles of hay and helped feed the animals. As the afternoon wore on, everyone pitched in to build a giant bonfire. At sunset, the fire was lit, and we roasted corn on the cob and hotdogs.

It wasn't until dusk that I began to get nervous. I knew Mumma and Daddy didn't know where I was, and I always had to be home before dark. I imagined Mumma calling for me at the top of the hill and getting no response. As day turned to night and the fire burned brighter, we played hide and seek in the dark, but by then my heart wasn't in it. I knew I should be going home, but how? I asked Linda's mother if we were leaving soon but got no answer. The later it became, the more I worried. With a sinking feeling, I knew I was going to get it when I got home.

Finally, around ten o'clock, we piled into the station wagon and thirty minutes later, we pulled up in front of the diner to see police cars parked in front. Mumma and Daddy were sitting on the bottom steps that led to our apartment. Mumma's face looked white as a sheet, and her eyes were red. Daddy sat with his head in his hands, looking like he was going to be sick. Policemen were walking up and down the street.

When I hopped out of the car, Mumma and Daddy and the policemen rushed toward us. "Where have you been?" Daddy yelled. I had never seen him so angry. Linda's mother explained how I was supposed to run home to get permission. I admitted to lying. Daddy grabbed my arm and pushed me up the stairs, warming my behind along the way.

Later when everyone went home, Mumma came into my bedroom. "What made you go off like that without telling us?" she asked.

"Daddy would never have let me go. I had to visit the farm, and I knew he would say no," I sobbed. Although I never knew why Daddy never let me go anywhere with friends, or eat with them, he changed after that night; and when I was in junior high, he let me go to sleepovers at my girlfriends' houses. But I still couldn't go to boy/girl parties until I was in high school.

Mumma and Daddy were glad to send me off to school the following Monday. Before leaving the house, Mumma said, "Come straight home today. I don't want you going anywhere except to school for a while."

Back to school

My fourth grade classroom was on the second floor of South Grammar because the fourth and fifth graders were the big kids of the school. Mrs. R, a tall, stately woman, was the wife of the police chief of Waterville and liked to warn us about undertaking a life of crime. "Obey the laws," she warned, "you don't want the police to come to your house." I didn't tell her that the police had already came to my house when I went to the farm, but she probably knew that. Maybe she was talking about me in her warnings. She was also interested in teaching us manners and describing her home in the Melchor, an apartment building next to the fire station and library. She was not a mean teacher, but not a grandmotherly figure like Mrs. M either. I didn't want to get into trouble with her and have her husband come after me.

Halloween

Because Mrs.R talked so much about her apartment building—a structure I had barely noticed before even though I went by it regularly on my way to the library—I decided on Halloween I would go trick-or-treating there. After rushing through my friends' neighborhoods with Georgie, I dropped her off at home and rushed to the Melchor, sure I would get the best candy. My idea didn't work out so well. I discovered lots of old people lived in that building. They gave out popcorn and apples instead of candy.

I didn't know which apartment belonged to Mrs. R until she answered the door. I had my Casper the ghost mask on, but she recognized me anyway. "What are you doing here, Kathy?" she asked in a brusque tone. "Trick or Treat," I mumbled incoherently. "What? It's too late for children to be out in the streets," she said, grudgingly placing a lollipop in my half-filled pillowcase. And as I turned to leave she said, "You know Halloween isn't a real holiday. Now head on home." I walked down the hallway with as much dignity as I could muster as she stood in the doorway watching me. Once down the stairs, I exited the building with relief, and hurried home, afraid she would follow me. Because of my greed, I got less candy that year.

Winter arrives

As the days grew shorter and colder, we knew it wouldn't be long before it snowed. Now that we were older, we didn't have to spend most of the winter indoors. I still have a picture of me on Mumma's bed when I was two, surrounded by dolls, but I was never attached to any of them the way I was to the sled I received the Christmas I was nine. I started asking for one after the first snow, but I had to wait until Christmas. In the meantime, I went sledding with my friends, or used a piece of cardboard, like we had done in the summer. Cardboard didn't fare as well in the wet snow, though.

The hill that led to the South End was perfect for sledding. It was so steep that after a major snowstorm, the road would be closed, which meant it was open for sledding to any kid within walking distance. On the right side, going down, was a sidewalk, with houses lining the road. On the other side was an area of dense brush and shrubs filled with burdock and thorny nettles which were deceptively covered when it snowed. It was land that no one seemed to want, and we avoided it too. Speeding down on our sleds, we tried to steer straight ahead onto Kennebec Street.

As soon as the snow stopped, kids poured out of their houses with sleds, toboggans, saucers, garbage can lids, and large pieces of cardboard. One Saturday morning, after bundling into my zip-up snowsuit, mittens, and hat, I rushed to the hill. As I raced down Silver Street, screams of fear and laughter made me plow even faster through the knee-deep snow that hadn't yet been shoveled by the merchants in front of their stores. Mr. Charles, the grocer, asked me where I was going so fast. "To the hill!" I yelled with anticipation. When I arrived, Nancy and her brother Joey on their toboggan called to me: "Jump on!" We screamed as Joey steered toward the bumps at the bottom, making us airborne. Landing in a snowdrift on the side of the road with a face full of snow, we laughed and did it all again. Struggling up the hill was not easy; we had to walk on the sidewalk to steer clear of sleds, but the sidewalks would take most of the day to shovel, so we had to trudge through deep snow, making paths as we went. When we got thirsty or hungry, we ate snow. We didn't think of going inside to eat or to get dry mittens until we were starving, or our hands were numb.

The new sled

The first day after Christmas that the hill was open for sledding, I was there with my new shiny Speedaway. It wasn't a big one, but when I lay flat, only my feet dangled off the edge. Taking a running start and flopping onto the sled on my stomach, off I flew, the sled runners whooshing on the packed snow. Sometimes I'd run into someone, and we'd both spill into a snowbank. Sometimes, a kid would fly into the burdock patch and emerge with scratches and burrs. When we made it to the bottom without incident, we had to hop off our sleds immediately or get smashed into by a kid coming from behind. We all had minor injuries, bumps, and bruises, but a few had real accidents, broken arms or legs. I pitied all the kids who had to go school in a cast after a sledding, skating, or skiing accident, but I was lucky and never had broken a bone, although Mumma said she wished my head injury had knocked some sense into me.

Unlike some of the other kids, I tried to avoid the bumps at the bottom of the hill because they scared me. But one day I was going so fast I lost control, and went flying over a bump at the bottom straight into the iron fence that belonged to the first house on the street. Just like in the Tom and Jerry cartoons, I saw stars and blacked out for an instant. Coming to, I saw a man standing over me. "Are you ok?" he asked, helping me up. "You better go home and have your mother look at that lump on your head." I felt my head, and sure enough, a giant egg had formed. Grasping the rope, I slowly pulled the sled up the hill and went home. Mumma put me to bed and called

Dr. Daviou, who came to the house. He didn't think I had a concussion, but Mumma had to watch me all night just in case. The worst part was I couldn't go sledding for a week.

A path of money

One winter day, Georgie and I were lying on our sleds, pulling ourselves along the sidewalk on Silver Street with our arms, heads down, looking at the packed snow under the sleds. We were tired from a long day of sledding and were making our way slowly home. Although it was 4 p.m., the winter sun was already going down and the sky was a deep gray. The streets were nearly empty as everyone was anxious to get home before it started snowing again.

Suddenly, I noticed coins on the ground. Nickels, dimes, quarters! We followed the path of money picking up this treasure as we went along. I was so engrossed in picking up the money, I didn't see the man until Georgie grabbed my arm and I looked up. The man up ahead was dropping the coins so we would follow them. Sensing danger, I grabbed Georgie's hand and we jumped off our sleds and raced past him toward home as fast as our heavy, waterlogged snowsuits allowed. We left the sleds in the street. As we approached the diner, I put the coins in my snowsuit pocket and, gasping, we sat in front of the taxi stand to catch our breath. I didn't dare to go back and get the sleds. We knew we had to go inside, but before we went upstairs, we counted the change and stopped in the grocery for Hershey bars. We didn't tell our parents, but I worried about our sleds all that night. Did the man take them? The next day when we went out to play, there they were, leaning against the door at the bottom of the stairs.

The long winters in Maine gave us ample opportunities to play in the snow. After one long day of sledding, I left my sled in my friend Susan's back yard because I was too tired to push it up the hill. When I went to retrieve it the next day, it was gone. Her family didn't know where it was. I walked home crying, but Mumma was not sympathetic, "Too bad. You shouldn't have left it there." I never got another one. Even with pictures to remind me, I don't remember my dolls or Teddy bears, but I mourned the loss of that sled.

Chapter Fourteen
Books, New Friends, and More Adventures

Georgeanna was always more domestic than I was. She liked helping Mumma do housework and never seemed to mind when we had to stay inside. I, on the other hand, always wanted to get out of the house. Not really a tomboy, because I did like getting dressed up, but playing outside was far better than being cooped up in our small apartment. I hated cleaning and had no real desire to learn to cook and sew.

So even if we had no plans to go anywhere, or friends were not around, I loved escaping the apartment to walk down Main Street and look in the shop windows. Mumma still took us shopping with her when we needed shoes, but with three of us, we didn't linger in the shops anymore like we had when I was little. So, George and I would go downtown and pretend to shop. Woolworth's was our favorite. We'd look at the hair bows, bobby pins, and cheap dime store jewelry, linger in the toy aisle, picking out the dolls we wanted, and if we had a nickel or a dime, we'd buy a Hershey bar or peanut butter cup and share it on the sidewalk in front of the store.

Sometimes I bought comic books. I had a collection of *Little Lulu, Casper, the Friendly Ghost, Donald Duck, Richie Rich* and *Nancy*. I read them all until they fell apart. Huey, Duey, and Louie, Donald's nephews, convinced me to eat mashed potatoes. Someone put mashed potatoes in their ice cream cones, and I thought that was a great idea, so I told Mumma I'd eat my mashed potatoes if I could put them in an ice cream cone. It worked, and she was glad she got me to eat something because I was still such a picky eater.

Discovering Trixie Belden

Then one day, in the magazine section of Woolworth's, on a metal circular shelf, a display of hardcover books with shiny covers caught my eye: *Trixie Belden and the Mysterious Visitor, Trixie Belden and the Red Trailer Mystery, Trixie Belden and the Mystery off Glenn Road*. Opening one of the books, the smell of ink hit me, and I started to read. I was hooked. I loved reading at school and loved it when the teacher read stories like *The Boxcar Children* to us. I could go to the library to borrow books, but at home, except for tattered Golden Books from when I was little, and some Scholastic book paperbacks, I had few books of my own.

All the books on this particular rack were fifty-nine cents. I raced home and begged Daddy for the money and soon was in possession of the first in the series. I loved Trixie because like me, she had a younger sibling she had to babysit, and like me, she often complained but did as she was told most of the time. She loved horses like me, and her family also could not afford to buy her a horse. Unfortunately, that's where the similarity ended. Lucky for Trixie, her best friend Honey was rich and owned horses, so Trixie helped her exercise them. I had no rich friends and none that owned horses. Trixie's life was never boring because there was always a mystery to solve. As my collection of Trixie Belden grew, I read them over and over again, and they came with me wherever I moved throughout my life.

While George and I roamed the city, discovering new things to see and do, Mumma stayed home taking care of baby Jimmy. But he wasn't the only child she looked after. While some people took in stray pets, Mumma took in stray kids. I often brought kids home for lunch and if they looked hungry, she fed them before they left. One girl, Rosie, who I had met playing in the street, lived around the corner with her mother, brother, and twin baby sisters. There was no dad. She was only allowed out to play once in a while after she finished her chores because she had to help her mother with the babies. When she came over to my house, Mumma made sure she ate before she went home. For Mumma, Rosie set an example for me. "Look how good Rosie eats," she said. "You should eat like her. She doesn't waste anything." Rosie ate her mashed potatoes without ice cream cones.

Johnny Appleseed, as Mumma called him, was a little boy from my class who lived in the trailer park down the hill. He was from Alabama and was one of Mumma's favorites. He only lived nearby for a few months before his family moved on, but I'd bring him home for supper, and Mumma got a kick out of his accent and his polite, southern, "No, ma'am, yes, ma'am" every time she spoke to him. He also didn't wear shoes unless he was in school. I envied that and copied him one day, taking off my shoes on the way home after he dropped his off at his trailer. Proudly walking past the taxi stand holding my shoes, Aunt Maria saw me from the window and strode outside before I got to the stairs. "Why are your shoes not on your feet?" she asked with a frown.

"I'm not wearing shoes, like Johnny," I answered tentatively, not sure now it was such a great idea.

"In Waterville, we wear shoes. This is not the country. Now put your shoes back on your feet. What if you step on a cigarette? That won't feel good, will it?" I hadn't thought about that. My barefoot days ended as soon as they began.

Abandoned kids?

Mumma befriended a woman in the diner who had a little girl, Janie, George's age, and a boy, Michael, who was Jimmy's age. They often came up-stairs, and the kids played while the women had cof-fee. The woman asked Mumma if she'd babysit her kids while she and her husband went on a week-long trip. Not wanting to refuse her new friend, Mumma said yes, so then she had five kids to watch. George and Jimmy played with them during the day, while I pretty much stayed out of the way outside somewhere, but the nights were chaotic. We had to share our beds, and the boy cried most of the time for his mumma.

As the week came to an end, Mumma, tired of cooking, cleaning, and trying to keep enough diapers clean, was anxious for the parents to pick up their kids. Sunday came and went with no pick-up. Monday, Tuesday, and Wednesday came and went with no sign of their parents. Daddy was furious and Mumma was frantic with worry. The phone number the parents left was no longer in service. Mumma hadn't known the woman for very long, and had no way of contacting her, nor did she know any of her family members. Daddy's angry voice boomed at Mumma, scaring us all. "Didn't you ask these people where they were from? Where did they live before they came here? Don't you know anything about them?" Mumma had no answers.

The police were called. Then one afternoon I came home from school, and they were gone. "Where are Janie and Michael?" I asked. "They had to go to live with someone else," Mumma answered sadly. That's all I ever found out, and we never saw them again.

Uncle Tony

At least once a day, Daddy stopped by Yiayia's house in Winslow, the next town over, across the bridge. Often I'd go with him. Daddy never stayed any place longer than five minutes. Even when he was sitting down, his legs were always moving, ready to jump up and go at a second's notice. After having a cigarette, we'd leave. Sometimes I stayed behind to play. Daddy's brother, my Uncle Tony, was a special-needs grown-up who acted like a little boy. Mumma said he had Downs Syndrome and was born that way. Tony couldn't talk very well, and he never went to school. In fact, he never went anywhere, spending all his time playing in the yard, except when Daddy or another family member took him for a ride in the car, his favorite thing to do, or Grampie took him to the pool hall on a Sunday morning when it was closed. When he saw Daddy's car in the driveway, he always went to sit in it, waiting patiently to go somewhere. So after talking to Yiayia, Daddy rode around the block a few times, then dropped Uncle Tony and me off and left to go back to work.

Tony was one of my first playmates. He liked to shoot hoops into the basket on the side of the garage, and he was pretty good at it. After trying to make a basket with the heavy ball and failing to get even close, I usually left him to play and wandered through the yard.

Yiayia and Grampie owned a large duplex house. They lived on one side that had two stories, and the other side was converted into two apartments, upstairs and downstairs. Uncle Tommy and Auntie Dee lived in the bottom apartment, and another couple lived upstairs. We always entered Yiayia's house through the back door, into a small glassed-in porch where we left our shoes before entering the kitchen. We could go in the den because the TV was there, but the living room with plastic-covered furniture was off limits. Usually everyone sat in the kitchen, but I didn't spend much time inside the house because I loved being outside in the big back yard.

The front of the house was just a few feet from the road, but the back had a flower and tree-filled yard where it only took a slight breeze to send plant perfumes floating through the air. Behind the garage, three giant old pear trees bloomed every spring, rewarding us with juicy pears in the fall. The lawn gave way to flower beds, with tiger lilies taller than me, sweet-smelling roses, and lilac bushes, along with apple and cherry trees. The lilacs were my favorite. In the spring, I liked to crawl under the lilac bushes, close my eyes, and inhale. Besides the smell of books, it was my favorite smell in the whole world.

Behind the flowerbeds, Grampie grew a large garden. He planted vegetables and herbs like they did in the mountains of Greece, in square patches instead of rows. Squares of corn, beans, cucumbers, tomatoes, peas, lettuce, and scallions covered every inch of the property along with herbs like oregano, dill, chamomile, and parsley. Grampie always cut a stem of dill for me to chew, and I savored the exotic flavor. On warm days when Daddy could be persuaded to sit for a few minutes in the yard, he'd pick a juicy tomato, cover it with salt and pepper, and share it with me.

Walking to Yiayia's

One day, bored with sitting on the stoop in front of the taxi stand, I decided to walk to Yiayia's house. George was inside playing with Jimmy, so by myself, I set out for Winslow. I'd ridden in the car enough times that I knew how to get there: turn right on Main Street and walk one block past the hardware store. Then I crossed the street and walked past Levine's, a men's clothing store. Past the clothing store, the Crescent Hotel made a V on the corner, one side on Main and the other on Front Street. Cars whizzed by in a circular rotary in front of the hotel. On Front Street, I waited at the crosswalk until it was safe to go and headed toward the bridge that separated Waterville from Winslow. I approached the bridge with trepidation. Here's where I'd have to decide to go on or turn around and go back. The sulpher from the factories along the river stunk like rotten eggs, and as I got closer to the bridge, the smell intensified. I could see why. The Kennebec River seethed and rolled over the Ticonic Falls, churning a sickly yellow, like a giant had vomited his breakfast.

I almost turned around before stepping onto the bridge, but I inched forward. Taking a few steps, l could see over the concrete railing further upriver. Above the falls, a logjam covered the water, looking like a wooden floor. Men were actually walking on the logs, separating them with long metal poles. A footbridge, the two-cent bridge, connected Waterville and Winslow. Made of wooden slats, it swayed back and forth and some people dared to walk across. Not me. No way would I ever get on that bridge. This cement one with a sidewalk was bad enough. I slowly made it to the halfway mark feeling the bridge shudder whenever a truck whizzed by; then I increased my pace until I was running, and I finally made it across!

Glad to have made it this far, I now had to climb up Clinton Avenue, which began as a steep hill. At the top of the hill, I only had four or five blocks to go, and there I was. Leaving my sneakers on the back porch, I entered the kitchen. At first Yiayia was not surprised to see me, and looked out the window, expecting to see Daddy's car. Then, "*Kahti...*" in her Greek accent. "Where you father?"

"He's home. I just walked."

Her eyes got big. "Your Mumma know you here? How long it take you?"

"No, I just decided when I went outside. I don't know."

"I call the taxi." We didn't have a phone upstairs, so she let Aunt Maria, in the cab office, know where I was.

"Sit. Eat some *yaourti*," Yiayia said. She always tried to make me eat yogurt with spinach. Grampie made his own yogurt. When I got a bit older, I discovered we were the only family that ate yogurt. No one even knew what it was. I liked it, but it was so tart it made my mouth pucker and gave me goosebumps. Yiayia put it on top of spinach or other greens. I was used to the strong taste though and as usual, ate a few bites to make her happy. Then I ran outside to play in the yard until Daddy picked me up. By then they were used to my wandering, and I didn't even get a scolding. Probably they didn't notice I was gone. After that day, I often walked to Winslow when I felt like it, but I never lingered on the bridge.

Joyce Ann

The summer before fifth grade, when we left Little Grammie's house, Joyce Ann came home with us. She wanted to move to the city and finish her last year of high school at Waterville High School. She was a grown-up teenager now. Every morning I watched her put her dirty-blond hair up in a pony-tail with a scarf around it. She wore poodle skirts and saddle shoes with white socks, and finally, before she left the house, she put on red lipstick. I think she was happy to be living in the city because she made a lot of new friends, and it wasn't long before she had a boyfriend.

By the time she graduated from high school, Joyce Ann was engaged. After her graduation, she got married and moved into a small apartment in the North End of Waterville where her husband's family lived. When she had her first baby, I liked to visit and hold him while she did housework. I was only nine and too young to babysit, but sometimes she left me with the baby while she ran to the corner store to get soda and snacks. This was my first time watching a little baby. A few years later, babysitting would be my main source of income to buy clothes and school supplies.

Fifth grade

At the beginning of fifth grade, we all had our eyes checked in school, and it was determined that I needed glasses. Mumma said I had ruined my eyes by all that reading. Aunt Maria wore glasses too, so it didn't bother me that I had to get them. Daddy always said I was going to be a teacher because I was so bossy with my sister and brother, but now that I had glasses he called me "little teacher," which I liked. I didn't have to wear them all the time, just for reading until I got older and my eyes got worse.

For the first time, we had a young teacher, Mrs. Weymouth who we all adored. I wanted to be a teacher like her and worked hard to please her. It wasn't always easy. Arithmetic was hard that year. She gave us word problems and fraction problems and long-division problems to work on in class. Once we finished our work, we could read. It always took me a long time to finish. We had to go up to her desk to have her check our work, and if it was wrong, it was back to our desk to try again. I had to do those problems over and over and over, erasing so many times the paper ripped. Frustrated to the point of tears, I kept at it until I either got it or it was time to go home. Except for arithmetic, everything else about fifth grade was perfect. We read all kinds of books and poetry too.

Loving poetry

We had to pick a poem, memorize it, and recite it in front of the class. I looked through all the books in our classroom until I found the perfect one. I loved trees—the fruit trees in Grampie's yard that smelled so wonderful in the springtime, the elms that lined Silver Street dressed in their fall colors until the leaves floated down all around us and formed piles for us to play in, and the Christmas pines that filled our apartment with the scent of Christmas. So I chose the poem "Trees," by Joyce Kilmer:

> I think that I shall never see
> A poem lovely as a tree.

A tree whose hungry mouth is prest
Against the earth's sweet flowing breast;

A tree that looks at God all day,
And lifts her leafy arms to pray;

A tree that may in Summer wear
A nest of robins in her hair;

Upon whose bosom snow has lain;
Who intimately lives with rain.

Poems are made by fools like me,
But only God can make a tree.

We had taken turns reading from our books in our reading groups, but this was the first time we had to stand in front of the class and recite from memory. One boy recited a few verses of "Hiawatha" and then it was my turn. "Trees," by Joyce Kilmer. Although I knew my poem by heart, I was so nervous my voice quaked and I rushed through it so fast no one could understand what I was saying. Mrs. Weymouth told me to try again, slowly. My heart beating out of my chest, I tried to slow down and managed to get through it. She smiled as the class clapped. I wasn't sure if I did a better job the second time or not because I felt just as nervous the second time. (My fear of public speaking has remained with me all my life.) I never got over the anxiety that I would be judged, or worse, laughed at. Mrs. Weymouth was kind and I wanted to please her, but every time I got in front of the class, I wanted to turn and run.

The end of ballet

I was still going to ballet after school, but not for long. One day after class Miss Jeannette gave me a sealed envelope and told me to give it to my mother. I didn't know what it was and when I asked Mumma, she didn't say anything. Then a few weeks later another envelope came home with me. And after the third time, Mumma asked me, "How would you feel about quitting ballet?"

"Can I still take tap?" I asked, not sure what she meant.

"No, I mean quitting tap and ballet."

Mumma looked worried, so I could tell she wanted me to quit. "I guess so," I said. I would miss the recital in a few months, but something felt wrong.

"Daddy thinks it's too much exercise. You are not gaining any weight," Mumma said. I knew I was skinny as a rail; family members never failed to point out this fact, and everyone always tried to feed me. Miss Jeannette was very thin too. Maybe dancing did that.

When I didn't appear for dance class in the following weeks, my friends at school wanted to know why. I told them what Mumma told me, but eventually I discovered the real reason. Notices arrived at our door, and one day I overheard my parents talking about the dancing school bill. It was sent to a collection agency and Daddy had to pay it or go to court. So that was why my dance career was cut short. I missed those dance classes and the recitals.

A year or so later I ran into Miss Jeannette downtown one afternoon, and she looked truly pleased to see me. She told me that she missed me in class and that I was a wonderful dancer. I blushed, embarrassed, and said, "Thank you."

Chapter Fifteen
The Queen of Christmas

One cold December day, I was itching for the school bell to ring. Despite the below freezing temperature, I was anxious for the school day to end so that I could see what Aunt Maria was up to next. When the bell finally rang, I wasted no time getting into my snow pants, boots, and coat, and hurrying out the door. Christmas break was just a week away and things were happening in downtown Waterville.

Rushing up Gold Street, I slid along the recently shoveled sidewalks past snowdrifts piled on the corners. My breath, colliding with the frigid air, created a cloud in front of me, leading to Silver Street and home. Just a couple of months before, the elm-lined street had been covered with leaves, and I shuffled my way home through the knee-deep crisp colors, taking my sweet time. But now, snow and ice replaced the leaves, and although I'd probably slip and fall at least once on the icy patches, I didn't care. I was impatient to get home. Aunt Maria was decorating the taxi stand.

Downtown was magical during the holidays, and this year was no exception as the storefronts transformed into Christmas. Garlands hung from street lamp to street lamp all along Main Street; the windows of Montgomery Ward's and Woolworth's were lit with rotating pink and silver trees. Christmas lights shone in every shop window making the town sparkle, especially since fresh snow covered the older, dirtier drifts darkened by the factories' pollution. Waterville wore her Christmas best and with Perry Como and Bing Crosby crooning, "White Christmas" and "Silver Bells," from inside the buildings, shoppers couldn't help but be in the holiday spirit.

Aunt Maria spent her days answering the phone, "City Cab, may I help you?" as she dispatched Leo and Phil on the two-way radio to pick up their fares. Her small office with a large plate glass picture window faced Silver Street so she could see what was happening outside. Not to be outdone by the large department stores, Aunt Maria started decorating early, soon after Thanksgiving.

She took her time, adding more decorations each day. Earlier that week she had spray-painted fake snow, creating a border around the window. The next day when I came home from school, she had attached blinking colored lights around the border. Then came snowflakes, but not so many that shoppers passing by couldn't see her. When she stood in the middle of the window, she was perfectly framed so that it looked like she had stepped into a magical Christmas card. Christmas music played continuously, and when customers opened the door to the waiting room, the songs overflowed into the streets. In one corner stood the small silver Christmas tree that I had helped decorate the day before with lights, silver tinsel, and different colored glass balls. What would we do today? Was she done?

Maria made our lives exciting because we never knew what she would do next. She never married. Her two older over-protective brothers tried to control her, but she had a strong streak of independence, causing arguments to erupt when she didn't listen to them. She attended Colby College for a year, but had no real ambition. So Grampie put her in the taxi stand to work, hoping some Greek man would spy her and carry her off, although that wasn't likely since we were related to most of the Greeks in town. A few times a year we all went to visit relatives in Massachusetts where many Greeks lived, but no luck. Maria was destined to be single.

Like most spinster aunts, she had her quirks and eccentricities. And either despite of or because of her brothers' attempts to control her life, she rebelled and sometimes got into trouble, frequenting bars with her friends and partying late into the evening. She loved the latest fashions and spent money on clothes from Alvina and Delia's, the most expensive women's dress shop in town. And she drove way too fast on the highways. Mumma always threatened to forbid us from riding in the car with her, after we all, at one time or another, came home with egg-sized lumps on our heads due to her last-minute braking for people or lights.

Maria had straight black hair that she curled in pin curls every night, except for once a week when she went to the beauty parlor for a professional styling. Her brown eyes sparkled playfully most of the time, at least when she was with us. Her features were exaggerated: her chin was too long, and she had the "Greek beak" of a nose. At one point Maria decided she was getting too fat and went on a major diet. She lost weight, but it wasn't enough, so she started taking a diet drink called Metrecal. When she lost too much weight, the family became worried. My aunts tried to make her go to the doctor, but she didn't listen.

Maria may not have looked like the movie stars on the pages of the magazines she kept in the waiting room, but she had an outgoing personality and many friends, and she was fun. So, when she wasn't on the phone, she stood in front of the window waving at all the passersby. "How are you today, Mrs. So-and-So? Beautiful day isn't it? Are you getting ready for the holidays?" People she knew stopped in to chat even when they didn't need a cab. I never heard her complain, but sometimes I caught a sadness in her eyes as she watched the world pass by in front of her window.

It took about fifteen minutes for me to walk home from school. My hands and feet were numb, and I kept breathing into my mittens to thaw my red nose. Despite my discomfort, all I could think about was what Aunt Maria had in store for today. Lights, snow, tree, music, what more could she do?

I passed the gourmet food store that sold strange food from other countries in glass jars, then the cleaners, the beer joint, the alley, the State Theatre, and there I was. The smell of fried onions and hamburgers wafting from the diner made my stomach growl, and I could hear "*City sidewalks, busy sidewalks, dressed in holiday cheer...*"

Then I stopped and stared. Aunt Maria stood in her Christmas card window, waving to me, and I couldn't believe my eyes. This was the best yet! She had had her once-black hair teased high, framing her face, but it was now RED! Red hair sprinkled with silver sparkles. Aunt Maria had decorated herself! I jumped up and down. She looked like a Christmas ornament and a Christmas princess all in one.

Daddy, working in the diner, saw my delight, but I didn't get the usual welcome-home smile. I knew right away that Aunt Maria was in trouble.

"Do you like it, Koukla?" she asked, laughing. (Daddy called me Katura sometimes, which I think was a made up name, and Aunt Maria called me Koukla which was Greek for doll.) I liked it when they called me those special names.

"Yes! You look just like Christmas!" I exclaimed.

"I thought so too, but Papa and your daddy don't think so. They want me to fix it."

"Can you?"

"I don't know," she chuckled again. "It's dye. If I try to remove it, my hair might fall out."

"Can't you just leave it for Christmas?"

"We'll see," she answered as she turned and waved to people she knew.

I spent the rest of the afternoon in the office with her, watching the expressions of shoppers as they noticed her hair. Some looked truly shocked, others laughed, and a few gave her strange looks. We just laughed.

The Crayola-red hair remained for a while, and Aunt Maria became a sort of celebrity in town that Christmas. When word got around, people made a special trip to wave to Aunt Maria, and her hair created so much foot traffic that it became good for business on Silver Street. Daddy listed Christmas specials for the days leading up to Christmas Day, and Mumma made Christmas cookies with red food coloring.

However, Aunt Maria wasn't one to rest on her laurels. The next week I came home from school to find Aunt Maria's red hair a thing of the past. It was replaced with light pink that sort of looked like the color the older ladies got from the Miss B's beauty parlor.

"How do you like my new color?" she asked.

"It's good, but I like red better. Are you going to do any other colors?"

"Maybe I'll do your favorite color, Koukla."

"Purple?"

"Yeah, it is Advent," she laughed.

The heightened foot traffic continued throughout the Christmas season. Now everyone wanted to see what color Maria would be next. Before her hair returned to her normal black color, she experimented with white and different shades of blonde, but none were as dramatic as the bright red. I was sad when the holiday was over and dull January arrived, always the longest month in Maine.

Chapter Sixteen
Cinderella for a Week

Spring must have arrived early that year when I was ten, or Greek Easter must have been much later, because by the time Easter arrived there was very little snow on the ground, which was unusual. One afternoon, I came home from school to find Aunt Maria upstairs holding a large rectangular box. I stared in awe as she removed the cover, and under the tissue paper there was what I imagined must be the most beautiful dress in the world. "For me?" I asked, incredulous. White organza covered with pale blue flowers and layers of petticoats, this dress would make me an instant princess when we attended Greek Easter celebrations in New Bedford. My parents, grandparents, aunts, and uncles would be traveling to Massachusetts to attend services at the Greek Orthodox Church with our family there.

After carefully packing my dress in the suitcase, we were on our way for the five-hour road trip. Easter was and is the most celebrated holiday in the Greek Orthodox religion, and everyone stayed up for the midnight service, even us kids. After many prayers in Greek, we lit our candles, replacing the darkness for the light as we watched the procession of the body of Christ three times around the church. Incense filled the church as the music and hymns reverberated through our bodies, creating chills as we proclaimed, "*Christos san esti, Christos san esti,* Christ has risen, he has risen indeed."

That weekend was the best Easter of my life. We ate Greek lamb and pastries; we played "crack the egg" with red-dyed eggs, and the most fun of all, we did the Greek dances at the home of our great-aunt and uncle. In the midst of the celebration, I twirled and whirled through the rooms in the circle dance with my girl cousins, dress flaring, like Cinderella at her first ball, and feeling so unlike my bashful, introverted self, I never wanted it to end.

All too soon the weekend was over, and the diaphanous dress was once again packed into the suitcase for the drive home. But once at home, I could not bear to put it away in the closet for another holiday. "I'm going to wear my Easter dress to school tomorrow," I announced, as Mumma was about to hang it up.

"It's not a school dress," she commented.

"I want to wear it."

Too tired to argue with me, she draped the dress over the foot of my bed, where I found and promptly donned it first thing the next morning, with my black patent leather shoes and white ankle socks.

Normally when I arrived at school, I'd sit at my desk quietly waiting for the teacher to begin. The other girls came in in twos or threes because they lived in a neighborhood and were all best friends. No one else lived downtown over a diner, taxi stand, and pool hall like I did. But that day was different. I waltzed into the classroom, aware of all eyes on my dress. As I slid regally into my seat, hands folded together in front of me, I could see the stares out of the corner of my eye.

It seemed forever until recess, but the bell finally rang and we were released for our fifteen-minute break. As we headed toward the playground all the girls in my class followed me like ladies in waiting. "Where did you get that dress?" they wanted to know.

"It's my Easter dress." Instead of running toward the swings as we usually did, I sat on the brick windowsill of the school's basement window. Positioning my body, I carefully spread out the skirt of my dress, creating a throne effect as all the girls surrounded me.

"But where did you get it?" They wanted to know, as if I didn't deserve such finery.

I told them my story. "My aunt took me to Boston, shopping. We stayed in a big hotel called the Parker House where fancy waiters served us cake and tea in the afternoon. Then we went shopping at Filene's, and I got to pick out the prettiest dress in the shop. They had a million beautiful dresses, but this was the one I chose." I knew about the Parker House and Filene's from my Massachusetts relatives.

"I would have picked that one too," one of the girls said, and the rest nodded in agreement.

"Well, I almost gave it to another girl who was shopping at the same time and wanted it, but my aunt said I had found it first, so I could buy it if I wanted to."

"Was the other girl mad at you?" someone asked.

"No, but she was famous and could have had as many dresses as she wanted."

"Who was it?" they all asked in unison. "Who?

Who? Tell us!" they begged. And suddenly, there was the bell to end recess.

"Oh, there's the bell," I said. "I'll tell you tomorrow." I carefully lifted my dress and jauntily paraded into the building, my entourage following close behind.

The next day, Mumma once again tried to convince me not to wear the dress, but I absolutely had to wear it—the thrill of fame had taken hold and there was no going back. At recess we took our places, me on my throne in the window and my classmates surrounding me as I continued, "After we bought the dress, I put it on, and we went for a carriage ride with horses. My new friend came with us. When we were tired, we stopped for ice cream."

"Who was she? Are you going to tell us?"

"Well, have you all seen the movie *Pollyanna*?" When they all nodded, I exclaimed, "It was Hayley Mills!"

All jaws dropped. All mouths went silent. Reveling in my newfound popularity, my imaginary adventures with my dress continued that day and through days three, four, and five. Each morning Mumma tried to make me wear one of my school dresses, and when I cried, she gave in, saying it was the last day and she didn't want to hear any more about it. I had a meltdown if she even threatened to wash it. Each day's embellishments outshone the day before, with sleepovers, horseback riding, and fancy dinners with my new friend Hayley. She even asked me to be in a movie with her, but I said no since Hollywood was too far away.

After five days, my dress was showing wear. The flowers were covered with mustard from my bologna sandwich, along with a few drops of chocolate milk.

A tear on the side where one of the ties was coming loose created a small hole that was getting bigger. The white was beginning to look gray. The blue flowers were fading.

Finally, on that last day, I knew my newfound fame was over when the bell rang and all the girls ran to the swings, ignoring me and my dress. Anyway, by then my imagination had run dry, and it was becoming increasingly difficult to make up stories. Dragging myself up the stairs that last afternoon, I looked more like the Little Match Girl than Cinderella. I took off my dress for the last time and gave it to Mumma to clean and repair. My reign was over.

Years later, when I told my sister Georgeanna that story, she laughed. "I told a whopper too. After the Christmas holiday, I went to school and told everyone I got a doll from Santa that could talk. The story got more and more outlandish, until the teacher said I could have special permission to bring it to school. How was I going to bring an imaginary talking doll to school? The doll quickly met with an accident, and that was the end of her."

Neither of us knew why we felt the need to make up stories. Was it the influence of the movies on which we spent so much time? Did we crave the attention? Whatever the reason, we both took solace in our imaginary worlds. And the attention we received enlivened our daily lives, even if it was short-lived.

Cinderella dress, age 10

Chapter Seventeen
Lessons from Yiayia

One afternoon Daddy left me at Yiayia's, as he often did, and I immediately raced out to play in the backyard. My Uncle Tony was sitting in his usual spot on the glider swing. Lilacs perfumed the air as I sat beside him. Out of the corner of my eye, I checked to see if Yiayia was watching us. Getting up off the seat, I asked, "Want to go faster, Tony?" I took his smile as a yes. He sat on one side of the wooden glider swing with opposite facing seats while I stood with legs outstretched between the two seats, pushing the rickety swing as high as it would go. In years, Tony was in his twenties, but intellectually he was younger than my ten years and his childlike delight in the moving swing propelled me to go higher as we both laughed.

"Kahti, Kahti, stop, now! Too fast! I get switch! You too rough! Come inside!" shouted Yiayia. Despite her broken English, I understood her perfectly, and knew I was in trouble.

I waited until the swing slowed down before I made my way to the door. "He likes to go fast; he was laughing," I said, trying to defend myself, but Yiayia, protective of her son, was having none of it.

Learning the art of spinach pie

"You too rough. Come inside and help make spinach pie. You, gel, need to act like gel. Learn cooking. You help Mumma?"

"No, she won't let me. The stove is too dangerous," I answered. Resigned to staying inside, I plopped in the chair by the kitchen table. Yiayia had spread flour over the entire top of the table and a large ball of dough sat to one side, ready for rolling. I watched as she lifted a four-foot long, half-inch thin dowel.

Yiayai said, "You need learn. Look to Yiayia; one day you make for you bebbies." Looking at the surprised expression on my face, she cackled, "Hoo, hoo, hoo," in her high-pitched laugh. "You make bebbies one day when you grow big." Sitting upright, I shifted my bony knees up to my chin, placed my arms around them, and watched as she cut a section of the dough and rolled it and rolled it and rolled it until the flat circle became larger and larger and larger until the dough was so paper-thin I could see the painted flowers underneath it on the porcelain table. Her huge hands, covered with wrinkles and calluses, moved steadily across the table. When the dough was ready, she deftly lifted the thin layer and placed it in a circular baking pan so quickly that the dough didn't have time to fall apart. She sprinkled some olive oil on the sheer layer and continued the process of making the thin dough circles until she had eight dough layers in the pan. I was mesmerized.

She broke the spell when she placed a small ball of dough in front of me, handed me the dowel, and said, "You try." I put some flour on the dowel and rolled it slowly across the dough. It was stretching. Feeling confident, I rolled the dowel faster until the dough took on a circular shape, sort of. Then it started to stick a little, so Yiayia added a little more flour, and I continued. A hole appeared. The dough was breaking apart. "Heeeheee, first time is hard," Yiayia retrieved the dowel, gathered up the dough, and we finished the last two layers together.

Checking on Tony, she brought the rest of the ingredients to the table. "Now we put filling. Break eggs in bowl. Beat." I cracked all six eggs in the bowl with only a minimal number of shells landing in the bowl and turned the handle of the eggbeater, beating until my arms got tired. "Good, now we mix one pound feta with two pounds spinach," she declared. She had already slightly cooked and drained the spinach, so we broke the feta into small pieces with a fork and added them to the spinach. Then the eggs were added to the mixture.

"Go to garden and pick dill," she ordered, "and hurry back!"

I grabbed my tennis shoes off the porch and raced out the back door to the garden. Tony was still swinging slowly, and when he saw me, his face lit up. I waved. He was still smiling as I hurried past him toward the garden.

I picked a handful of my favorite herb, inhaling its pungent scent and chewing on the stem before returning to the kitchen. Yiayia chopped the dill, added it to the spinach, feta, and egg mixture, and poured the mixture over the bottom layers of dough. She was

163

ready to add the top layers.

Cutting another section of dough to make more circles, she checked on Tony before she started the whole rolling process all over again. We talked.

She peppered me with questions. "How you school? You get high marks? You listen to teacher? You smart gel." She carefully lifted one layer of filo dough onto the spinach filling and sprinkled it with olive oil.

I shrugged. "I like school, except for arithmetic."

She then changed the subject. "You get big now, almost eleven years. Your mother tell you some ting about every month?" Another piece of dough slapped on the floured table as she continued rolling.

"Whaaat?" I faltered as my cheeks went pink with embarrassment.

"Every month, you get periods. You know about? You mother tell you?" Flip. Another layer positioned expertly.

No use pretending ignorance. "I know about it; Mumma told me, and we learned about it in school, too."

"What? They teach in school? What kind of school you go? Hee-heee." More rolling. More flipping.

"We got a book called *Growing Up and Liking It.* It's all about our bodies and stuff." Please, no more questions, I silently begged.

A look of confusion flitted across her face, but that did not stop her interrogation. "You not make some ting with boy? Very bad. Make bebbies. I too young when marry Papou. Too young." The final layer flipped on top of the pie.

My faced was now flushed with full-out embarrassment, and I sat silently for a moment, remembering when the school nurse showed us a slideshow about our changing bodies. I didn't remember them telling us about making babies, though. I guess periods and making babies went together. "Are we done, now?"

"Yes, done, I put in oven. Go get Tony. We eat some ting. You too skinny, gel. Need to eat more."

I was so glad to be out of the house that I did cartwheels across the lawn toward the swing. And from the window came Yiayia's voice, "Kahti, stop! No do that! You get nail in head! Act like gel!"

I didn't know it at the time, but our daily stops at Yiayia's would soon end. Fifth grade was almost over and for the first time I wasn't excited for summer. I didn't want to go to the races and wait for Daddy to win big. Not only that, this would be my last year at South Grammar because sixth grade was in junior high. I would miss Mrs. Weymouth and South Grammar. Not only would I be going to a new school, but Daddy and Mumma had been talking about moving out of our apartment, and maybe we would be living in a new apartment somewhere. I wasn't excited about leaving downtown either.

When Daddy picked me up at Yiayia's a few weeks before school ended, I was still playing in the yard when I heard Daddy and Grampie yelling at each other through the open window. I had never heard them yell that loudly before. I covered my ears, but watched as Daddy, who always talked with his hands, flung his arms toward the sky and cursed in Greek. I knew he was swearing because he always said those same words when he was furious. Grampie was doing the same. I had no idea what they were saying, but I knew it had something to do with

Daddy spending his money at the races. I found out later that Daddy had quit the diner.

That must have been why we were moving away from Silver Street. A few minutes later, Daddy came out of the house, slamming the door. "Get in the car," he ordered. That was the last time I saw Yiayia and Grampie until Christmas.

Chapter Eighteen
The Summer of Freedom

Just before the school year ended, Daddy came home and bounded up the stairs with exciting news: "We're going to the lake for the summer!" Mumma smiled happily at the news and the excitement was contagious, even though we had no idea where we were going. "We'll have our own camp on the lake and you can play in the water every day!" he said. We all jumped up and down and danced around the kitchen. We then prepared for what would be both the longest and shortest summer of my life.

A week later, with the car packed, we left Silver Street for our summer at the lake. That first night of summer 1960, the moon rose over Great Pond, one of the Belgrade Lakes, which was about fifteen miles from Waterville but seemed like another world. The moonlight created a trail over the water leading to the rocks where we sat mesmerized by the trees on the opposite shore as they faded from green to gray to black. With sunset, the mosquitos feasted on our bare legs and arms, not as badly as the mosquitos in the north woods had been, but irritating enough to force us inside on the porch. Mumma sprayed around the screens and Daddy waved his cigarette in circles around our heads, attempting to keep the bugs at bay.

In the morning, Daddy began his new job as the cook at Camp Abena, an all-girls' summer camp. Mumma was the pastry chef. Camps in Maine then were actually cabins, so even though some were rustic, it wasn't the same as camping in a tent. Our small cabin had two bedrooms, one with three bunks for us kids and the other with one bed for Mumma and Daddy, a bathroom without a shower or tub, and a screened-in porch with enough holes for mosquitos to join us inside. This was our shelter at night, but the lake and the woods became our home for the summer.

That first night away from the city, the strange sounds of the frogs and fish jumping for their dinner lulled us into silence, an uncharacteristic stillness for me at ten, Georgeanna at six, and Jimmy at four. Suddenly, the spell was broken by the what sounded like a blood-curdling cry of a woman in distress echoing across the lake. Daddy bolted out of the porch rocker, cigarette ash floating behind him as he banged open the screen door.

"Christ Almighty! Someone's in trouble!" he yelled.

To our astonishment Mumma laughed. "Come back in! It's a loon, George; it's just a loon."

"What the hell is that?" Daddy asked, laughing now too.

"A bird that lives on the lake."

"I never heard anything like that in my life."

As we had no television or radio, we quickly grew accustomed to the loon's melancholic cry, calling to its mate, lulling us to sleep every evening. After settling into our bunks, we dove under the blankets to drown out the whining mosquitos floating above our heads. Our summer of freedom had begun.

While Mumma and Daddy were busy in the kitchen, we had free rein to explore. Mumma emphasized the only two rules: don't go near the water without an adult, and don't bother the campers. We awakened each day to the chattering of chickadees outside our windows. Early mornings were chilly, and without heat and running water, we washed our faces quickly in the lake, all goose-pimply, watching the mist rise over the still water as our shivering parents bathed. In the mess hall, workers prepared breakfast for the campers, while we ate Rice Krispies on an old picnic table by the back door. Every day the sun rose to a new adventure. I'm sure it must have rained that summer, but I don't remember a single rainy day.

Like feral children, we circled the areas where campers would soon be engaged in their structured activities: horseback riding, theatre, crafts, boating, and swimming. Hearing the kids approach, we'd scatter into the woods with our own "horses," made from the best branches we could find. Mine I named Black Beauty, and pretended I was Elizabeth Taylor from the movie. Riding through the woods, I discovered Lady's Slippers and Jack-in-the-Pulpits, and picked a handful until Mrs. Tinker, the camp owner, explained that they were endangered, which meant I had to leave them alone and watch where I stepped with my horse.

Each day we explored farther into the woods, the dense trees muting the campers' voices. One day we cantered out to a point where, next to large glacial boulders, we discovered bushes ripe with blueberries. We gorged ourselves on the sweet berries until we lost track of time and missed our lunch check-in at the back door. No one noticed that we left our peanut butter and marshmallow fluff sandwiches untouched. The blueberry patch became our fort in the woods. Early on, we gave up wearing shoes, and galloping through the pines every day, our bare feet were covered in pinesap that never washed off during our evening swim.

Black Beauty and I sometimes trotted out alone, leaving my sister and brother to play by the back kitchen door. On those days, I'd sit at the water's edge with a handful of blueberries and watch minnows circling in front of me, the silence broken only by a stray bee, or a rock I tossed into the lake, or birds calling to each other from the tall pines that leaned over the water. Here, in this quiet place, it was easy to lose track of where I ended and the natural world began. I blended with the landscape feeling utter contentment.

I never bothered the campers, but the smell of horses lured me toward the stables where I watched riding lessons, making sure I kept my distance. From the hill above the stable, I carefully observed reluctant campers, some of whom refused to get on their horses. I mimicked their movements on my wooden horse. One day, the instructor, who noticed me paying attention as she tried to coax a fearful rider to mount, called me over. "Would you like to show Anne how to post?" she asked.

Incredulous, I could only answer, "Me?"

"Yes, come on over and get up." She gave me a

boost from the step stool. "Now show her how to post."

I couldn't believe I was on a real live horse and so far from the ground. With eyes wide, I felt the campers watching, but my determination to ride was stronger than my fear. I had to prove I could do it. Clucking my tongue on the roof of my mouth, I gently nudged the giant creature, and much to my surprise, she moved to my commands. Up in the stirrups, down on the seat, up and down we circled the paddock. I wished it would never end. Coming back to the starting position, I got off, gave "my" horse a hug and went trotting off on my wooden Black Beauty. I never knew whether the instructor got in trouble for letting me get on the horse, but that was my one and only real ride that summer.

Some days, after exploring, I lolled in the hammock, reading one of my Trixie Belden books or a Nancy Drew mystery that I had discovered on one of the bookshelves in the dining hall. Sometimes, time would stand still as I dozed off to birdsong and the pungent scent of sun-warmed pine.

The natural world was not our only entertainment, however. At the end of the first two-week camp session, the three of us had our first experience with live theater when the campers put on a play. The cook (Daddy) and his family were the guests of honor, sitting in the front row. How we loved the entertainment! Rumplestiltskin came to life on the stage, and at the end, we joined Daddy in giving them a standing ovation, calling "BRAVO!" over and over again.

Sometimes I felt jealous because I couldn't be a part of their plays or sing-a-longs or riding classes. Other times, I felt sorry for the campers. They had so much to do every day while I was free to roam the woods. Mostly, though, I was just content.

Reality returns

The only time we went to the races that summer was when Daddy had a day off between camp sessions. And after those days off we were glad to be back at camp, and I think Daddy was too. He was happy there. It was the first time he seemed content to be somewhere, to not be so anxious to go, go, go someplace else, only to turn around and go again. Every evening after the dining room was cleaned for the day, we went swimming. None of us could swim, but we could dog paddle, and we made sure we didn't go over our heads. Daddy always stood at the water's edge, made the sign of the cross three times before diving headfirst into the lake and then popping up a few feet away to shake the water out of his hair. Then, cigarettes in hand, Mumma and Daddy would sit on the rocks talking while George and I dove underwater to collect shiny rocks from the bottom and Jimmy would throw his homemade fishing line in the water, sure he would catch a fish.

"One day we'll have our own camp," Daddy said. "And we'll come and spend the whole summer." Mumma just laughed.

"What? You don't believe me? You just wait and see," he said. "When I hit a big one, we'll buy the biggest camp on the lake and we can live here all year if we want to."

"Are we moving to a new house after we leave camp?" I asked, beginning to worry about where we would live.

"Don't you worry about a thing," Daddy answered. "Don't you worry about a thing."

That would be the only summer I spent at the lake and the only one when we didn't spend most of the time driving from racetrack to racetrack. It was by far the happiest summer of my childhood. Daddy got other jobs and resumed his gambling habit. We returned to our "feast or famine" days, not knowing which it would be until he came in the door at night. But from then on, it would be mostly famine.

Many years passed before I returned to that lake, but now every summer I return to the Maine woods. The breeze waves scents of pine and hemlock over the cool lake water, the soft carpet of needles caresses underfoot, and the silence of the evening is broken only by the call of the loons, beckoning me home. There's a sign in the camps where we stay that says it all: "If you're lucky enough to vacation at the lake, you're lucky enough."

The Summer of Freedom

Middle Years:
1960 – 1968

"It's not true that life is one damn thing after another; it's one damn thing over and over."

Edna St. Vincent Millay

Don't Worry About A Thing

Chapter Nineteen:
The Move

Life changed after Camp Abena. We were moving out of the city, leaving our downtown apartment to live in another upstairs apartment in an old, converted farmhouse in the country, and life would never be the same.

No one explained why, or how, or what our new home would be like, so I was left to imagine life in the country. Would there be horses to ride like in my books? I doubted it. Woods to explore like at camp or the dense woods like Grammie's upcountry? Maybe. Did other kids live nearby? I hoped so, and with the resilience of childhood, I tried to view it as an adventure, with visions of finding my own best friend like Trixie Belden's best friend, Honey. In my daydreams I pictured us trotting along winding country roads, solving our own mysteries.

But the truth was, I was worried. I worried how I would get to town or to Yiayia's house when Daddy was working or at the races. How would I get to the library? How would we get to the store if we needed something when Daddy was gone? How would I go to the movies? We would be too far away to walk anywhere. And not only would I be attending a new school, but now I'd have to ride a bus

I carefully packed my Trixie Belden books and wrote my name on the box with a large black Crayola. Before we left, I begged Aunt Maria and Daddy for enough money to buy some new books. On a lucky day, there would be a new Trixie Belden book on the shelf. There were some other books also, Janet Lennon of the Lennon Sisters and Donna Parker, both teenage series, and I bought a few of those after I had purchased all the Trixie Belden books. Handing the cashier the fifty-nine cents plus tax, I rushed home to add the book to my box.

The farmhouse apartment

Although the new apartment was only maybe five miles or so from our place on Silver Street, It might as well have been in another state. On moving day I discovered that the old farmhouse where we were to live had two apartments. The owners, an older couple who looked more like grandparents than parents, had two kids and lived downstairs. Upstairs, our new place was larger than our town apartment, with a kitchen, living room, and two bedrooms, but it felt empty because we didn't have living room furniture at first. Georgeanna, Jimmy, and I shared a bedroom, sleeping in three twin beds on the linoleum floor. We didn't have a bureau, so we put our clothes in Mumma's maple dresser. My brother's bed was against an inside wall, and my sister and I had ours next to the two windows. My window was in the front of the house and looked out onto a long-mowed lawn.

I think the best part of that room was the ancient maple right in front of my window that hid my view of the road. I placed my box of books under my bed.

Although Marleen, thirteen, and Robert, eleven, lived just downstairs, it took a long time to get to know them. They were friendly to us at first but couldn't come out to play very often because they always had chores to do, Robert more so than his sister. There were no horses, but they had chickens, thousands and thousands of chickens crammed into a two-story chicken barn behind the house. The woods were far back, beyond a meadow, and too far away for us to explore. When the wind blew a certain way, all we could smell was chickens—no lilacs like at Yiayia's or pine scent like at camp. And the closest farm, a half-mile away, raised cattle. At certain times of the year, in the middle of the night, we could hear the frightful screams of the cows as they knew they were being led to slaughter. On those nights, lying in bed listening to the death cries of the cattle, I longed for the screams of sirens in the city streets.

Still, at first it was an adventure. I got used to no cars honking all night, no lights from cars or snowplows shining in the windows, and no police or fire sirens. Instead, we heard the sounds of wind moaning in the large maple and the crows screeching first thing in the morning. We played in the creek that crossed the meadow, wading and catching frogs and on windy days, danced around silky milkweed seeds as they burst from the pods, filling the air. It never felt like the countryside I imagined in my books, or idyllic scenes of the movies, but we accepted our new life.

When it rained, I stretched out on my bed by the window with one of my books, a jar of Aunt Doris's mustard pickles, and a box of saltines. I read and re-read my favorites, *The Secret of the Mansion* and *The Gatehouse Mystery*, wishing I were Trixie, imagining I was there, riding the trails with Trixie and Honey as they found clues to solve the mystery.

At first, I only noticed the huge maple outside my window as background, subconsciously aware of the wind rustling the leaves. I watched the sunbeams play hide and seek in the branches, and I could almost touch the limbs as they reached toward my window. But I was more interested in the pages of my books.

With autumn's frosty mornings, however, the tree took on a new life of color that was difficult to ignore. Bright crimson and persimmon took the place of green, and as the sun toasted the day, an earthy, decaying smell floated through the window. Sometimes I'd give up my book and lie under the tree's canopy, staring as the leaves floated downward, covering the ground. I remembered in fifth grade when I had had to recite "Trees" in front of the class. There was something about a tree that gave me a feeling of calm, of safety in an uncertain world.

All too soon, the color faded and bare branches lifted toward the heavens, sometimes leaning to one side in a nor'easter, sometimes stiff, with icicles dangling from the limbs like frozen fingers pointing downward, scolding Mother Earth. Its trunk, rough and strong, withstood the winter blasts like a coat of armor. I marveled at its strength. I still read by the window, but now I was bundled in blankets, completing my homework until the words blurred into black.

Sometimes I wondered what Mumma did at home alone all day while we were in school. When we got off the bus, we would find her sitting in the kitchen near the oil stove, a cardigan wrapped tightly over her dress, smoking and drinking instant coffee. The apartment never felt warm enough. She listened to my grumbling and our bickering, never complaining about being alone all day. Every morning as we left the house to walk down the long driveway to the bus, she told us to behave ourselves and listen to the teacher. She didn't have to worry about that. We were good kids.

Riding the bus to school

I got used to riding the bus into Waterville where I was a sixth grader at Pleasant Street School. Every morning I looked forward to seeing our driver, Mr. B, a kind man who joked with us. And through that long winter, on many days, the warmest place to be was on that bus with the heat blasting.

The school bus would inch along the icy roads, but I didn't mind that it was so slow. On one particular day, around 3:30 in the afternoon, the sky hung heavy with another impending snowstorm. Dusk was already creating streaks of gray across the wintry sky. Soon it would be dark. We were almost home, and I'd have to remove my feet from the heater next to Mr. B and face the frigid winds on the quarter-mile walk up the driveway. On days like this I missed our old apartment on Silver Street more than ever. Even though I used to walk home from school, I didn't remember it ever getting so cold in the city.

By the time I made it up the driveway and climbed the ice-covered outside stairs into our tiny kitchen, my feet and face were numb. As I entered the kitchen, I noticed right away the oven door was open, but the heat coming from the oil stove did little to warm the kitchen. When I went into my bedroom, the warmth from the kitchen didn't follow me. I looked at Mumma. "Why is it so cold in here?"

"The electricity got turned off. Daddy forgot to pay the bill," she said.

"It's freezing. We'll freeze to death!"

"It's going to be ok. I'm heating up some chicken soup to warm you up. Then you can hop in bed under Grammie's quilts and you'll be warm."

After eating a bowl of Campbell's chicken noodle soup, I wrapped myself in one of Grammie's heavy quilts and lay on the bed next to the window trying to complete my fractions homework. The wind howled, whistling through the cracks in the window corners, as the nor'easter drifted snow where the driveway had been. When it got too dark to see, Mumma lit candles, and I used a flashlight to read my library book. What if I didn't finish my book? I was assigned to talk about it the next day in school.

Georgeanna and Jim fell asleep early, burrowed underneath piles of blankets, but I continued to read until it was too hard to see, even with the flashlight. With everyone quiet, I could hear laughter coming from downstairs. Marleen and Robert were watching TV.

The sound of laughter made me angry, as if they were laughing at us. Getting out from my warm blankets I hurried past Mumma to go to the bathroom. I could feel the cold floor even with my knee socks on. "Jesus H Christ," I swore aloud.

Mumma looked surprised, hearing me. "What's gotten into you?"

"I want to go back to Silver Street. I hate it here. When is Daddy coming home?" She didn't answer.

Climbing back under the covers, I fell asleep with the sounds of TV playing downstairs. When I awoke in the middle of the night, I could hear whispering in the next room. Daddy was home.

"Did you win anything today?" I heard Mumma ask. "We need to get the lights turned back on. The kids are cold."

"Don't you worry about a thing," Daddy answered. I knew what that meant: He didn't have any money.

Early the next morning, I awoke to Mr. M plowing up and down the driveway so we could catch the bus. I lay in bed until the last minute, dreading getting out from under my warm quilts. Only the thought of getting into the warm bus motivated me to get moving. The main roads had already been cleared overnight. As Georgie and I left the apartment, we met up with Marleen and Robert at the foot of the stairs as they came out of the house.

Downstairs neighbors

I liked Robert, but he was quiet and always had a sad look on his face. Mr. M made him work in the barn all the time, and sometimes I heard him crying before he went to clean the chicken coops. When we had first moved in, they showed us the chicks growing under the lights, and while they were cute, we knew they were destined for the kitchen table. The noise of the chirping inside the barn competed with the smell of chicken caca, and poor Robert had to spend hours cleaning up after them. Marleen was a few years older than me, and I thought she was nice at first, but she always bragged about her things and thought she was better than us. What I hated the most was the fact that she knew about the electricity being shut off. Our secret was out and there was no way I could hide it.

"What did *you* do last night?" Marleen asked slyly, as we headed toward the bus.

"Nothing."

"Didn't you watch *The Dick Van Dyke Show*? We laughed so hard."

I know, I thought to myself. *We could hear you.* "No, I had to read my book."

"Really, you were reading?" she smirked.

The arrival of the bus kept me from throwing snow in her face.

After school, she started in on me again. "Are you going to watch TV tonight? I'm watching *Dr. Kildare* after I finish my homework. He is so dreamy. Do you like Ben Casey or Dr. Kildare?"

"Neither." That was true. I didn't like doctor shows. And I had just about had it with Marleen.

The sun had come out about midday, and although it was still cold, the wind was not biting, so we didn't rush up the driveway. I wished later that I had run straight up to the apartment before I got myself into trouble. Just as we reached the stairs—and unable to stop myself—I blurted out, "Well, anyway," I said spitefully, "I know something about you that *you* don't know." As soon as the words were out of my mouth, I regretted them. Without looking at her, I ran into the apartment. I knew it was the meanest thing I'd ever done and immediately felt guilty. I had almost spilled someone else's secret. Before we left Silver Street, I had told my friend where we were going. Her mother overheard me talking and told me a secret about the people we were renting from that I must never tell anyone. I almost blurted out that secret. That night I wasn't just cold, I was sleepless because I knew I was going to get in trouble the next day. I tried to convince myself Marleen wouldn't say anything to her parents. But then, wouldn't I want to know what someone knew about me? She would tell her parents and then I was doomed.

The next day the snow was melting a bit, but icicles still hung from the windows, and parts of the driveway were turning to slush. Marleen was quiet. Every time I looked at her, she looked away, but at least she didn't talk about TV or anything.

That afternoon dark clouds were building in front of another impending storm. We jumped off the bus to be met by Mr. and Mrs. M and Mumma and Daddy at the end of the driveway. My heart sank. I knew I was in deep trouble.

Mrs. M called me over. The adults surrounded me as the other kids watched from behind us. "Kathy, what do you know that Marleen doesn't know?" she asked tentatively. I looked up at Mom and Dad. "Nothing." Snow started to fall, and I just wanted to get inside where the cold didn't seem so bad anymore.

"If you know something we should know, we'd like to hear it," Mrs. M continued as I tried to walk away.

With legs shaking and voice quivering, I couldn't see any way out of it. "My friend Linda's mother told me that Marleen and Robert are adopted," I blurted before running off. "Jesus H Christ," I whispered to myself as I turned and left them all standing with mouths wide open.

Marleen and I stayed away from each other after that, but I continued to feel bad about not keeping the secret. My big mouth was always getting me into trouble. But then, I had other things to worry about. The heat was back on, but Daddy was never home, and food was getting scarcer by the day. We were living on macaroni and canned tomatoes. At least if we had to eat the same thing every day when I came home from school hungry, macaroni and canned tomatoes tasted pretty good. I remembered the good old days when I was a picky eater and refused to eat what Mumma made and she would fix something else. I thought of that awful corned beef hash from the cafeteria. If someone gave it to me now, would I like it?

When I complained about our situation Mumma told me to stop the fussing, saying she had it much worse when she was my age. She told us stories about the hard winters when she was a kid. They were so poor they had nothing to eat for the entire winter except buckwheat pancakes. Pancakes for a whole winter! Mumma never made us pancakes because the smell of them cooking made her sick. Macaroni and tomatoes weren't so bad, really, but that didn't stop me from complaining. I craved hotdogs with ketchup and mustard, and Mumma's Sunday roast chicken with peas and mashed potatoes made my mouth water just thinking about it. One thing I discovered about being hungry though, I would eat whatever was in front of me. No more fussy eating for me.

Searching for God

In December I missed being downtown to watch the shopkeepers decorating for Christmas. I knew Aunt Maria probably had the taxi stand already decorated. She picked me up for church on Sundays, but then took me straight home. The children's choir was practicing Christmas hymns.

Everyone at church was so sure about God and Jesus, no one questioned whether God was real. I knew grown-ups would tell you things they didn't even know themselves, so I didn't want to ask anyone. Was Jesus really born in a manger, in the hay? Did the three wise men really hear an angel telling them to follow a star to Bethlehem? How do we know it really happened? I decided I didn't believe any of it, but I still wanted to find out if it might be true. I started praying again. Maybe this time it would work. Only I decided on a different prayer. Every night, burrowed in my blankets, with my knee socks on that did little to warm my freezing toes, I prayed: "Dear God, I need to know if you are real. Do you exist? If so, please let me know so that I can talk to you. Things are not good here, and I'm not very good either, what with making enemies with the kids downstairs and everything, so please let me know if you are real. Amen." Some version of that prayer was said every night in all earnestness. The hunger inside of me to know the truth was so strong it was all I could think about.

One afternoon when we got home from school, Mumma asked me what I wanted for Christmas. She said they couldn't buy much this year, but what one thing did I want. I immediately told her a record player, the small 45rpm record player I saw downtown one day. I didn't know how much it cost, but that was the only thing I wanted.

In those final weeks and days that led up to Christmas, I never fell asleep without my nightly prayer. I never told anyone. I decided if I never found out, it would be my secret. I knew we were going to have a poor Christmas that year, so I was surprised when I got home one afternoon, the day before Christmas and Mumma had her box of decorations on the living room floor. Daddy was bringing home a tree. Even though I wasn't sure it would happen, I hoped, and when we saw Daddy taking a tree out of the trunk later that day, we all jumped up and down with excitement. Mumma put away the groceries he had brought and started making a spaghetti sauce while we decorated. She saved the silver icicles from previous years and they were the last thing to go on the tree. We stared at the sparking silver tinsel and knew that Santa would be coming.

Our bellies full of spaghetti, we went to bed early, excited for Christmas morning to arrive. I didn't forget my prayer: "Please God, let me know if you are real and baby Jesus is real." I was more concerned about finding out if this holiday was legit than about getting presents in the morning.

I don't know what time it was when I fell into a deep sleep, my prayer on my lips, when I thought I was awakened by a beautiful angel shrouded in white light who gently touched my forehead. Instantly I felt an inexpressible love permeating my body. Taking my hand, she flew me swiftly through a multi-colored tunnel, floating through space until we landed in a tiny village. Ahead we could see what looked like a shed that was open on one side. Animals, shepherds, and angels were staring toward a light that emanated from a bed of straw where a baby lay. Jesus. Angels were singing the most beautiful hymns, and the light surrounding the baby expanded until we were surrounded by a ring of love that absorbed every part of my body. I wanted to stay there forever. But all too soon the angel took my hand and we returned to the tunnel. I glanced backward once more and the next thing I knew, I was back in bed.

I tried to speak to say goodbye to the angel, but I had no voice. Jesus appeared, as a grown- up now, looking down at me, and said, "If you ever need me, just call out to me. I am always with you." Then he was gone.

I tried to sit up, to reach out to Him, but my body wouldn't move. I began to panic when I could see that my arms and legs were paralyzed, stuck to the bed. I wanted to scream out, but all I could do was breathe. I think it lasted only a few seconds, but it seemed like a long time. Eventually my legs and then my arms came back to life and I could sit up. I looked around the room. Everything looked the same, but everything was different. The love I had experienced still embraced me and I felt euphoric. Eventually I faded back to sleep, hoping my experience would repeat itself. When I awoke, it was Christmas morning.

Mumma and Daddy noticed how happy I was that morning as we opened presents and I got the record player. They must have assumed I really wanted that record player badly, but I couldn't tell them what had happened in my dream. They would never have believed that I spent Christmas Eve with Jesus. My prayers had been answered, and for days I basked in the memory of that dream even while life went on and our situation stayed the same.

A new maturity

That winter, just before my twelfth birthday in February, I started my period. I was lucky. It happened at home one morning when I got up and noticed blood in my panties. I was relieved because one of the girls in my class started in school and there was blood all over the floor. I worried that would happen to me. Mumma was expecting it because she had pads for me, and a new Kotex belt. The thin elastic belt went around my hips. She showed me how to attach the two ends of the pad onto the metal clasps that hung off the belt. It was uncomfortable, and if I sat the wrong way at my desk in school, those metal clasps would dig into my behind. I hated having my period. Every month I got cramps and had to take Midol that made me jittery because of the caffeine. One month I felt so sick I fainted. Mumma said I was now a woman, but if this was what being a woman was all about, I wanted none of it.

Isolation

Living way out of the city was boring. Most days there was nothing to do. With no money, and no way to get to the store anyway, we spent our time at home waiting for Daddy. People rarely came to visit. Aunt Maria picked me up on Sunday to go to church, but that was about it. Daddy and Grampie still hadn't made up from the fight they had had the previous spring, I think Grampie had to bail Daddy out of his gambling debts, and he was finished with him. When Grampie stopped supporting Daddy's habit, we all suffered.

Spring, at last

Finally in March, the icicles melted and the last of the snow mixed with the softening mud in the driveway. Mud time, Maine's "fifth season," had arrived. It was impossible to avoid the mud ditches as we ran along the edge of the driveway to catch the bus, and by the time we got on the bus, our boots were covered. Along with gray skies and brown earth replacing the snow and ice, spring arrived with the sound of the stream overflowing in the meadow and the occasional chattering of chickadees building new nests in the maple. A few shoots of spring growth appeared here and there, giving me hope that winter would soon be gone.

One sunny spring Saturday, I decided I was going to walk to town. I wasn't exactly sure what I would do when I got there, but going to the library was definitely on the list and I figured I would then stay in the taxi stand with Aunt Maria. I asked Mumma how far it was. She thought it was about three miles to Silver Street. Mumma told me to stay home, but I was restless and had to get out of the house. Uncle Spike's house was on the way, so if I got tired, I knew I could stop in there. Uncle Spike was Daddy's younger brother. He and his wife Gerry had three kids, my cousins, Tony, Tim, and baby Kelly. We didn't see them very often, mostly at church on Sunday or holidays at Yiayia and Grampie's. I think they spent more time with Aunt Gerry's extended family than they did with Uncle Spike's Greek side. I didn't know why.

Walking along the side of the country road turned out to be harder than I anticipated. If a car or truck came speeding down the road, I had to jump in the water-filled ditch to get out of the way; so between getting sprayed by the vehicles and wading in the ditch, my coat and snow pants were splattered with water and mud. I almost turned around a few times but was too stubborn to admit defeat. I ambled on with heavy mud-splattered coat, water-filled boots, and tired legs. I was sure it would not be much farther.

After trudging along for what seemed like forever, I made it to Uncle Spike's house, sweaty, exhausted, hungry, and thirsty. Aunt Gerry wasn't very pleased to see me and I could see why. I looked like I had fallen in the creek and rolled in the mud. My cousins were playing in the playroom basement, so after I removed all my outer layers and left them in the mudroom, she told me I could go downstairs and play until their naptime. My stomach was grumbling. I wanted to ask her for something to eat, but I couldn't bring myself to say the words, so I asked for a glass of water instead and then went to play. Soon after, she piled us all in the car and drove me home. It was the only time I tried walking to town.

A scare

One morning I woke up and saw that Mumma was sick. I watched her, scared, as her face lost all color. I asked if she was okay, and she nodded yes, but as she got up from the chair and tried to make it to the bed, she fainted. Panicked, I rushed downstairs to use the phone. I called the taxi stand to have Aunt Maria send the driver to take her to the hospital before she died. "Mumma fainted!" I screamed into the phone. "Come quick!"

By the time Leo arrived, Mumma had revived and was mortified because the neighbors downstairs now knew what had happened. They insisted on calling the doctor. I was in the other room when he examined her and heard him say, "When was the last time you ate?" Now everyone knew about our predicament. Daddy still wasn't home, but Aunt Maria brought us groceries later that day. Someone went looking for Daddy, and he finally came home. After that, things got a bit better, except for the shame. Mumma and Daddy even laughed about me calling the taxi. I didn't think it was funny. Everyone knew we were poor and hungry.

We lived in that apartment through the summer, before Daddy got behind in the rent, and then we had to find a new place. I didn't know where we were going, but I was glad to be leaving a place that was so far from downtown.

Don't Worry About A Thing

Chapter Twenty
A Fish Out of Water

Before seventh grade ended and before we moved away from the country, all that the girls in my class could talk about were the coming summer days at their camps on the lake. They looked forward to campfires, boating, and swimming, but most of all, they were excited to have slumber parties. I remembered my summer at Camp Abena and knew how lucky they were.

I had been in classes with most of the girls through elementary school, and we were in Girl Scouts together too. When I got an invitation to Ellen's end-of-the-year party at her camp, I couldn't believe it. Although I felt like an outsider, I was thrilled to be included, especially since we didn't have a camp to invite friends to. (Daddy let me go. Although he did make sure there would be no boys there.) I didn't have a sleeping bag, but I brought blankets and my pillow, my bathing suit, and a change of clothes, and waited for my ride to pick me up.

"Get changed into your suits," Ellen ordered when we arrived. "And meet me at the dock. We're going to swim to the float." Evenings in June could still be cold; the water had not warmed up for the season yet, so we knew it would be freezing. It didn't bother my friends who, one by one, jumped off the dock. As I watched all seven girls dive into the water and swim to the wooden float further out in deep water, I tried to summon the courage to follow. Standing at the edge of the dock chewing my nails, filled with fear and embarrassment that I was twelve and didn't know how to swim, I wondered if I could dog-paddle all the way to the float. I had to. It was my own fault I hadn't learned to swim. The previous summer I had signed up for swimming lessons at the Waterville Municipal Pool, but after the first class, I quit, but not because I didn't want to learn. I refused to go back because I had put my watch, a birthday present I had received the previous February, in the pocket of my shorts and left it by my towel. When I returned after the lesson, someone had gone through the pockets and stolen my watch. I was so upset I told Mumma I was never going back there, and I never did.

So, there I stood on that sunny June afternoon, shivering on the dock in my green one-piece swimsuit, praying for the courage to just jump in and swim, while wishing I could turn around and go home. Neither seemed an option, but I had to do something. China Lake and the float, a far-off island, loomed in front of me. I told myself it wasn't that far. Swallowing my fear, I watched with apprehension as, one by one, the girls made it to the float and climbed the ladder, warming their shivering bodies in the sun.

Before following the others into the water, my friend Jane had paused and asked me before jumping in, "Are you sure you want to do this?" She was being kind, sensing my hesitation, but my pride was stronger than my fear.

"Sure, you go, I'll follow."

"Ok, see you there."

I couldn't back down now.

I sat on the edge of the dock and inched into the cold water. Goose bumps made the hair on my arms rigid as I raised them over my head and waded out neck deep. The ridiculous thought entered my mind that because I was a Pisces, maybe, like a fish, I would miraculously swim like one. This was it. Inhaling a deep breath of pine that wafted from behind me, I floated forward.

Paddling a few yards away from the dock, I could see that Jane made it to the float, pulled herself up and plopped onto the warm sun-drenched boards. She must have been glad to be out of the cold lake. Should I re-think this and turn around? Out of the corner of my eye, I saw her lift her arm in a slight wave, watching as I flopped gracelessly through the water. *Keep going*, I told myself bravely.

My arms were getting tired, but I still wasn't halfway there. I tried to breathe deeply, but my breath caught in my throat, the air stuck somewhere inside. Panic arose as my limbs flailed about, not making any forward progress. Float! I told myself. But I was too tired. My muscles ached, and my leaden legs sank into the water. I tried to turn around and relax but went under as the panic intensified. My arms and legs ached, and I couldn't breathe. I was in trouble.

Struggling to keep my head above water, I lost count of how many times I went under. I could only see blurs of green and blue and yellow where the girls were sitting on the float. The lakebed was a crazy quilt of rocks, sparkling mica, and black, white, and gray quartz, along with clam shells, barnacles attached. Then surprisingly, my fear evaporated as I floated to the bottom. Minnows darted around me and time stopped. As panic evaporated, a silent peace settled inside of me, and I accepted what was to come.

Just as I was preparing to die, I looked upward toward the light at the surface of the water. A voice from somewhere, deep inside? Outside of myself? I don't know where it came from, but it was clear. "GET UP! IT IS NOT YOUR TIME TO GO!"

My arms and legs moved as if an unknown source propelled me upward, and my head bobbed to the surface. Someone placed an arm around my neck and swam toward the shore towing me in. The next thing I remember, I came to, vomiting on the dock as Ellen's mother hovered over me.

Visibly shaken, she asked angrily, "Why didn't you tell us you couldn't swim? Thank God Sarah went after you, young lady, or you would have drowned! What got into you to try to swim to the float?"

My stomach hurt, but not as much as the shame and embarrassment. Sarah looked embarrassed too. She didn't say anything.

The rest of the party was a blur. We grilled hotdogs and hamburgers, made a campfire and s'mores when it got dark, and scared ourselves with ghost stories, but I didn't say much. I remember sitting there, alone in the group. But not alone. Who was it that saved me? Was it God? The essence of what I had felt in the water was an overwhelming love and peace.

Inside the screened porch, in our pajamas, we all got cozy in blankets and sleeping bags as night settled around us. I hitched myself up on my elbows to watch the last embers of the campfire die, and beyond the fire, I could see the waves lapping against the rocks along the shore. Where earlier a shimmering light had pierced the water, now all was black, with only a reflection of the half-moon on the surface. From a distance, the eerie call of the loon echoed across the lake like a woman mourning her lost child, melancholy, like an aching inner sadness.

Although we could only slightly feel the heat of the campfire, the scent of the wood smoke floated up and encircled us on the porch, comforting in its familiar scent.

Jane broke the eerie spell when she dropped her sleeping bag beside me. "I glad you're ok," she said, smiling.

"Thanks. I thought I could make it, but I guess I could have died."

"My sister almost died," she confided. "She was rushed to the hospital, and they discovered she has diabetes. She has to have shots all the time."

"That's so awful. I hope she'll be ok."

"Me too." We looked out onto the lake, settling quietly into our own world.

Don't Worry About A Thing

Chapter Twenty-one
Back to the City

In contrast to my friends' summer at the lake, our childhood cycle of feast or famine continued. I didn't know why it was so hard for Daddy to keep up with the rent, but I knew it wasn't a question I could ask him. For us it was normal to be packing up our things once again. When I watched Daddy and Mumma sitting in front of the TV, drinking coffee and smoking and laughing, I was glad everything was once again okay for now. Anyway, none of us was unhappy to be leaving the chicken farm to go back to the city.

With our car filled to overflowing with our possessions, we arrived at our new home, an old brown clapboard house on Lublow Court. For the first time, we'd be living in an actual house instead of an apartment, a rental that looked out of place across from a tractor sales store. Our new neighborhood, just past the railroad tracks on upper Main Street, was mostly rental properties; but for six-year-old Jimmy, having rows of tractors across the street was a dream come true. One day he even managed to start one of the tractors. Sitting in the seat with the ignition running and the tractor shaking, he screamed until we all ran outside and laughed while Mumma rescued him.

As I looked up the hill from the corner of Main and Lublow, I could see that each consecutive street off Main had fancier and larger homes, and although I lived at the bottom, it didn't bother me one bit. As far as I was concerned, we had stepped up in the world. We were back in the city, and this house, with its strange hodgepodge of rooms, had one room that was all mine!

Like my bedroom in the country with the maple tree outside my window, my new room looked out over the side yard where two large elms guarded the house. Their huge trunks gave me a sense of strength and a feeling of protection. Once again trees were watching over me. On days when I moped about, when my moods grew dark, just looking at these ancient giants with their limbs reaching for the sky consoled me.

A bed, a small bookcase, and my 45rpm record player on top of a metal TV tray, made up my prized possessions. I spent a lot of time in my room listening to records and reading teen magazines, especially during my period when I was crampy and weepy. A large poster of Greece covered one wall, and on my worst days, I dreamed of the day when I'd be old enough to travel far away from Maine. I'm not sure which was stronger, my dream to travel and see the world, or my longing to escape Maine. I was sure leaving Maine was the answer to my problems.

I especially wanted to see where Daddy was born. He had come to America when he was thirteen, but never talked very much about the old country. He had lived a completely different life in a foreign country and, to me, a mysterious place. Maybe if I went there, I would understand why he tried so hard to make us rich by his gambling that never worked. I knew we were never going to win big, and I knew if he did, it would all go back to feed more horses. We'd always be poor. But what if he had stayed in Greece? I wouldn't be here. Mumma from the north woods of Maine and Daddy from half-way around the world, and then me. How did that happen? Was it God's plan, or just random? I wondered if there was a reason or purpose to life, and if so, how would I discover what that purpose was?

The unique house

In the meantime, we settled into our new home, not sure how long we'd be here. This house was a bit unusual, as if the builder had figured it out haphazardly as he went along. Unlike most homes, this one had no front door. As we entered by a side outdoor porch, we came into another glass-enclosed porch, just big enough to put our wet boots. From there we entered into our dining area, with table and chairs, but the fridge was also in this room in the corner. Off the dining area was the kitchen with the stove and sink, a small oblong room with high ceilings, almost like an afterthought. The back door was off the kitchen, which led to what was supposed to be another porch but was only a floor without any railings. We liked it that way because it was a perfect stage that George and I would use to perform when we created our own plays and talent shows. We charged five cents and set up chairs in rows in front of our "stage," choreographing new dances to music from my 45 records in our old dance costumes.

Also from the kitchen, a door opened to stairs that led to two bedrooms, George's and mine, and the bathroom, an attic-like room with a slanted ceiling. Jimmy's room was downstairs off the dining area. The living room was also off the dining area, and beyond that, another bedroom (which was really supposed to be a den) where Mumma and Daddy slept. They had a curtain in the entryway to the room because there was no door for this arched entry to the room. And that was it, our first real house.

Little Grammie visits

The first winter in the new house, Little Grammie came to stay with us for a month. Hauling wood to heat her house was becoming too difficult for her, so she would take turns over the winter staying with her kids for a month at a time. It was a long month for both of us because, unfortunately, our relationship didn't improve that winter.

In the early sixties girls were wearing skirts above the knee, and Grammie did not approve. She thought the way I dressed was scandalous. Convinced I'd become a hussy by wearing short skirts, she let me know how she felt every day as I left for school. "I don't know how your mother can let you leave the house like that. You should be ashamed of yourself. Parading out in public like that." Mumma never argued with her. I had a feeling Mumma didn't always agree with her, but she never said so. I wished just once, though, she had taken my side. "Jesus H Christ!" I fumed as I left the house on more than one morning, slamming the door behind me.

In home economics, we had to sew a jumper. Colored denim was all the rage that year, and we had our choice of colors. I chose red. After buying the required amount of fabric and a pattern, we learned how to put it together. At least some of us did. For me, nothing worked out as it was supposed to. Laying the pattern on the material, cutting the material, and sewing it together turned out to be more difficult than I could have imagined. It was just a straight shift so it shouldn't have been so hard, but why couldn't I get it right? Most of the other girls were whizzing along on the sewing machine, while I was still trying to fit the material with the pattern, which made me rush, which in turn made the cutting uneven. Then the worst part, the actual sewing. Two minutes in and the machine jammed, and the bobbin thing popped out. It happened over and over again, making me so frustrated that I didn't care whether I ever finished that dress. Finally, the teacher grew tired of watching me struggle and helped. I got a C minus on that project.

All the girls in the class decided to wear their jumpers to school when we were done, so despite the raggedy appearance of mine, I wore mine too. Grammie had a lot to say about that. "Are you wearing that outside in public? The seams are all uneven. The shoulders don't even look the same. And that hem is way too short!"

I left school questioning my choice to wear the jumper, but I wasn't going to give her the satisfaction of changing before I left. The other girls all looked fine in their different colored denim jumpers that they continued to wear for the rest of the year. Thankfully no one made any comments about mine, but that was the only day I wore it. It hung in the back of my closet until our next move, when it got thrown away.

Some of the other girls got help at home. If Grammie and I had gotten along, she could have helped me because she knew how to sew, crochet, knit, embroider, and do anything else with a needle. Mumma was like me. We were hopeless.

Babysitting

Shortly after moving back to town, I began babysitting regularly. One of my first jobs was for Uncle Tommy, babysitting my cousins Dino and Tina Marie. I didn't actually get paid money. Uncle Tommy worked for a vending service and replaced 45s in jukeboxes. When he put new records in, the old ones were piled in the back of his station wagon. "Take as many as you want," he offered. After rummaging through the piles of vinyl, I collected quite a few records, mostly from the 1950s. Lots of Elvis and lots of country music, and the Motown sound. Anyone driving by the house could hear us along with the neighborhood kids, singing and dancing to "The Loco-Motion" and "The Twist" and all the songs of the Supremes. I was more a fan of rock and roll though, and it wasn't long before the Beatles and the Rolling Stones were added to my collection.

Eventually my babysitting jobs expanded to include taking care of my teachers' kids and those of Colby College professors. I was making money, but I had no idea how to manage my earnings. Spending was more fun than saving; the instant gratification of Humpty Dumpty potato chips and Pepsi and Whipper's pizza was more enticing than putting the dollars in my savings jar.

The money came in handy because the fridge was frequently empty, and we were never sure if there was going to be dinner. I'm sure it occurred to my parents that kids needed to eat every day, but after paying the rent, lights, and heat, there never seemed to be enough money. Unless Daddy won at the races. He said, "Don't worry about a thing. All we need to do is hit a big one and our problems will be over." I hated those words. Worshiping on the altar of luck, he believed at some point his luck had to change. I didn't believe it. Luck was not going to buy us groceries or keep us in a home.

Mumma wasn't really a gambler like Daddy. She liked to play cards for fun, maybe with pennies sometimes, but that's all. So, when she discovered that Bingo was every Friday night at the American Legion Hall, she started going and loved it. Sometimes she only had a few dollars to play, but unlike Daddy, she was lucky, often coming home with money that she used to buy groceries.

The favorite sweater

Eventually I learned that in order to buy myself new clothes, I'd have to save some money. When I had enough to buy a skirt and matching turtleneck, it felt good to pay for it myself. Because I only made fifty cents an hour, it took forever, so I didn't own many outfits. At the beginning of the school year, we always had to remind Daddy that we needed money for school clothes, and if he won money at the races, he gave it to us. But it was hit or miss.

I knew it wasn't my sister's idea to borrow my favorite sweater. I don't think she would have thought of it. And I was right, as I soon found out. The sweater was a soft off-white wool with a macramé design around the shoulders. I only wore it on special days because it had to be dry-cleaned. It was the most expensive article of clothing I owned, a one-of-a-kind sweater that I had agonized over buying in the store because I knew it would take all of the money I had saved. I'm not even sure how long the sweater had lain in my bureau drawer with the large chocolate stain on the front before I discovered it. The sweater not only had a large chocolate stain, but had been shrunk to one third of its previous size.

"NOOO! Who ruined my favorite sweater?" I shouted, throwing it on Mumma's lap.

"Georgeanna wanted to wear it to school one day and I didn't see any harm in letting her borrow it," she said.

"How could you? It's ruined. I can't believe you let her have it!"

"I didn't think anything would happen to it. And I knew you wouldn't let her borrow it."

"No, I wouldn't have. And this is why, pointing to the stain. You took it and thought I wouldn't find out." I stared at Mumma in disbelief. She didn't even feel sorry, probably because she thought I was selfish for not sharing. I was selfish and why not? Was I supposed to buy clothes for my sister too because she was too young to babysit yet?

Forcing back tears so she wouldn't see my hurt, I screamed at them both to never step foot in my room again. Stomping to my room, I slammed the door.

When my anger dissolved, I was left with sadness as I realized that my anger was not because of the borrowed sweater. I felt betrayed. I knew George would never have taken the sweater herself. It was like the feeling of homesickness I had felt when I was younger. The feeling of not belonging, but not sure where I did belong. The sweater wasn't all that important, and I realized, neither was I. My feelings didn't matter. And that was that.

The world upside down

One afternoon in late November of 1963, we had just finished lunch and were getting settled in Miss Buzzell's eighth grade English class. I sat in the last row (alphabetical order as always), in the next to the last seat. David, the boy who sat behind me and liked to pull my ponytail, was getting on my nerves when I glanced up at the front of the room and noticed Miss Buzzell was crying. The class stared silently when the intercom broke the stillness. In a quiet but somber voice, the principal informed us that President Kennedy had been shot in Dallas, Texas. We were dismissed early and everyone paraded out of the classrooms through the eerily silent school. Some kids were crying, but no one spoke as we left the building.

I raced home and burst into the house. "President Kennedy has been shot!" I yelled. Mumma left the American chop suey simmering in the kitchen, and Daddy, who was working nights and had been sleeping, leaped out of bed and turned on the TV.

Walter Cronkite, in his serious tone, announced that it was a sad day for America. Like most people in our town and across America, we camped out in front of the TV for the next forty-eight hours watching history unfolding in front of us. I couldn't comprehend how such a terrible thing could happen to our president and his family. Our problems suddenly didn't seem nearly as important. The world was turning upside down.

Boys

Eighth grade was also the year I discovered boys, or at least my hormones discovered boys were not another species. My first crush, Danny, was a new kid who had dark hair and blue eyes. We flirted and joked in class but were both too shy to acknowledge we liked each other. I couldn't vouch for my own face, but his was permanently red from blushing. I was in love. Then another girl in my class decided she liked him. Sally quickly moved in on Danny, and when she had her 13th birthday party, I was not invited. It wouldn't have mattered if I had been invited. Daddy was strict when it came to boys, so I didn't know when or even whether he'd ever let me go to parties with boys.

The Monday after the party, Sally appeared at school with hickeys all over her neck. She had a turtleneck on to cover them, but she couldn't keep it to herself, announcing to everyone that they had played spin-the-bottle at her party and then pulled her collar down so everyone could see her neck. I was shocked. Danny's beet-red cheeks were a dead give-away that she wasn't lying. I was both disgusted and crushed. When he tried to joke around with me, I ignored him, and he got redder. As far as I was concerned, our non-boyfriend/girlfriend relationship was over.

I went home that day and appeased my broken heart by eating popcorn and watching *Days of our Lives*, my favorite soap opera. The love story was about a priest who had fallen in love with one of his parishioners and he was torn between his love for the woman and his love for God. I was rooting for the woman.

Learning about religion

One Saturday all the churches in Waterville, in the spirit of ecumenism, opened their doors and welcomed all the citizens of town to come and visit their houses of worship. My friend Anne and I decided we should visit all the churches in town. Because she was more precocious than I, she knew what questions to ask, while I basically tagged along, not really comfortable speaking with all those priests, ministers, and a rabbi. I learned that Methodists didn't use real wine for the blood of Christ. We even tasted the warm grape juice. The Congregational Church, with its plain pews, was decorated sparsely, with just a simple wooden cross in the front of the church. And on we went, marching through town, mingling with the adults who showed up, two young girls searching for answers. I was sorry Anne didn't get to see the inside of a Greek church, which I thought was far more beautiful than any of the others, with its icons and large gold-leaf panels of the saints and the Holy Mother with the Christ child. The ornate crystal chandeliers emanated a candlelight-like glow that made it a far holier place, in my opinion, than the others. I was convinced the Greeks, just like with everything else, did religion right. Too bad Waterville didn't have a Greek church.

Still searching for God

That spring I attended confirmation classes at St. Mark's Episcopal Church. The church was within walking distance of home, so I didn't need anyone to drive me. At the end of April, the bishop arrived for the ceremony. I was in the junior choir and wore my choir robes as I was presented to the bishop. Father Montgomery gave me a gift that I still cherish: a copy of the *Book of Common Prayer.* On the inside cover he wrote: "To Katherine Louise Yotides from her friend and rector, David K. Montgomery, April 22, 1964." Father Montgomery was my first adult friend, a kind man who believed in the goodness of people. He was a man of God, far above me, but I never felt as though I were judged and found wanting. I think he truly felt everyone was good, including me.

My relationship with God was a combination of wanting to believe tinged with a good bit of skepticism. After all, why had He not saved the president? Why did He let people suffer? I had never forgotten my dream about seeing Jesus on Christmas Eve. Daddy blamed God for his bad luck, but even I knew that wasn't God's fault. At first I prayed a lot, mostly that Daddy would win at the races and we'd be rich, but those prayers were not answered. So, as I got older, I didn't bother asking for things, unless I needed a miracle to help my math grade, which seemed to actually work sometimes. In spite of my questioning, I did believe He existed, a force that made me accountable to something.

Don't Worry About A Thing

Chapter Twenty-two
Back to the North Woods

Another school year was over. Starting the summer after eighth grade I would leave home for all or part of the summer break to stay with extended family or to work. I was spending less and less time with my own family.

Our week in the country with Grammie was coming to an end, and Daddy was on his way to get us when my cousin Roberta asked if I wanted to stay with her for a few weeks instead of going right home. We looked forward to seeing each other every summer and neither of us wanted me to leave this year. So, when Mumma and Daddy and the kids left, I stayed. Aunt Ruby and Uncle Bob already had six kids, who were a mixture of red heads with freckles like Aunt Ruby, or brunettes with pale complexions like Uncle Bob. Uncle Bob was injured in the war and received disability, so he was always home except when he had to go to the VA hospital. Even though they had six mouths to feed, they welcomed one more.

Speaking like a Mainer

At first Roberta's brothers and sisters were curious about another kid in the house, but it didn't take long to integrate me into the family. I was used to different accents in Waterville—like the French-Canadian elders who, like my Greek grandparents, retained much of the old world in their speech and lifestyle, so it was easy for me to fall into another accent of the North Woods. All the "ain'ts" came easily. "I ain't gonna close the do-ah!" They would say, but to be high and mighty, I would correct them. "Ain't isn't a word; it isn't in the dictionary." Which made them laugh at my city talk. G's were left off the ends of words, and H's and R's were added. "I ain't lyin." Or "That ain't a good idear." Or "Git in the cah." And "Git out in the doahyahd to play."

But it was the cussing that got some getting used to. With that many kids in the house, most of them quick-tempered like their mother, fights often broke out, and arms started flying, along with words. Not that I didn't hear cussing at home, but we understood only adults used certain words. When Daddy swore in Greek or Albanian, we knew to make ourselves scarce, and when Mumma yelled out, "Jesus H. Christ," someone was in trouble. But here, the kids, even the little two-year-old, would let fly a stream of cuss words, some I'd never heard before. "Son of a ho-ah," "goddamn bahstad," "friggin son of a bitch," flew from angry faces as easily as the water gushing forth from the pump in the "doah yahd." It wasn't long, though, before the shock wore off, and if the little ones could curse, so could I. Ayuh, I could cuss like the rest of them. Aunt Ruby warned me not to use those words in front of Mumma and Daddy, or she would get in trouble.

Although it was the 1960s, living with my cousins was like going back in time. Their black clapboard, weather-beaten house stood on top of a hill, just down the road from Grammie's. If we wanted a drink, we took the tin dipper from the nail inside the door and pumped water from the black iron pump in front of the house until the cold clear liquid filled the dipper. On hot days nothing felt better than a cold drink of water. It took me a while to prime the pump because my skinny arms were weak, but it wasn't long before I got the hang of it. The bathroom, just like at Grammie's house, was an outhouse behind the barn.

Inside, the kitchen and living area made up the largest room. All the boys slept in the bedroom to the left, including Uncle Bob, and all the girls slept in the bedroom to the right, including Aunt Ruby. Roberta and I slept upstairs in a room that was unfinished. Someone started to build rooms, but the sheetrock had not been put up yet. We could see all the way through the length of the upstairs from our bed.

Since it was summer, food was bountiful from both the garden and nearby apple orchards. The kids, especially the boys, were always hungry even though Aunt Ruby was always cooking something on her large wood stove. One afternoon Cousin David came in the house carrying a huge yellow onion. "What are you going to do with that?" I asked. Looking at me as if I had lost my mind, he said, "Makin' a sandwich; whad ya think I'm doin'?" I watched as he sliced the onion, tears streaming down his face, put it between two slices of white bread, and crunched into it with relish. I always remember that day when I'm slicing onions.

Aunt Ruby cooked large pans of homemade dishes like New England baked beans, which were my favorite. The first time I had her beans, she warned me to take it easy, but I had seconds, and then paid the price. After running back and forth to the outhouse, I worried I'd have to spend the night out there. Finally, as darkness set in, I appeared in the kitchen looking peaked. They all laughed, thinking it was uproariously funny. Aunt Ruby chuckled, "I told you so! Guess you got cleaned out good." I didn't think it was so funny, but despite my embarrassment, I laughed too, relieved I didn't have to sit out there with the skunks and raccoons that came out at night. From then on, I ate only small portions of her beans, afraid of a repeat performance in the outhouse. Roberta knew how to cook too. She made the most delicious homemade chocolate cake. Barely able to tell the difference between a cake and pie tin, I watched as she put it together from scratch, and for the first time, I took an interest in cooking.

Unlike at home, where Mumma liked to go to the races with Daddy, many times at a moment's notice, Aunt Ruby's days were set with a routine that never wavered from week to week. Mondays were wash days and it took all day to heat the water on stove, put it in the old wringer washer and after the washing and wringing out, doing it all over again for the rinsing. Roberta and I then carried the clothes out to the clothesline where the breezes on top of the hill dried them in no time, making everything smell as fresh as the outdoors. Ever since we had moved back to town, Mumma took our laundry to the laundromat, where she could wash and dry all our clothes at once while she sat and read movie magazines.

Aunt Ruby was one of my earliest teachers, not because of what she said or what she did, but because of *how* she did things. I always thought a chore was just a chore to be finished and done with, but watching her work, whether it was scrubbing clothes, or washing dishes, I saw that there was another way, that the act of doing was just as important as getting it done. She had to pump the water, boil the water, and mix it with some of the cold water, but it was still so hot when she added the soap that her hands were beet-red when she took them out of the suds. Each dish was carefully scrubbed in the basin with a dish-cloth and placed on the rack where Roberta and I dried them. I loved to watch her as she carefully washed each dish, taking her time as if there was nothing more important in life to do. We talked as she washed and we dried, a communal ritual that repeated after every meal.

Beating summer heat

That summer was a scorcher with no way to cool off except to sit under the shade of a large tree and hope for a breeze. The kitchen was hot from the wood stove, which had to be lit to cook and heat water to wash dishes and to bathe, so none of us stayed inside.

Then one day Aunt Ruby decided we'd go swimming in the river. We put on our oldest clothes and hiked through the woods to the swimming hole. Bugs swarmed around our heads as sweat trickled down our necks, but we didn't complain because we couldn't wait to jump in the cool water. The river was not very wide, but it did have a current, so we were warned not to go too far out. Our feet squished in the riverbed and, holding our noses, we went underwater to escape the bugs. We splashed and jumped off the bank until our skin looked like shriveled-up apples that had fallen from the trees in the orchard we passed on the way to the river; we didn't want to leave. By the time we got home later that afternoon, we were covered in mud, grass, and bug bites. Aunt Ruby put the water on to boil and then added it to cold water in the round tin tub in the middle of the kitchen floor. One by one, from youngest to oldest, the kids got in the soapy water and washed the river scum off their bodies. Roberta and I took smaller basins of water up to her room where we took sponge baths, away from the boys.

Grocery shopping for a crowd

Once a month, when the disability check arrived, we all packed into the car and drove to Lincoln to do a month's worth of grocery shopping. Aunt Ruby and Uncle Bob took the two youngest ones inside with them and the rest of us—Roberta, Connie, David, Johnny, and I—waited in the car. Two hours and two carts full later, they finally appeared and packed the trunk, but not before taking out a pound of bologna and a loaf of white bread. Passing around the bread and bologna, the car full of hungry kids devoured the sandwiches in the back seat. Then best of all, we stopped at the ice cream place and all got vanilla ice cream cones.

Roberta and boys

Roberta was sixteen that summer, and boys started to come around. She started to like the boy who lived just down the road. At fourteen, as far as boys were concerned, I was ambivalent. So far, except for Danny, all my crushes were movie stars like Troy Donahue and Paul Newman; later, when I was fifteen, I fell madly in love with Omar Sharif in *Dr. Zhivago*. But that summer I had no boy interests at all.

I felt left out when she rode through the countryside, while I stayed at the house with the other kids. A couple of times I walked to Grammie's house. She missed Mumma and Joyce. I was probably a poor substitute for them, but she didn't seem to mind my company. I guess we had reached a truce of sorts because we never really argued again. I asked her about her life and what it was like when she grew up, but like Mumma, she never shared very much about her past. Everyone seemed to have their secrets.

One day, sitting around the front steps, waiting for Roberta to come home from her boyfriend's house, I got restless and decided to borrow her bike to ride to the corner store, the only store in Macwahoc Plantation. I knew it was a long way, but I figured with the bike it wouldn't take so long. I had a few dollars I brought with me and intended to buy some penny candy for everyone. I made it to the store, made my purchases and headed back. But I didn't notice the glass bottle until I ran over it, and sure enough, the back tire went flat. "Son of a bitch! Friggin glass! Goddammit!" I shouted, using every cuss word I could think of. When that didn't help, I grabbed the bike's handlebars and began the long trek home. It was nearly dinnertime when I arrived at the house, hot, exhausted, and hungry. Aunt Ruby was standing at the top of the hill, a worried look in her eyes, and I knew it took a lot of self-control for her temper not to flare up. I didn't fare as well with Roberta. She let me have it for taking her bike. Lucky for me, she got over her anger quickly, like her mother. Just like when my sister took my favorite sweater, I never should have taken that bike.

In spite of all the kids, Aunt Ruby managed to give each one-on-one attention. She was generous with hugs and even I was included. With hair as red as her name, and the temper to go with it, Ruby was someone none of us ever dared to cross; but her anger left as quickly as it came, and it wasn't long before her loud laughter could be heard throughout the house. I also think Aunt Ruby liked me. I think we were alike even though we were only related by marriage. Both of us spoke our minds and didn't hide our feelings, especially anger. I loved the way she made me a part of her family.

When I went home, I missed her and my cousins, but I was happy to be back in the city, and with babysitting and getting ready for high school, I had plenty to do.

Chapter Twenty-three
High School and Other Disasters

Growing up, we all heard stories about walking miles to school in the winter during a blizzard, uphill in the snow. And how lucky we were to have cars and buses to take us to school. We rolled our eyes when our parents told us how difficult it was for them to get through the long northern winters. But unless you lived through it, you didn't realize how bad it could be. This is one of those stories.

The blizzard

During my freshman year in high school, we lived less than two miles from school, so I had to walk. When the weather was good, I met a few friends along the way, our arms filled with our schoolbooks. As soon as we had received our books in the fall, we had to cover them with brown grocery bags that we marked with artwork and doodles. Some of the girls drew hearts around their boyfriends' initials.

Snow, however, added another dimension to the morning walk. We all looked like an alien army of hunchbacks with our books and notebooks clutched in front of our chests, covered with thickening layers of snow. Although the roads were plowed in the middle of the night, the sidewalks were not. By midwinter, the trek became more difficult due to the drifts on both sides of the road. And by February, we had to make our way carefully around the snow piles to avoid getting hit by oncoming cars. When we got to school, we were half-frozen and tired from fighting the wind and flurries.

Unlike elementary school when we wore ski pants and took them off in the hallways, in high school, girls didn't wear pants. Because skirts were now shorter, I rolled my wool skirts at the waistband a couple of times baring my knees. Striped turtlenecks that matched the skirts, nylons, or knee socks, and high boots completed my outfits. Not the warmest of clothes, as my knees were only covered with nylons; by the time I got to school, my knees were bright red and numb with cold.

One morning, awakening in below freezing temperatures and a nor'easter in full swing, I begged Daddy to drive me, "Please Dad, it's too cold out there." Mumma never got her license, so she couldn't drive. I tried to shake him awake, but he just turned around, grumbling, "I just went to bed a few hours ago. I'm not getting up now."

I persisted, knowing it was worse than normal. All night the wind had roared as the lights from the plows flickered across the walls of my room as they drove up and down the street, but the snow was coming down too fast for them to keep up. Peering outside my window, I could see the plow's tracks were already covered again. Groaning aloud, I was instantly aware I'd have a problem. Dad worked past midnight, and I knew he was tired, but I decided to try once more as I headed out. "Dad!" I yelled from the doorway. "What?" he mumbled, eyes half open. "Are you taking me or not?" No answer. Sighing in resignation, I got ready to face the storm.

Wrapping my scarf around my face so that only my eyes were visible, I buttoned up my coat, put on gloves and with books and notebooks grasped tightly in front of me, I approached the door. "OK, I'm leaving. If they find my body in a snow drift, it'll be your fault!" I warned before storming out.

The arctic winds blew the snow sideways, stinging my eyes. I trudged into the street, my body bent against the onslaught, lifting one leg and then the other, higher than normal, trying to keep the snow from falling into my boots. My nyloned legs exposed to the wind and snow immediately turned scarlet. After the first hill, I turned the corner to cross a bridge. The gale was now pushing me sideways, making it more difficult to keep my balance. Tightening my grip on my books, I prayed they wouldn't slide out of my arms and into the snow. My teeth chattered. My feet and legs were now covered with snow that had seeped into my boots.

The other kids who usually met me at the bridge were not there. Why hadn't I stayed home? Fear of missing something important? Not wanting to be bored at home? I didn't question. I had to go. A few cars slowly made their way by me, fueling my anger. "As soon as I'm old enough to get out of here, I'm going south and never coming back to this damn burg," I muttered to myself, vowing, not for the first time, to leave Maine.

Crossing the second bridge over the river, the gusts increased and the frigid air went clear through my clothes all the way to the bone. My legs were numb. Waterville High School was just ahead and finally, with relief, I arrived at the front door. Mr. Trask, the principal, whisked me into the office and pulled up a chair next to two other students thawing by the heater. Mrs. Smallwood helped me remove my boots and wrapped a blanket around my feet. The clock revealed I was twenty minutes late. When my legs finally tingled with life, I left for class.

The storm over, walking home that afternoon was easier. Dad was in front of the TV, drinking coffee before he had to leave for work. "The principal made me go into the office to dry off this morning. I nearly froze to death," I exaggerated dramatically. He looked at me guiltily. After that, every time I wanted a ride to school, he didn't refuse, dropping me off at the front door so he could wave to the principal.

My attempt at popularity

When cheerleading tryouts were announced, I, along with a couple of my girlfriends, decided to try out for the junior varsity squad. I thought that If I made the squad, overnight I would miraculously become one of the popular girls wearing cute uniforms in purple and white. Pom-poms. Football games. Maybe even a boyfriend. I could only dream as we practiced every day in the gym. In my fantasies, I waited anxiously for the PE teacher to call out my name, and sure enough, she did, making me instantly part of the "in" crowd. That would be the life.

A group of us learned the cheers together, and we went into try-outs in threes. My voice was not the low bass required by the thundering cheers. It was too high and shrill. My arms went in the right direction, but my legs didn't, and when I attempted the jumps, my skinny legs never landed like they were supposed to. To give credit where it's due, no one laughed at my attempts, but deep down, I suspected I wasn't meant for the cheering world.

On the day the coach posted the names of those who had made the squad, some of my friends, who also didn't make it, burst into tears. Surprisingly, after the initial disappointment came a sense of relief. Did I really want to go to all those games and freeze out in the cold? Did I even like football? I was more humiliated that I wasn't good enough than sad about not cheerleading. I just didn't want to fail. I guess I wouldn't be popular after all. With my cheerleading dreams ended before they began, I was free to go to games when the weather wasn't freezing; but on the frigid days, my school spirit was usually tempered by how uncomfortable I'd be sitting on the bleachers.

Even before I entered high school, I had begun to think about going to college. From early on, Daddy always said I was going to be a teacher because my head was always in a book and also because I was so bossy. "Ok, boss," he called me when I ordered my sister and brother around. "Listen to the boss," he laughed when I thought I knew it all. But the idea had taken root, and I decided that I was going to be an English teacher. I loved English and could imagine myself teaching literature and writing. I decided on my own to go into the college track, the other choices being business/secretarial, or vocational. I had no idea how I would actually go to college, since we had no savings, but that was my plan.

I liked my classes, but always worried about not doing well and failing at that too, like the cheerleading fiasco. At first, I was intimidated by Shakespeare's language, "In sooth, I know not why I am so sad ... and such a want-wit sadness makes of me, that I have much ado to know myself." (*The Merchant of Venice*) But before long, it was surprisingly easy to translate. I loved *Romeo and Juliet* and all the other novels we read, like *Silas Marner* and *Ivanhoe*. Because I took Spanish in junior high, I continued in high school. An overachiever, I managed to get good grades in everything but algebra, which became my nemesis. No matter how hard I tried, I didn't get it. Finally, I took Mrs. Smith up on her offer to help me after school, and two afternoons a week, I, along with a few others like me, sat in her classroom as she reiterated what she had taught in class. It didn't work. I never really did understand the concepts but was able to memorize enough to get by. And I did, finally. By the end of the year, I was able to pull my D up to B and that was when I realized that if I worked my butt off, I could succeed.

The heavy snows continued, but they didn't stop the neighborhood kids from going outside on weekends after the storms. The sun-drenched snow was blinding as we escaped the house for a few hours. Bundled up in as many layers as we could tolerate, we stayed outside until we were too wet or too cold. Our house in this neighborhood, unlike our others, was not near a hill to go sledding, so we tunneled through the tall drifts, making forts to prepare for snowball fights. Jen, across the street, had a rope swing that hung from a tree in front of her house. We loved swinging and flying off into the high snowdrifts. And that winter, I got ice skates for Christmas, blue with white fur around the top. We went to Alfond Arena at Colby College, an indoor rink, and for someone with no athletic abilities, I became a reasonably good skater, which meant I could skate around the rink without breaking my leg.

Many of the kids who attended Catholic schools through eighth grade now were attending Waterville High School, along with kids from other parts of town, so I made a few new friends that year. Some were girls who, like me, couldn't afford to go skiing at Sugarloaf every weekend. We met at the corner and walked to school and sometimes ate lunch together, but rarely saw each other on weekends. I never invited friends to my house, except for once, and that turned into a disaster.

Bragging will get you no where

"What is your favorite meal?" Susan asked me one day on the way to school just before the Thanksgiving Holiday.

"My memere's *tourtiere* pie," Mary Ann quickly answered. "It's the best. We have it at Thanksgiving and Christmas." I had heard of that French Canadian pork pie but had never had it.

"Mine is turkey and stuffing. All our family is coming over and my mother is already baking pumpkin and squash pies," Susan said.

"My favorite is roast lamb with potatoes and vegetables. Daddy is cooking the lamb and my mother is making pies and chocolate cakes and my grandmother is making baklava and spanakopita," I added. And then, not to be outdone: "The cupboards are full of food to make pies, cakes, cookies, and all the fixings."

Of course, that was a lie. Why did I have to exaggerate so much? Would they not like me if they knew? My prevarications always got me in trouble, but I couldn't seem to stop, and they caused more shame than if I just let things be, without making them worse. This time was no exception. We would probably have Thanksgiving at Yiayia and Grampie's, but there was no food in our house. The racetrack wasn't open in the winter, so we usually were a bit better off; but after paying the rent, heat, and lights, there was not much left for food. And if there were emergency repairs on the car, we were really in trouble. More often than not, Daddy made a big pot of bean soup or Mumma fixed American chop suey if we had hamburg in the house.

Then one day soon after our conversation, on our way home, Susan and Mary Ann asked to come inside to use the bathroom. I hesitated, but couldn't think of a reason to say no. Because I had overdone it with my bragging and lies, Mary Ann opened the refrigerator: ketchup, mustard, and margarine sat alone on one shelf. Embarrassed, she quickly shut the fridge, and they left. That was the last time they came into the house.

School, and glee club

The long winter dragged on, but I looked forward to school every day, and that was mainly because of Glee Club. Mrs. Nickerson, our music teacher—blond hair piled high in bun, a perpetual tan even in winter, and gold bangles covering both arms—sparkled and shimmered with sophistication, reminding me of Glenda the Good Witch in *The Wizard of Oz*. I remembered her from elementary school when she came to our classes periodically to give us lessons in music appreciation. She brought her record player and introduced us to classical music, like *Peter and the Wolf*, instilling in us the love of song and music. Now, I looked forward to Glee Club every day. Right away in the fall we began preparing for the Christmas concert. I was second soprano.

The Christmas program was the much-anticipated highlight of the year. After weeks of practice, we performed part of Handel's *Messiah*. Before the "Hallelujah Chorus" at the end, Mrs. Nickerson turned and motioned for the audience to rise. We performed this every year, but it never failed to send goose bumps up my spine. I could see Daddy and Mumma in the audience looking at me with pride.

At home, I added new posters to my bedroom wall, mostly of the Beatles. The night they came to America, I sat on the linoleum floor in the living room waiting for the Ed Sullivan Show to begin, and like millions of teenagers my age, I swooned over the fabulous four. I was in love with John Lennon. Mumma and Daddy, on the couch smoking and drinking coffee, had never seen anything like it. They got a kick out of the spectacle of screaming, fainting teenage girls. I longed to be in that audience. I'd be screaming and fainting too.

Before it got warm enough for the snow to melt in early spring, pollution from the paper and textile factories turned the gray plowed drifts at the end of the streets to black. No one wanted to be outside. Eventually the days became warmer and the melting snow turned to dirty slush as we maneuvered through the ruts made by cars, hoping the last of the storms were over.

The spring talent show

That spring, Mrs. Nickerson directed the music for the school talent show. In between the solo acts, groups of us would perform song and dance routines. She gave us carte blanche to come up with our own acts. The best acts were the ones where kids could really sing well. I could carry a tune in the chorus, but never could have pulled off a solo, not only because my voice wasn't that great, but I would have died of stage fright. So in between the talented singing acts, dance routines, and piano solos, my friends and I were allowed to lip sync and dance to whatever tunes we could come up with, and unless we were exceptionally bad, we were in. Mrs. N was more concerned we had the stage experience than how excellent we were. Except when it came to the *Hallelujah Chorus* at Christmas. If we were off, she made us do it until we got it right.

"What should we do?" Deb asked me and four of our girlfriends, anticipating the spring event. Judy had an idea. "Let's create a dance with 'Walk Right

In' by The Rooftop Singers."

"Yes, when the song goes, 'Everybody's talkin' 'bout a new way of walkin', we can come up with a new walk!" Lib suggested.

"Let's have three of us come on stage left and three from stage right and meet in the middle," I offered my two cents.

"Let's do it!"

During rehearsals, I didn't think much about being nervous, but on opening night, as I watched backstage as the audience filled, my heart started fluttering. "I don't know if I can do this," I whispered to Deb who was watching beside me.

"What's the worst thing that can happen? You could fall on your face."

"Thanks, I didn't think of that! Or I could pee my pants," I remembered my dancing school days.

"What?" she laughed.

"Never mind." We giggled, the nervousness forgotten for a minute.

The music began. That was our cue. One, two, three ... we were on! Before I knew it, it was over and clapping followed us as we danced off, stage right and stage left.

Laughing with excitement and not a little relief, we hurried backstage to prepare for our next acts.

The closest I came to a solo was a comedy routine that Sue wrote, a Rocky and Bullwinkle skit. I was Rocky, the foil. She did most of the talking, and at the end, I had to escape while she was in the middle of her monologue, but she caught me when she produced a cane, wrapped it around my neck, and dragged me back on stage. Judging from the laughter, or lack of it, our act was not a hit. Comedy was not our thing, evidently.

"What went wrong?" she asked sadly at the end.

"I don't know. Maybe no one likes Rocky and Bullwinkle."

Later in the show, nineteen of us sang "America" from *West Side Story*. I felt like Rita Moreno, twirling around the stage pretending to live in the tenements of New York City.

Finally, just before the finale, eleven of us did a Charleston dance routine. Evie's mother had made us matching costumes with white fringe in different colors. Mine was blue.

School year ending

After spending weeks preparing, rehearsing, and performing, life seemed anticlimactic when it was over. Those glee club shows were some of the most fun days of my high school life despite the stage fright. It's like there were two Kathys. Kathy number one, who wanted to be out there on the stage, dancing, singing, entertaining, and Kathy number two, nervous, frightened, and insecure. To her credit, Kathy number one didn't let Kathy number two stop her completely.

Near the end of the school year, when threats of snow had finally passed, the entire Glee Club went on a field trip to Boston for the weekend. I could hardly wait to get on the bus for the four-hour ride to the city. Riding south on I-95, away from Waterville, the excitement of leaving town rivaled my anticipation of what I would discover in the city. I always felt that driving south, away from town, I was escaping to a place where life was better and happier. Grampie, Yiayia, and Daddy moved away from Greece to find a better life, and in my mind, leaving Maine had the same allure. I couldn't imagine what it was like in the old country if they had had to come to this place. It was exciting to be going into the unknown.

The trip to Boston

With some babysitting money, twenty dollars from Aunt Maria along with her small brown suitcase she let me borrow, we left on Friday morning to go to the Parker House, where we would stay for two nights. First on the agenda was shopping in Filene's bargain basement. As we descended into the bowels of the large multistory building, the contrast between the perfume-scented, flower-decorated first floor and the basement was stark. Before the escalator reached the bottom, I could hear the canned music from above replaced by women yelling, sounding more like a men's locker room than a place to buy clothes.

"Where do we begin?" I asked Debbie, who had been there before and knew what to expect. The huge bins filled with clothes of every size were overwhelming.

"Just pick a bin and go through it until you find something. Look there's bras over there. Want a bra? And over there, lots of blouses. I think I'll check that out."

Women unabashedly were trying on brassieres, slips, blouses, and skirts right there on the floor because all the dressing rooms were full. It was kind of embarrassing, but funny too. Women grabbing underwear as if their lives depended on it.

I hadn't brought enough money to buy clothes, so I followed behind Debbie until she got tired of searching. Then we were happy to ride up and down the escalators until we reached the floor that had a gourmet food section. Staring at the chocolates through the glass cases, we knew we had found heaven. After much deliberation, we chose a few chocolates with maple, raspberry, and coconut fillings, eating them right there.

Before we left the store, I bought a new pair of nylons, not because I needed them, but because I had to have something from Filene's. Now I could say I really bought *something* from Filene's unlike when I was ten and had made up the story of my Cinderella dress.

On Saturday, we attended *My Fair Lady* in new Technicolor at the Saxon Theatre. Even though it was a movie, they handed out playbills with information about the cast just as if it were a live performance.

Later that evening, dressed in our Sunday best, we attended the Metropolitan Opera at the Prudential Center, the real reason Mrs. Nickerson had brought us to Boston in the first place. Entering the foyer, we were awed by the limos discharging men in tuxedos and women in furs and long evening gowns. Mrs. Nickerson told us to look closely, we might see someone famous, but we never did. That year we saw Puccini's *Turandot*. Since it was in Italian, we had a difficult time following the story line, but the music, the costumes, and the sets, kept us entranced. Some of us, me included, dozed off, having stayed up most of the night before, only to be awakened by the bravos and standing ovations at the end.

Leaving Boston on Sunday, we made one more stop at an ice cream smorgasbord shop where we lined up to make our own sundaes. We could get lunch and dessert, but my cash was almost gone, so I went straight for the ice cream, making a delicious hot fudge sundae with coffee ice cream and hot fudge sauce.

The end of freshman year was fast approaching. While I was glad algebra was almost over, I had become fully engaged in my education and extra-curricular activities. The summer months loomed ahead with not much to look forward to but warm days and cool nights, and hopefully a lot of babysitting jobs. However, not long after school let out, I had the chance to travel out of Maine again.

Don't Worry About A Thing

Chapter Twenty-four
The Grass is Always Greener?

Daddy's first cousin Ellen invited me to stay in Massachusetts with her family for a few weeks. I was glad we had relatives who didn't live in Maine and thought of Massachusetts as a special place where life was better—even though I had only been a few times. I'm sure Ellen knew about Daddy's problem and thought a trip to Massachusetts would be a nice escape for me.

Arriving in my cousin's suburban neighborhood, I thought I'd landed in Oz, where the Yellow Brick Road morphed into quiet streets with names like Shady Lane and Blueberry Terrace. The houses, New England capes, were surrounded by white picket fences and all had backyards with swing sets. Flowers and shrubs lined the walkways. Kids were everywhere, riding bikes up and down the street. I could see right away that everything was different here. Fathers left in the morning to go to work, leaving the mothers to take care of the kids and socialize with their neighbors over coffee. On weekends, friends got together for a backyard barbeque or to play cards.

When Greek family members visited, Ellen played Greek music and everyone danced and feasted on hamburgers and hotdogs from the back-yard grill. I was surprised to find that, like me, my cousins didn't have a favorable opinion of Maine. "Your grandparents should have moved here. Maria would have been much better off if she lived here. There is nothing in Maine," Ellen repeatedly stated throughout my stay with her. Ellen and Aunt Maria were first cousins, and she liked to compare her life with Aunt Maria's in Waterville. Aunt Maria's life always came up lacking. Hearing them denigrate my grandfather's decision to settle in Maine made me want to defend him, but there was not much I could say. The contrast was stark. My life in Maine couldn't compare to this, but I wondered if it would have been different for us if Mumma and Daddy had moved to Massachusetts. I wondered if Daddy might have stopped gambling. I listened to the criticisms of my family, secretly torn between loyalty and betrayal.

Sometimes we went to the beach at Cape Cod for the day, had a picnic lunch, and stopped for ice cream on the way home. On Friday or Saturday night, I babysat Ellen's two little boys while she and her husband went out to dinner or a movie. There was always enough food, and no one seemed to be worried about money. That would be nice, I told myself. Here was a place where, when Daddy said, "Don't worry about a thing," it could really come true. Yet, I didn't feel that I fit in here, and it was my fault. This world was alien to me, too normal, too secure, too stable, too perfect, in other words, too strange.

The girls in the neighborhood who were my age were mini versions of their mothers, spending hours playing cards. Every day they got together on some-one's back porch and tried to teach me to play canasta and bridge, a futile attempt because I had no card sense. So mostly I listened to them gossip about their friends, and then they acted nice when the "friend" appeared. Their mothers did the same when the neighbors came for coffee. For example, one might say, "Did you hear what Mrs. Samson did?" Another could offer, "Sally Jamison does not know how to cook. Someone should show her how to make a decent meal."

I was aware that I was an outsider, but I didn't attempt to try to fit in. On some level I understood that I was too different, or maybe out of their league. As those summer days passed, I realized something. I was bored. Every day was the same as the one before. At home I could go to a friend's house, walk to a movie, go downtown, or walk to Yiayia's house. Instead of playing cards and listening to all the gossip, I would put cousin Ellen's youngest son in his carriage and stroll up and down the streets, exploring the neighborhood. Even that got tiring because every street looked the same and when the streets ended, the countryside with farms made it impossible to walk any further.

There were obvious advantages to life here, as Ellen often reminded me. The kids didn't have to worry about money, food was always plentiful, and the bills got paid so families were not evicted. I was still glad I didn't live there, although I did appreciate that this was what life was like when one had enough. I kept expecting Ellen to run out of food, but every time she needed something, we got in the car, drove to the grocery, and bought it. No problem. Every day wasn't a struggle to make ends meet, waiting for a paycheck before they could buy something. Everyone had time and energy for games and gossip and fun.

Before I left, Ellen took me to one of the large factory outlets in New Bedford that made kids' clothes and bought me enough outfits for the new school year. I came home with jumpers and blouses. Jumpers were in fashion then, but I was so skinny they hung on me like plaid sacks. I appreciated her generosity, but never liked wearing the clothes, and as soon as I got back to babysitting, I bought new ones.

When it was time for me to leave, I felt conflicted. Waiting for Uncle Tommy and Auntie Dee who were coming to get me, I stared dejectedly out the front door. Ellen, standing beside me, said, "Don't cry." I couldn't help it. When I got into the car, I burst into tears. No one knew, though, that it wasn't sadness that caused the outburst. I realized then just how unfair life was, and I felt angry more than anything else. I didn't want to go back to feast or famine, not knowing if we'd have to move again, worrying about everything. Life wasn't fair and maybe it never would be.

Back at home I settled into my old familiar life, getting ready for school, babysitting, and hibernating in my room, becoming increasingly overcome by adolescent moods. It was a time of watchful waiting, not knowing when, but knowing for sure that another change was imminent.

Chapter Twenty-five
Here We Go Again

The more things change, the more they stay the same. That was true about our life. Like my 45 rpm records when they got scratched from repeated playing and the needle got stuck on repeat, we were caught in a rut. On repeat, our song of life played over and over, Daddy continued to gamble and got behind in the rent. When he couldn't catch up, we were evicted. Again. But God only knew where the needle would stop this time and where we would be living.

Moving again

The day arrived when we had to be out of our house, but Daddy was nowhere to be found. Desperate, Mumma found us an upstairs apartment in an old run-down house in the north end of town, so we reluctantly left.

Moving day was a blur. Mumma got one of her brothers to help us move our stuff, then we were left in our new apartment surrounded by boxes. Too tired to unpack, the three of us kids fell asleep on a mattress on the floor in one of the bedrooms. Sometime in the middle of the night, Daddy finally showed up, though I don't know how he found us. He had been drinking and was furious at Mumma for moving us to that run-down low-rent apartment. We could hear him yelling at her as if it were her fault. She was tired and crying, and I'd had enough.

Getting up off the mattress, I stormed into the kitchen where they were sitting, my face red with anger, "Why are you yelling at Mumma? Where were *you* when we had to leave? Why didn't you get us a new place? It's not her fault you are never home and don't pay the rent!"

At first, he was as stunned as I was at my outburst. It was the first time I had ever challenged him. *Holy hell*, I thought, *I'm going to get it.* Even though I was fifteen, and he was never physically violent, I still had a healthy fear of his anger.

"Get back to bed!" he ordered. And that was that. We heard no more that night, and the next day, Daddy moved us to a new apartment in a better neighborhood, two streets up from our old house, off Main Street on Boutelle Avenue. It wasn't a house this time, just a downstairs apartment, but we still had our own rooms. This place was much smaller than the house, but I liked my bedroom that faced the road and had a window seat where I could sit and read. And like all the other times when there was a crisis in the family, things settled down for a while and we enjoyed a semblance of normalcy. While it lasted.

By now I had no illusions about Daddy winning at the races. I still really hoped he would win. Why couldn't he win a big one just once? But I didn't trust him when he said things would change when his horse won big. He knew by the way I rolled my eyes and sarcastically said, "Sure it will," that I didn't believe him. When things were okay, I forgave him. When things were not okay, I'd get angry, but not for long. Most of my anger I directed toward Mumma. I couldn't understand why she always accepted the way things were. Why didn't she fight him? Why didn't she do something? When I challenged her, she said you can't change people. One of her favorite sayings was, "You make your bed, you have to lie in it." I guess she was okay with the way things were, or she was resigned. That's just the way Daddy was and there was nothing we could do about it. It seemed to me if he cared about us at all, he would stop gambling. The older I got, the more of a kid he seemed to be. I know he loved us; he just couldn't take care of us the way most fathers did. And that was that.

On to sophomore year

Like during freshman year, life during sophomore year settled into a routine of school and babysitting. Mumma and Daddy believed I was smart enough to go to college, but they had no plans to help me get there. It was one thing to hear that education was the way out of poverty, but it was another thing to figure out how to get that education. They were proud when I brought home good grades, but pride wasn't going to pay for college, and I suspected I wasn't all that smart anyway. My friends were all much smarter than I was. I had to study for those grades, and it wasn't easy, especially for math. I survived algebra, mainly because of the kindness and help of Mrs. Smith, and now I worried I'd have the same problems with geometry. But to my relief, geometry made sense so I didn't have to stress out about passing math.

On weekends, if I didn't have a babysitting job, I spent most of my time in my room, reading or listening to music, but my life really revolved around school. Georgeanna and Jim were still old enough to play outside, but I had lost interest in kids' games. Sometimes I went to Joyce's apartment to play with her little ones, or to the library, and sometimes on Sunday to church, but I no longer sang in the choir and I stopped attending regularly. I wasn't interested in God anymore. He wasn't showing much interest in us, that's for sure. My Christmas eve visitation with Jesus a few years before was now relegated to a childhood dream. But to hedge my bets, when I awoke in the middle of the night worried about life in general, I snuck in a prayer here and there, just in case He decided to listen.

Christmas and another birthday

For Christmas that winter, I got a desk and typewriter. Rarely leaving my room, my favorite albums played continuously as I completed schoolwork. Besides the Beatles, I loved the Rolling Stones, the Byrds, the Supremes, and Vanilla Fudge, whose song, "You Keep Me Hanging On," I played over and over until Mumma threatened to get rid of it. My room was always neat and clean with everything in its place. I became attached to my few possessions and if George or Jimmy came into my room, I went ballistic. My room was my security blanket and keeping everything in its place was the only aspect of my life I could control.

My sixteenth birthday, at the end of February 26, 1966, coincided with our weeklong mid-winter break. No school for a week was my present by default, and usually it was a non-event because without fail, a blizzard would ruin any plans that I might have made. That year though, for my birthday, Aunt Maria arrived at the house and told me we were going out.

"Where?" I wanted to know. Mumma shrugged, having no idea herself.

"Come on, hurry up, we have an appointment," Aunt Maria urged.

More confused than ever, I left the house with Maria and we went to a doctor's office. I stopped in front of the door, too nervous to proceed. "Okay, okay, here's your present," she said, handing me a small Tardiff's Jewelry box. Inside were fourteen-carat gold studs. Aunt Maria was giving me pierced ears for my birthday!

Pierced ears were in style then, but not all the girls at school had had theirs pierced yet, so for the first time in my life, I felt like I was stylish. I returned to school with my below-the-shoulder ironed hair behind my ears so that everyone could see the shiny gold earrings. And just in case no one noticed, I flipped my hair back every now and then to make sure they would.

Right away after the mid-winter break, we began rehearsing for the spring talent show. A large group of us sang and danced to "Put on Your Sunday Clothes" from Hello Dolly and "Nothing Like a

Dame," from *South Pacific*. And just like the year before, it was the highlight of the year. On our Boston trip we saw *The Sound of Music* at the Gary Theatre and *Pique-Dame, The Queen of Spades* at the opera. I wish I could say I fell in love with opera, but I'm afraid I would have disappointed Mrs. Nickerson if I had told her I was bored; maybe I was just tired after running around all day. I tried not to, but just like the year before, I couldn't help nodding off during the long performance, only to wake to the sound of loud applause. On the other hand, I could have watched *The Sound of Music* every day. Movies were still my favorite. Life was good that spring, and I was so involved in school I stopped worrying about everything.

I began to think that maybe we'd be staying in that apartment on Boutelle Avenue for good.

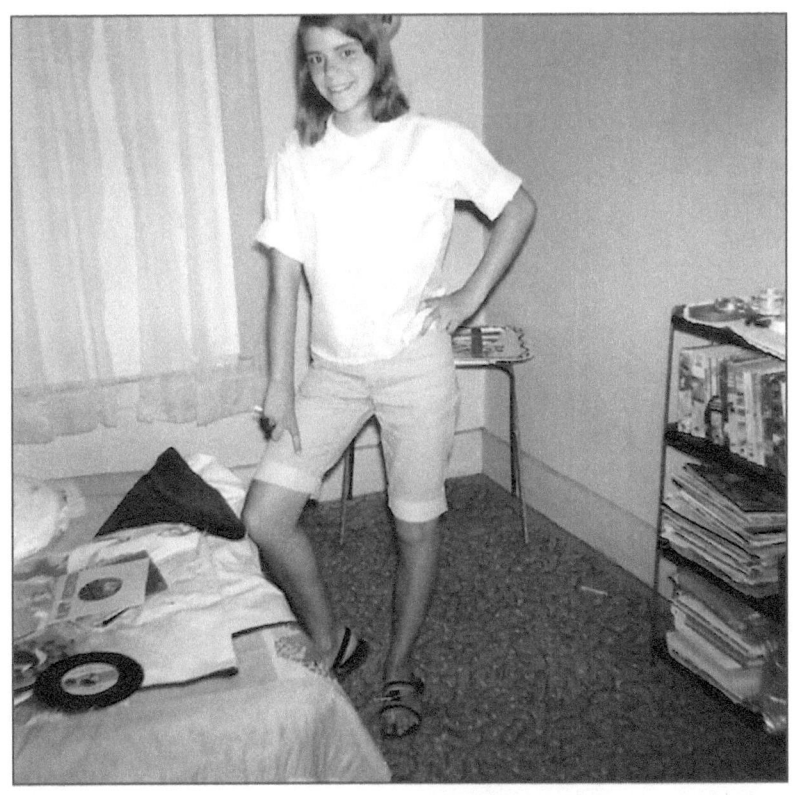

Back to the City

Don't Worry About A Thing

Chapter Twenty-six
My First Real Job

Before the school year ended, my guidance counselor called me into the office to talk about a job opportunity for the summer. Camp Somerset, a summer camp for girls, mostly rich Jewish girls from New York City, was hiring waitresses. Would I be interested? Without hesitation, I answered yes. The camp director came to interview us and soon thereafter, I received a contract and a code of behavior that I would also have to sign. The letter stated, "I was very impressed by you and I know that you will not only make a wonderful contribution to our camp, but that you will have an enjoyable summer as well." I was beyond excited until I read further. I would need three or four pairs of navy blue shorts; a half a dozen white shirts or blouses; white, red, or navy sweaters; a white poplin jacket; two pairs of dungarees; a sweatshirt or two in navy, gray, or white; white socks; three sheets, two pillowcases, and four towels; and two or three blankets, along with a raincoat and two bathing suits! The laundry went out once a week and was back in three days.

My heart sank. Did they think I was made of money? Even if I had had a stash of babysitting money put away, which I didn't, there's no way I could buy all that. After the initial shock, undaunted, I decided I was going anyway. I bought a few shorts and white tops, folded my one pair of sheets and some towels, a rain jacket and sweatshirt, and packed it all in Aunt Maria's little brown suitcase. It would have to be good enough. My pay would be $150 for two months, from June 19 to August 26. That was more money than I'd ever seen all at once and room and board were all included. The only expense would be my laundry at $1.25 per week. I couldn't wait to go!

The waitresses' dormitory was a cabin next to the mess hall. We had to be in the dining room a half hour before the meal to set up, then serve it, and then clean our tables. Each waitress had the same four tables every day, and I was given the youngest campers, ages six to eight. I loved the sweet little girls I served every day and became friends with their counselors, who were previous campers at Somerset.

That summer I learned how the very rich lived. Little girls were sent away to boarding school in the winter and then to camp all summer. Most were from New York City, but some came from as far away as Chicago and Los Angeles. They only saw their parents on holidays or special visiting days. When they first arrived at camp, many of the girls appeared at the breakfast table with red, swollen eyes after a night of homesickness for their parents, or in many cases, for their nannies, but after a few weeks, the camp staff and the counselors became their new family.

Visiting Day at camp

When we had been at camp for a month, chauf-feur-driven limousines lined the road to get into the camp parking area as parents arrived for visiting day. Campers waited impatiently behind a roped off area and parents listened for the signal to disembark from their cars. Our job was to keep the campers from sneaking under the rope barriers and racing toward the cars, but it was futile, and we stared when parents and children raced toward each other laughing and crying. Trying to hold back my own tears, I felt sorry for these girls, especially my little ones, who rarely got to see their parents.

When our mess hall duties were over, the wait-resses, the kitchen crew, and the grounds crew hung out together. I hadn't brought a bathing suit because I had run out of money buying my work clothes. So, while some of the staff spent afternoons swimming and boating when the campers were doing other activities, I sunbathed in my shorts, walked in the woods, and sat around talking to my new friends.

One of those friends was Henry who worked in the kitchen. Not much taller than I was, he had a long thin face and wore wire-rimmed glasses. His outer demeanor reflected an inner serious nature. He attended American University in Washington, D.C., but was from Waterville, Maine, and had grown up a few streets away from where we now lived. Worldly wise and well-traveled, he immediately made an impression on me. Five years older, and unlike kids my age, he was concerned about the state of the world, global poverty, and human rights. I knew little of the world outside my town, so I enjoyed his stories about his life experiences. He found me a good listener. And I loved that he called me Katherine. Not even my parents called me by my real name. Henry wasn't a swimmer or boater, so we spent many afternoons chatting by the lake.

Sitting on the dock one sunny afternoon, Henry was about to light a cigarette when he turned toward me offering me one. I nonchalantly took the cigarette and put it in my lips as he struck the match to light it. I inhaled, watching the end burn red. Luckily for once I didn't make a fool of myself, not even by coughing, but I'd been inhaling Mumma and Daddy's cigarette smoke all my life. That day, I was instantly hooked. Smoking made me feel like a grown-up. With a cigarette between my fingers, I'd wave it in the air as I talked, and when I was trying to think of something to say, just pausing to inhale always helped. I loved the crutch that made a little girl feel like a woman. In the movies, the bad girls, the edgy ones, the ones with a devil-may-care attitude always smoked. I don't remember Doris Day smoking, or Gidget, and I wasn't sure which of those types I wanted to be, but I did know smoking came naturally. Most of us smoked that summer, and since Henry had access to a car, I tagged along when he drove into town to buy our cigarettes.

Unlike some of my girlfriends who had experience making out, I was a cliché: sweet sixteen and never been kissed. That was to change. The boys' camp was across the lake, and sometimes we'd get together with its waiters and staff. Ricky was my age and kind of funny looking with big ears, but one afternoon when he asked if I wanted to go for a walk, I said yes.

"Let's go down by the stables," he suggested. Taking my hand, we strolled to the horse stables. As we stared at the horses, pretending to be interested, he asked, "Do you like to ride? My sister has horses and that's all she talks about."

"Yes," I replied. "I love horses." I didn't mention that with the exception of the one time I rode at Camp Abena, my only horse experiences came from books. Anyway, he didn't seem too interested in horses.

He acted nervous, but I didn't read the signals until he turned to me blushing a deep red and asked, "Would you mind if I kissed you?"

Taken aback, I nonetheless couldn't help thinking how polite he was. Should I refuse? He did ask so nicely. They never did that in the movies, but what did I know? "Ok," I assented. So, he pulled me close and kissed me, putting his tongue in my mouth. How awful! Gross! Pulling away, I began walking back to the dining hall, trying to hide my disgust and embarrassment. As we approached the mess hall, he turned to me with a smile, oblivious to my feelings, but still blushing, "Thank you. Can I see you again?" Maybe it was his politeness that made me lie. "Sure," I stammered as I made my way to the door. "Bye."

Back to work in the mess hall, 1 set up for dinner, and when the campers filed in, I was still re-living my first kiss. Was I supposed to like it when a total stranger kissed me? I felt nothing but embarrassment and determined then and there that I'd have to be "in love," whatever that meant, before I kissed a boy again. Not paying attention to what I was doing, I began serving from a tray of glasses filled with chocolate milk. I lifted one of the glasses from the tray, and instead of placing it on the table, missed the table completely and it crashed to the floor, chocolate milk going everywhere. Harriet, the counselor at my table, stared at me in surprise. My expression must have been one of horror because she started laughing, and then the campers laughed, and finally I joined in. Trying to forget my first kiss, I focused on my work.

Ricky called every day for a week, leaving messages until he got the hint and finally stopped. I often didn't take Mumma's advice because I was usually determined to make my own mistakes, learning the hard way she always said, but when she told me to be careful because boys were only after one thing, I decided she was right. If I didn't like the boy, I certainly wasn't going to let him have that one thing until I was ready. I'd much rather spend my free time with Henry, with whom I had interesting conversations. (When camp was over, Henry and I dated for a while that winter, and we did make out; I liked him, and it wasn't at all disgusting.)

The summer ended far too quickly. Everyone cried as we said goodbye to our new friends, leaving names and addresses so we could keep in touch. Except for Henry, I never did.

Chapter Twenty-seven
Things Start Looking Up

Junior year got off to a great start. Everything was going well at home, and Mumma, especially, was the happiest I'd ever seen her. She got a job working in the snack bar at the new Mammoth Mart that opened within walking distance from our apartment. Daddy had a fit at first, but she was bringing home money, so he stopped complaining. Mumma made a new friend, a co-worker named Anne, a young girl in her twenties, who often came to the house for coffee. Anne was a hoot and she kept Mumma laughing. She was engaged to a Marine on active duty, and many of their conversations had to do with Anne's upcoming wedding night, not talking outright about what was to happen but laughing at the anticipated night of sex. I don't remember when our house had ever had so much laughter. Sometimes I joined them in the kitchen.

Taking up smoking

I had been smoking all summer, but Mumma didn't know it yet. One afternoon, sitting at the kitchen table, I asked, "Can I have a cigarette?" Without batting an eye, she handed me one of her Marlboros.

"You sure you want to smoke?"

"Sure, why not? My friends smoke; I might as well too. Everyone smokes."

"You're going to have to tell Daddy."

"Do you think he'll care?"

"Probably not. Maria still has to hide her cigarettes from Grampie. Your father sneaks her smokes all the time."

"Grampie can't smell it?"

"Probably, but the taxi stand is always full of smoke."

"How come Grampie and Yiayia don't smoke?"

"When Grampie was forty, the doctor told him that if he didn't stop smoking, he'd die of a heart attack."

"What? Why?" I let that sink in.

"I don't know; guess he has a weak heart. I've never seen Yiayia smoke. My mother, on the other hand, loves her smokes almost as much as she loves her kids. Maybe more." We laughed. Then, seriously, she said, "They don't call them cancer sticks for nothing. It's too late for me; I can't quit now, but you sure you want to start up?"

I inhaled and nodded. "Guess I'll die young," I added flippantly.

I had Tareytons in my purse but didn't admit it. She either knew I was already smoking or figured she couldn't stop me. At any rate, after our first cigarette together, she knew that I knew what I was doing. She never tried to tell me not to smoke. Mumma loved her cigarettes, and even if someone had told her how unhealthy smoking was, she would never have been convinced that cigarettes were bad for her. So, we smoked together at home, but we didn't tell any of our other relatives.

Smoking must have affected my voice because in Glee Club that year, I was moved to the alto section. I wasn't happy about that because I enjoyed the soprano parts more, but there was nothing I could do about it. I wasn't going to quit now.

Besides Glee Club, I joined the yearbook staff that year, along with a variety of other clubs, including Future Teachers of America, and Spanish Club. I also ran for Junior Class Historian and won.

At first, my socializing occurred mostly in my classes and clubs, but eventually a small number of us gravitated toward each other. We were a group of six at first, three girls and three guys, and then a few others joined our clique. We'd get together on weekdays after school at the Villager Restaurant and split a few orders of fries with gravy, sip coffee, and make plans to go to the movies or hang out at someone's house on the weekend. Sometimes we went to the dances at the YMCA where we danced to "Louie, Louie" by The Kingsmen—two long lines of girls on one side and boys on the other.

We were all trying to figure out who we were and where we fit in the world. Not part of the popular crowd, we found our places with each other. We laughed about being the odd ones, and our sarcastic, cynical attitudes made us feel like we mattered. Much of our sarcasm came from our view of the state of the world, the country going to the dogs, the escalating war in Vietnam. We, like most kids, could smell hypocrisy a mile away. We didn't believe for one minute that the war was making the world safe for democracy.

Sully, also a part of our group, and I started dating, but it was more for convenience for both of us because I had a crush on Mark, although Mark was more interested in my best friend Karen. And Sully was not dating anyone else, so the four of us double-dated, going to the movies and dances at the YMCA. Sully and I became good friends. Sam and Maureen were a couple, Sarah wasn't dating anyone, and Tony and Diana were single too, but it didn't matter. Sometimes we all hung out in someone's basement or rec room, smuggling in beer, listening to rock music, and making out. Most of us had parents who had issues of their own, and for the most part, were glad we were out of their hair.

As a group, we were trusted because we all excelled in school. It wasn't that my friends and I consciously tried to be deceptive. No one really noticed or cared what we did, but if we had gotten into trouble, living in our small town, everyone would know about it. So we tried to stay under the radar. We never got caught drinking and later smoking pot as we became more rebellious. We believed most of the adults we knew were making a mess of things in the world as we embraced the ideology of our "hippy generation." By day we were honor students with leadership roles in the school, and by night we were hippies wanting to dismantle the status quo and the establishment that was sending us to a war that could not be won. We fluctuated between a desire to create a better world and a resolve to tune out completely. Our group gave us the space to speak our truth and bounce ideas off one another.

Some of us could talk about personal issues without fear or shame, but that was difficult for me.

I could never share stories about my home life. When the others laid their souls bare, I remained quiet, choosing to keep my secrets. As much as I cared for my friends, I realized that it was still possible to be alone even in a tight group. I still believed my life was different from others and that everyone else had, if not a perfect life, at least a better one. I tried to envision a perfect life, one with stability and security, while at the same time condemning the status quo of a society ripe for change. My life felt like a paradox.

Henry

Henry was still in the picture. He had transferred to Boston University, so he sometimes came home for a weekend or the holidays, and we'd go to a movie and then back to his house. His parents were retired and always off on some trip, so he had the house to himself. On the phone, he'd ask me to come to a party at his house, which always turned out to be a party of just the two of us. After trying to ply me with his parents' whiskey, which I hated, he gave that up but continued with his attempts at seduction. If he tried anything, I would back away and our dates would become a game of him chasing me around the house until, eventually, exhausted, he would give up and call time out. I wasn't afraid of him because I sensed that it was just a game. He never stopped trying and I never gave in, but he was good-natured about his failed attempts, and we remained good friends. "You can't blame me for trying," he would always say. Then we'd spend the rest of the evening sitting in his VW Beetle in my driveway talking. I was flattered by his attention and enjoyed his humor and the philosophical discussions we had.

Then Henry decided he was not going back to school for the spring semester. I knew our dates were going to end because he talked about wanting to see the world.

"When is Henry picking you up?" Mumma asked.

"I don't know. He's usually late, but I think it's going to be a short night. I won't be seeing him much anymore."

"Why not?"

"He's going to travel around the world."

"Well, you're only seventeen, and there's a lot of fish in the sea." Mumma loved her clichés.

"Right on time," Mumma noticed as Henry arrived. "Hello, Henry. Are your toes freezing today?" It was the same question she always asked when he showed up in the dead of winter in flip-flops. Henry, with his insatiable appetite for serious discussion with everyone he met, always made my mother laugh. He was a strange bird to her, but I think she liked him.

"Well, hello Mrs. Y. No, my toes are good," he would say, and off we'd go in his beat-up Beetle, with its rusted-out floor, which made maneuvering into the passenger seat a balancing act.

Usually, we settled into a booth at the back of the coffee shop and ordered our usual: regular coffee and an order of fries to share. The Beatles were playing one of their newest hits, "I'm a Loser," and Henry seemed caught up in the song.

"How appropriate," he said.

"Why do you say that?"

"I've made my decision. I'm leaving BU to go to

India for six months. My parents are going to disown me, I think. They think I'm a loser."

"Can you just take a semester off and then go back?"

"That's what they said when they couldn't talk me out of leaving. I told them I couldn't play the establishment game any longer. I have to see the world. I have to figure out where I belong."

"And it's not here, I guess."

"No, at least not now. I don't expect you to wait. I'll keep in touch, write letters from my travels. But you won't be able to write to me because I'll be moving around a lot. When I return, we'll see where you are."

"Oh," I smiled at him, trying not to get teary, surprised at myself for caring so much. "You know, you could have just broken up with me. You don't have to travel to the other side of the world to do it."

Snorting coffee, he laughed. "That's one of the things I love about you, Katherine. You always make me laugh. And most of the time I'm pretty down."

"I know. I hope you find what you're looking for. I don't know what I want out of life either, but I'm just a junior. Guess I have more time to figure it out. Anyway, I think you're brave to give it all up to go to the other side of world. As much as I would love to travel, I don't think I'd have the courage to go alone. I just hope I can get enough student loans to go to college. That's enough for me now."

"Love is Blue" came on the jukebox. We looked at each other and smiled.

"So, tell me about India."

Henry did take the time to write long detailed airmail letters on thin onion skin stationary about his experiences in India. He was lonely, traveling solo, and having a difficult time with the extreme poverty he encountered. He also described the incredible beauty of the landscape that sparked a longing in me to travel and see the world myself.

After Henry left, still dating Sully but missing Henry, I asked Mumma one day, "How do you know if you're in love?"

Looking at me in all seriousness, she answered, "If you have to ask if you're in love, it's not love. You will know when it happens."

So that was that. Guess I wasn't in love with anyone yet.

Life for me at school continued to revolve around Glee Club. Our spring trip to Boston that year had an added bonus: Mark's older sister had an apartment in Boston, so we met up with her on our free shopping time, and she took us around the city, showing us her favorite places. That year the opera was *Aida,* and for the first time, I got lost in the story and was teary-eyed when it ended in the deaths of the two lovers. Later on that spring, instead of a talent show, the Glee Club presented the play, *110 In the Shade,* a musical based on the play *The Rainmaker.* I was too shy to try out for a part, but was happy to be part of the chorus.

The National Honor Society

That spring, my cynical demeanor was given a blow when my teachers nominated me for the National Honor Society. I did have the grades, but I never expected to be tapped, especially junior year, because there were only twelve students selected. At the assembly, the auditorium was silent as one of the seniors walked up behind my seat and tapped me on the shoulder. At first, I thought someone behind me was tricking me, but when she handed me the card with my name on it, I gasped. Later at the induction ceremony, we were honored for representing the three pillars: Sincerity, Service, and Scholarship. Although I along with my friends had become jaded about the world, this honor represented validation for the hard work I had done all through school. I was proud of myself and understood that if I worked hard enough, I could succeed at whatever I wanted to do. All that struggling with math had paid off. I was one step closer to college.

Summer camp?

The school year was winding down, and as summer approached, Daddy talked about getting a job at Camp Bomazeen, a Boy Scout camp on the Belgrade Lakes in Maine. In the army, he had trained as a cook, learning how to make food for hundreds of men, and I think he liked working in mess halls more than in restaurants. Even when he cooked at home, Daddy always made large pots of soup and stews that lasted for days. One of my favorite meals was his homemade bean soup.

Camp Bomazeen had a cabin for the cook's family, so they wouldn't have to sleep in tents like the campers. While the rest of the family looked forward to going to camp for the summer, I had no idea what I was going to do. If I went with them, I would not be able to get a job since I had no transportation, nor did I have my license. Unlike my friends who were anxious to drive, I didn't see the point since I wouldn't have a car anyway. And Daddy's old jalopy was untrustworthy. We never knew when it would break down and we'd be without a car until he could afford to get it fixed. I thought my only option was to go back to Camp Somerset and decided that's what I would do.

Chapter Twenty-eight
Summer at the Beach

Just when I had decided to work at Camp Somerset again, another opportunity for a summer job arose. My friend Donna invited me to her summer place at Weirs Beach in New Hampshire where she already had a job working on the boardwalk. Her parents owned a boarding house and rented rooms for vacationers. She asked if I'd like to come for the summer, rent a room from her parents, and get a job waitressing or working in one of the shops. Food was not included, so I would have to buy my own. She didn't have to ask twice. I wrote a letter to The Blue Anchor, a small restaurant in Laconia, New Hampshire, requesting employment. With a good reference from Donna's dad, the job was mine. Excited to be going away for the summer, we spent the last few weeks of school talking about the wonderful summer we were going to have.

"I have to warn you," Donna said as we walked to English class one morning. "You're going to work during Motorcycle Weekend."

"What is that?"

"All the motorcycle gangs from all over the country come to Laconia and take over for a weekend in

June. They have a contract with the city, and when I say take over, I mean TAKE OVER! They overrun the town, and all you can hear for forty-eight hours is the roaring of bikes, parties, and fights, with the police and fire departments on the sidelines, making sure the town isn't completely destroyed."

It sounded both exciting and frightening. I couldn't wait. While my family packed to go to camp for the summer, I packed my brown suitcase for Weirs Beach, excited to be traveling to New Hampshire and the new experiences that awaited.

First day at the Blue Anchor

Early in the morning of my first workday at the Blue Anchor, I woke up to the din of motorcycle engines coming from downtown Laconia. As I reoriented myself to my new surroundings, I covered my head with the pillow to muffle the noise. I was paying twenty dollars a week for a room I shared with another waitress while Donna stayed in the family quarters downstairs. Donna worked at the candy store on the boardwalk making taffy. While she had warned me about motorcycle weekend, I was seventeen, a nascent adult, and more than ready to be out on my own.

But now that I was here, the constant roar and backfire of engines was unnerving. Twisting my hair into two tight braids to keep it out of my face, I donned my white waitress uniform and carefully tied the bow of my apron, preparing for my evening shift at the restaurant. As I checked my lipstick in the mirror, I took a deep breath to calm my inner fluttering, then met Mr. Lane, Donna's father, at the foot of the stairs. "Ready?" he asked.

"Sure," I quaked nervously.

As he chaperoned me to work on that sunny June afternoon, he reminded me, "Don't leave the diner without me. I'll be here when you close at 1 a.m."

The Blue Anchor was a small diner run by Gus and Eula, a Greek couple who spent their summers in New Hampshire and winters in Florida. I had met them the day before and got a cursory training. Eula was a woman of enormous proportions, who sat on a stool in front of the cash register and kept watch over the diner. The place itself was a typical greasy spoon, six booths and a counter. Gus did the cooking and rarely came out of the back kitchen. Behind the cash register a small alcove held soft-serve ice cream machines and an order window. When we had a rush at the booths and counter in the front of the diner, Eula would tend to the ice cream window.

First shift at Blue Anchor: Motorcycle Weekend

My first shift was 5 p.m. to 1 a.m. Mr. Lane and I didn't attempt conversation as we walked down the hill onto the main street. It would have been futile anyway, for all around us the Devil's Disciples were setting up camp for the night.

Entering the diner, the jukebox was on full blast, but did nothing to lessen the clamor of the bikes. The sound of "Happy Together" and a cloud of heavy smoke engulfed me as I made my way past the rough, chain-covered bikers. Frightened but trying not to show it, I couldn't help thinking of the song, "Leader of the Pack" as Eula handed me my order pad and I went to work.

"Hey Chickie, over here; we need some food! We don't need no menus! We want some burgers. No beer here? What kinda #*&^@ joint is this? Hey, Snake, go next door and get us some beers. Weed is making me thirsty."

"Hey kid, what are you, ten? They hire babies around here? Where's my fries? I said bring me fries with my burger!"

The night became a blur of tattooed bodies in leather jackets, clanging chains, cursing, belching, and farting. The smoke and smells made me slightly dizzy, but I soon realized as I raced from booth to booth, they were generally satisfied once they were fed. After bolting down their burgers, they ignored the check most of the time and simply slammed the money onto the table as they left. I rushed to clean the booths before the next group arrived only to find cigarette butts had been put out on the table, in the dishes, and on the floor around the table. Devil's Disciples apparently had no use for ashtrays.

Finally, the last biker left. I sighed with relief as I watched Eula lock the door. The jukebox was quiet now, but the roaring of the bikes never ceased. My legs were sore, my hair had fallen out of the braids, my uniform was covered with catsup, sticky ice cream, and grease, and I was feeling nauseous. But we were not done yet. Tables, booths, stools, floor, all had to be washed. Eula let Mr. Lane in to wait at the counter while I finished my work. Then we rushed back up the hill. Motorcycle weekend had two more days to go. I'd have to do it all over again tomorrow. My upset stomach was now growling as I fell into bed and no wonder; I hadn't eaten anything since lunch.

The next day was a repeat performance, with even more blasting wheelies and vrooming engines as more Disciples arrived. As we hurried up the hill after the second night of work, we could sense something brewing. Sure enough, Main Street erupted into flames as they made a bonfire out of someone's car. Fights ensued. Police and fire trucks arrived from all the neighboring towns to help quell the riot. I was relieved to be in the safety of my room as I watched the flames light up the street below.

Summer calm replaces motorcycle chaos

My trial by fire was finally over and after that weekend, work at the Blue Anchor settled down into a calmer routine. I enjoyed the work, the tourists who were now allowed back into town and my bosses Eula and Gus. Every day Eula would give me a handful of dimes for the jukebox. She liked "I Fall to Pieces" by Patsy Cline, so I made sure to hit that first. Then I played some of my favorites, like "Happy Together," "Light My Fire," "I Think We're Alone Now," "The Letter," "Windy," and "All You Need is Love."

When I wasn't working, I hung out on the boardwalk with my new summer friends. Donna rarely joined us because her parents kept her busy on her time off. Some of us were here only for summer work, some were townies, and then there was "Richie Rich" aka Skeeter. He lived on Governor's Island, the wealthiest section of the lake, and owned his own convertible and a boat. We all crammed into one or the other when we wanted to cruise the highways and lake. Skeeter didn't have to work, so when I was free, I got to ride beside him in his cool car, the radio blaring. He was my boyfriend … for one whole week.

The Fourth of July holiday was approaching, so we made plans. When I checked the schedule for the week, I discovered with relief that I had the breakfast shift, which meant I was out of work by 2 p.m. A group of us were planning to get together on Skeeter's boat to watch fireworks over the lake that evening.

We all met on the boardwalk around 6 p.m. After we bought a six-pack of Pepsi and ordered fries, we settled ourselves on the boardwalk outside the pavilion to listen to the July 4th entertainment, which happened to feature Sam the Sham and the Pharaohs. As we listened to the music emanating from the pavilion, we all sang along with their hit, *"Hey there little red riding hood, you sure are looking good …"* Skeeter said he had a surprise for later, and we were anxious to get the party going. As time for the fireworks over the lake approached, we took our drinks and headed to Skeeter's boat, joining the other boaters on the lake. But instead of mingling with the other boats, we headed farther out on the lake by ourselves.

"Want a smoke?" he asked, flipping a Tareyton out of the pack to me.

"Yeah, thanks." I took the cigarette as he lit it from his, inhaling a deep breath.

"I can't have cigarettes at the Lane's, so I haven't been smoking."

"I'll bet you can't have beer either."

"Um, no, course not." Dave and Allison and I exchanged looks as he pulled out a six-pack.

"Happy Fourth of July!" We all clinked cans and sipped our beers as we cruised around the lake. At some point, Skeeter stopped at a marina and threw the empty beer cans away.

We were all feeling pretty good as the time for the fireworks approached. When we made our way back to Weirs Beach, our goal was to get close to the pavilion so we could hear the music. None of us saw it coming; a bigger boat inched in closer to us with a group of partying adults. Skeeter tried to slide in front of it, but missed, and rammed into their boat. Everything stopped for a second.

"Friggin' kids! You hit my boat!" screamed someone in the big boat. Without thinking, Skeeter backed out and we raced off. "Hey come back here! You hear me? Get back here!! Goddamn kids!"

The race was on. Skeeter knew every part of the lake. He turned off the lights and we sped out toward the head of the lake, passing other boating parties who were surprised when we nearly upended them in our wake. We could see the lights of the pursuing boat, but its driver could see only our wake.

"If we can make a good headway, I know a place we can hide!" Skeeter screamed as he maneuvered the boat. "If we don't run out of gas!"

We zigzagged around islands until we finally lost the other boat. Or maybe he just gave up.

"Oh, Christ," Dave moaned. "We're in a hell of a lot of trouble. You shouldn't have run."

"We were drinking," said Skeeter. "We'd be in more trouble if they had caught us. Anyway, that man looked like he was going to beat my ass. I had to get out of there. I'm going to let you off on the island and dock the boat at our marina. You can walk back to the beach."

"Oh my God, how far is it to the beach?" I complained after we had walked for an hour. We could see the fireworks over the water from the hill, but Weirs Beach seemed far away. Frightened sober, the excitement of the night was now replaced by fear.

"We've probably got a couple more miles to go," Dave replied with resignation.

By the time we got back, the fireworks were over, and I had missed my midnight curfew. Luckily, the door was unlocked, and I was able to make it up to my room without running into anyone.

The next morning at work, I had a visitor from the Laconia Police Dept.

"Can you tell me what happened last night on the boat?"

"It was an accident. Skeeter hit the man's boat, but the guy went crazy. We were scared, so we left."

"Is that it? Were you drinking?"

"No sir."

We later found out Skeeter's dad had paid off the man but was threatening to send Skeeter off to military school, so we didn't see him for a few days. As I worked the afternoon shift, I happened to glance out of the window to see Skeeter cruising past with the top down, Allison nestled beside him. The strains of "Happy Together" floated into the diner and faded out as they turned the corner. I knew that was the end of my fleeting romance with Skeeter.

After the first twinges of disappointment, I realized I wasn't heartbroken. Even though Skeeter was my age, he seemed a lot younger, and Allison, a pretty blond, was more his type. They made a beautiful couple driving through town in his convertible, and I remained friends with them. I then dated Dave, who worked on the *Mount Washington*, a small cruise ship that toured Lake Winnipesaukee. When our time off coincided, neither of us having much money, we'd sit in the sand at Weirs Beach, talking; or when Dave could get a six-pack, we'd walk into the woods and drink and make out before I had to be back at the house before curfew. As with Henry, I liked Dave; we had fun together, but I knew it wasn't love. Maybe I would never fall in love.

I liked the work of waiting on tourists while listening to music in the diner. On my break I usually had a cheeseburger and a milkshake for lunch or dinner, depending on the shift I worked, and many days the only time I ate was at work. We also got to listen to bands that played in the pavilion. Besides Sam the Sham and the Pharoahs, we got to hear The Turtles and Duke Ellington while sitting on the boardwalk outside the concert hall. None of us, except Skeeter, could afford to buy tickets, but we had better seats outside, near the water. When The Turtles came to town, they stopped at the diner for ice cream. I decided I'd give them giant cones but made the first one so big it fell over. Eula, laughing at my nervousness, rescued me while I gaped, star struck. My first encounter with someone famous, and I literally made a mess of it.

All too soon, one of my best summers, waitressing at Weirs Beach, was over and it was time to go home to Maine.

Don't Worry About A Thing

Chapter Twenty-nine
Senior Year, Hopes and Fears

I had high hopes for senior year. Everything seemed to be going smoothly from the start even though life felt bittersweet. I was both anxious for school to be over and fearful that it would end and I'd be left behind. I waited anxiously for my acceptance letter from the University of Maine. What would I do with my life if I didn't get in? I realized I'd miss being in the classroom. I would miss English class, when out of the blue, a line from Shakespeare or another poet would touch me at the core. I memorized lines of poetry by Wordsworth and Shelley and read the essays of Emerson and Thoreau. And the first time I read Hamlet's "tomorrow speech," I memorized it then and there, not realizing at the time how prophetic it would be:

> Tomorrow, and tomorrow, and tomorrow,
> Creeps in this petty pace from day to day,
> To the last syllable of recorded time;
> And all our yesterdays have lighted fools
> The way to dusty death. Out, out, brief candle!
> Life's but a walking shadow, a poor player,
> That struts and frets his hour upon the stage,

Don't Worry About A Thing

And then is heard no more. It is a tale
Told by an idiot, full of sound and fury,
Signifying nothing.

One of our English teachers, Miss Johnson, created an Independent Study Writing Class for a group of juniors and seniors who loved literature and writing. Our school had a model library with prints by famous artists, like Andrew Wyeth's "Christina's World" on the walls. We discussed art, kept journals, and wrote short stories from our interpretations of the art works. We read good poetry and wrote bad poetry. All my friends joined the class as well as a few new students. Miss Johnson even invited us to her house after school. We drank tea and coffee and talked about life and literature. She encouraged us to write and keep writing.

I had received a diary on my twelfth birthday but had made only a few entries in that first one. By the time I was sixteen, I was writing regularly in a journal, and now during senior year, Miss Johnson's encouragement validated my writing. I did keep journaling until writing became a habit. When life felt overwhelming, writing helped me to understand my own feelings, and it had a calming effect. I found if I bled on the page, I didn't act out my stronger feelings of anger, frustration, and sadness. It was therapy before I knew what therapy was.

Soon our class began a series of oral interpretations during which we did readings called "Philosophy of Life." Held in the library's circulation room, these readings attracted people who came to hear us read the works of Kahlil Gibran, Edward Lee

Masters, Henry W. Longfellow, and Matthew Arnold, to name a few. Senior year was turning out to be the best year yet.

College!

And it got even better. On November 27, I walked into the house after school to find Mumma and Daddy sitting at the kitchen table with a letter from the University of Maine at Orono perched between the salt and pepper.

"Don't worry about a thing," Daddy said as I shakily took the envelope and slit it open, not believing for a minute it would be good news. But right there in black and white, there it was. "I got accepted!"

"I knew it!" Daddy slapped his knee, cigarette ashes flying. Mumma smiled proudly while I read the words over and over. I just had to send in $50 right away with my signature to finalize it. I was in! I still couldn't believe it. For the next few months, whenever my insecurities took over, I took out the letter and read and reread it. Yes, it was real. I was going to college and life was good!

Until it wasn't.

As soon as things were going well, it seemed that something would usually happen to turn things around. Although I knew this about life, it never failed to surprise me. I should have been prepared.

Mumma and the C word

In January, the routine every-day-ness of being a student changed. One afternoon when I got home from school, I could sense something was wrong with Mumma. She looked worried. Instead of escaping to my room, I made a cup of instant coffee and sat next to her on the couch, expecting her to tell me we'd be moving again. But it wasn't that.

"I think I need to go to the doctor," Mumma said, looking pale and scared.

"Why? Are you sick?"

"My stomach has been bothering me, and now I can feel lumps." She pulled her skirt down below her belly and felt around until she could feel a bulge. "See?" She took my hand and sure enough, I could feel a lump. She did the same in another area, more lumps.

"Do they hurt?"

"I've been taking pain pills, so it hasn't been bad."

"I think you need to go to the doctor. Did you tell Dad?"

"No, not yet. You know how he gets when someone is sick."

She made the appointment for the following week, telling Daddy it was just woman's problems. After a few initial procedures, the doctor determined that she would need a hysterectomy. The C word was never mentioned even though I think Mumma knew. After the operation, we tried to carry on as usual. Daddy was convinced she was healed, and it would only be a matter of time before Mumma was fully recovered. We all were in denial, refusing to believe the worst.

Then Daddy stopped going to work to be home

with her, and once again we were falling behind in the rent, the telephone, the lights, and car payments, not to mention several loans and other bills.

Life went on at school. I came home one afternoon to find another letter sitting on the kitchen table from UMO and its Office of Student Aid informing me I had received an Educational Opportunity Grant and a National Defense Education Act (NDEA) loan for freshman year. Along with a work-study job, my education would be paid for. It was wonderful news. And alongside it, I tried to believe, like Daddy, that Mumma would get well and everything would work out.

While Mumma was recovering from the first operation, it was apparent to everyone that her surgery was not a quick cure, but not to Dad. Mumma had to have another operation so the doctor could get all the cancer.

Daddy and I sat in the hall chain-smoking outside the operating room of the Waterville Osteopathic Hospital, waiting for Mumma to come out of her second surgery. My throat was so dry it hurt, but smoking helped with my nerves and gave us something to do when there was nothing else we could do.

Dad couldn't find another job and talked about moving to Bangor to look for work after Mumma recovered from the operations. I didn't know how we could possibly leave Waterville but didn't comment on the idea. "I think, though, we'll go back to Camp Bomazeen this summer." It sounded like he had already made that decision. But what about work in the meantime, I thought; summer was a month away. I still didn't voice my concerns. "Mumma likes it at camp and the kids will have fun like they did last summer," he said. Was he trying to convince me, or himself? What was I going to do for the summer if they went back to camp?

Finally, I said, making the decision in that moment: "I'll be in New Hampshire again this summer." I added, to reassure myself, "My last summer before UMO. I hope I can make a lot of money."

"Don't worry about a thing," Dad said, but I know he didn't believe that anymore.

The doctor appeared from the operating room much sooner than expected. Daddy took that as a good sign that they got everything this time. "We did all we could," the doctor said tentatively. And before he could explain, Daddy sighed with relief. "Will she be home soon?" he asked expectantly.

"Yes, she'll be discharged in a week or so." Dr. A sighed and left us standing there.

We left to get Mumma something good to eat for when she woke up later. Mumma did come home a few days later and began the process of recovery from the surgery while she continued to deteriorate from the disease ravaging her inside. We refused to see it and refused to believe it. Her sister-in-law came to help around the house until she could get back on her feet, and we were all grateful she was there. After she left, George and I helped with the cleaning until she recovered some of her strength. Daddy did the cooking. Mumma rallied, playing along with the denial, hiding her pain, and protecting us.

Life went on as usual for a while. We tried to find some normalcy. For me, that included school, studying, a few dates here and there, and getting together with my friends. All of us pretended, and half-way believed, that everything was going to be okay.

Graduation, under a shadow

Graduation week was approaching, with parties and school events to look forward to. I received a Future Teachers of America scholarship during one of the senior assemblies, and I tried to feel excited, but was too anxious and unsure of the future. Mumma seemed to have reached a plateau. We all looked forward to my graduation.

After the ceremony, all the parents met in the gym to join their graduates. Mumma was the first of my family to get to me, making her way through the crowd, past other families that were taking pictures with their graduates. Tearfully, but smiling from ear to ear, she couldn't say it, but I knew she was proud of me. Like the first day of kindergarten when I detected her watering eyes, I felt her love for me. We had had many arguments throughout my teen years, words were said that we both regretted, but all of that was over now as I was about to start on a new journey.

Before she could ask what I was going to do, I said, "Will you take my cap and gown? A bunch of us are going to Sully's to celebrate. I'll probably be late." Nothing had been planned for me at home. Part of me wished my family had thought of some way to mark this day, but I didn't expect it, especially with Mumma's surgeries and all the time spent in the hospitals. But Mumma saw me graduate, and I left school that day hopeful that everything would work out.

Adulthood

Our anxiety does not come from thinking about the future, but from wanting to control it.

Trees are poems the earth writes upon the sky. We fell them down and turn them into paper, That we may record our emptiness.
                                    Kahlil Gibran

Chapter Thirty
Don't Worry About a Thing

Mumma, Daddy, and the kids left for Camp Bomazeen, while my friend Chrissie and I got a ride to Weirs Beach with her parents. We stayed in a different boarding house with ten other girls and most of us worked at Howard Johnson's. I didn't go back to the Blue Anchor because I thought I'd make more in tips at HoJo's and I did, but I didn't enjoy the work. I hated the large trays we had to carry, and waiting on fussy tourists was sometimes worse than the bikers during Motorcycle Weekend from the previous year. Time off wasn't nearly as much fun either. Sometimes we got beer from a friend and sat on the beach drinking, but mostly we worked or waited to go to work. But it was a job, and I couldn't complain.

One afternoon when I got home from the early shift, I found a message to call home. Expecting the worse, I was surprised when Daddy said everything was fine. Mumma was getting better. Not to worry. I believed him. Sighing with relief, I felt I could breathe again.

My relief was short-lived. In the first week of August, I got a phone call. Mumma was sick in the hospital again. I should come home. Chrissie's parents, who were not at all sure it was a good idea to let their daughter go so far from home to work, made it clear that when we wanted to come home, we could just call and they would come for us. They were in New Hampshire the next morning to pick us up.

Arriving at the hospital, I was shocked at the change in Mumma from just a few weeks before. She looked weak, frail, and drawn. Those last few weeks of summer she went downhill fast. I knew right away there was no hope. Her last days at Camp Bomazeen were pain-filled, and pills were not helping. Here, hooked up to an IV, she was receiving a steady supply of morphine. She was not eating. We gave her ginger ale through a straw or ice water, and sometimes she was too weak to sip. When we came to visit, she'd send us away telling us to bring her a coke with ice. When we returned later, she said, "No, no, I said root beer with no ice. I'm tired and want to sleep now." I don't think she wanted us there to see her suffering. We left, but once home, we always turned around and went back to the hospital. Despite what was staring us in the face, we still hoped for a miracle. Daddy always told us not to worry about a thing. Maybe he was right. Maybe this time...

That August, our days were spent in the hospital, either by her bedside or in the hallway smoking. We talked to the nurses who told us how she was doing every day, but the doctor was never around. I wondered, after it was all over, whether Mumma had said something to the doctor, because one day when I arrived at the hospital alone, Doctor A waylaid me in the hallway.

"Come into my office for a minute," he somberly ordered. I followed him, and he shut the door. "You have an impending tragedy in your family, and your father does not accept it." Once the words were out, I couldn't pretend anymore. Daddy could believe that someday he'd win at the races all he wanted, but he couldn't believe anymore that the outcome for Mumma would be anything other than death.

I didn't fall apart. Instead, his words created an inner stillness, as if the world continued to move around me, but I was trapped in a vacuum. It felt as if I were in a movie and playing a part. I asked, "How long does she have?"

"Two weeks, maybe more, maybe less. You have to prepare your father."

I left the office and entered Mumma's room and sat by her bed. She slept, blissfully free from pain as the morphine dripped into her veins, the drug easing her toward death and into the next world. If another world existed. I remembered a poem from Matthew Arnold we had read in English class, from "Dover Beach": it said:

> "...for the world, which seems to lie before us
>   like a land of dreams,
> So various so beautiful, so new,
> Hath really neither joy, nor love, nor light,
> Nor certitude, nor peace, nor help for pain;
> And we are here as on a darkling plain
> Swept with confused alarms of struggle and flight,
> Where ignorant armies clash by night."

Mumma had had her share of "struggle and flight," from childhood poverty, motherhood at sixteen, the death of two of her children, an earlier failed marriage, and finally, to life with Daddy, which was no picnic either. They had had their twentieth anniversary in January; and they both said those twenty years were the happiest of their lives. I hoped she had times of joy and peace.

When she awoke, I tried to give her water for her parched lips. I picked up the water and held the straw to her lips. She couldn't drink it. I was helpless to do anything. There was nothing anyone could do, and there was going to be only one outcome. I felt like screaming and crying and yelling, "Why don't you drink the water?" As if drinking the water would cure her. But I stood silently rooted next to her bed, and we stared at each other. Finally, I could see a smile curling the corners of her mouth, and I knew she knew that I knew. "I want you to get better, Mumma," I stupidly commented. Of all the things I could have said to her, I could only parrot what Daddy kept saying.

She looked at me and with difficulty said, "I'm sorry, Kathy. I'm sorry." Those were her last words to me.

Later that afternoon, after Daddy and the kids had visited, we drove home when visiting hours ended. Still in a daze, I was barely listening to Daddy when he said, "Don't you think so?"

"What?" I asked.

"Don't you think she looked better today?" Looking at me for confirmation as he was driving, I could only look away.

Finally, I said as quietly as I could, "No, she's dying. Dr. A told me we had to accept what was coming."

He blew up. "What the hell do those doctors know?"

Aunts and uncles and cousins arrived to say good-bye. Mumma's friend Anne, who hadn't seen Mumma for a few weeks, came to the house to visit, and when she was told Mumma was dying her face turned so white I thought she was going to faint. We spent that final week running back and forth to the hospital. We'd go into her room, sit for a few minutes, leave to go home, and once home, sometimes turn around immediately and go back. From eight in the morning until late at night we were constantly on the go, running, running, running, with nowhere to go, like crazy people, trying to outrun Death. The hospital, home, Yiayia's, Clinton (where Mumma's sister lived). Never staying in one place for more than a few minutes. Anywhere to keep moving. Daddy didn't want to stay in the house. People brought food, but we didn't eat.

One evening as Dad went into Cottles to buy some groceries, he was stopped by the sheriff who told him that he either had to pay a $60 bill he owed someone or go to jail. He told Dad he'd be at the house in a little while. I was in the living room with some friends who had stopped by to see how I was doing when I saw the sheriff's car pull into the driveway. Before he could come to the door, I walked outside to meet him. "Tell your father I need to speak with him," he ordered. Frightened, I answered, "I'll send him out." I prayed he wouldn't come inside and handcuff him. What would happen now? I went back in the house and pretended everything was fine even though I was quaking inside. A few minutes later, I saw the patrol car back out of the driveway and Daddy entered the house. I never knew whether Dad had given him some money or not, but at least he hadn't been hauled off to jail. Just like Daddy always thought when things were bad, I was beginning to think God was punishing us. What did we do to deserve this?

Losing Mumma

Then early in the morning, around 4 a.m. the phone rang. I heard Daddy pick it up expecting the worst, but it was Mumma. Energized by the drugs, she told Daddy she was sitting up and felt much better. Elated, Daddy hung up and drove to the hospital. "I knew she'd get better," he said before leaving. Despite what I knew, I still hoped.

When Daddy arrived at the hospital, Mumma was sleeping as if the phone call had never happened. I was still awake when he came home, looking beaten. The next day was a repeat of the days before, more running around. On one of the hospital trips, the doctor told us that Mumma's condition had deteriorated. It would not be much longer. Mumma's brothers and sister-in-law came to stay with us all night. Then once again in the early morning hours, the phone rang. Uncle Bob came into my room where my cousin Roberta and I were sleeping. He placed his hands on our shoulders and said in a quiet, sad voice, "Don't move. She's gone." On August 21, 1968, at 3:45 in the morning, Mumma had died.

Chapter Thirty-one
The Funeral

I am ashamed to admit this, but my first feeling was not one of sadness, but of relief. I thanked God she was out of pain. I don't know if I said it out loud, but that's the way I felt. I remember Mumma saying after one of the surgeries, "I didn't know anyone could survive such pain. I hope to never feel that bad again." At the end, she lived for the next morphine dose. I was glad it was over. I didn't know if there was really a heaven, but I knew that hell was what she had gone through. As if a movie reel were playing, I remembered all the good times and the bad times we had been through together, the laughter, the teenage rebellion, the attempts to understand each other, and my heart was broken for the loss of our relationship that would go no further than my eighteen years. Then I did what Daddy always did when the family was in crisis. He taught me well. I resorted once again to denial, placing my grief away, hidden some-where deep inside, where it would stay for many, many years.

The next few days were a blur of frantic activity. The phone was ringing off the hook. The undertaker came and we set the funeral for Saturday because

Uncle Harlan, Mumma's youngest brother, had to come from New York. Grampie had purchased four lots in Pine Grove Cemetery and Mumma would be the first to be laid there.

The day after she died, we went to the cemetery to see the burial plot, which was on high ground in a sunny spot. Next, we had to pick out the casket. Who was paying for this? Grampie, I think. We got a metal one with a copper-colored satin pillow and lining inside. We had to talk to the priest, Father Glendenning, a new priest at St. Mark's Episcopal Church, the church that I had pretty much stopped attending. Back in the car, we went to Yiayia's for lunch and then home to get changed for visiting hours at the Redington Funeral Home. I went to Stearn's and bought a black dress for nineteen dollars. It's strange how we carried on, doing what had to be done, moving like zombies through the day.

But the worst was yet to come. The time had come to go to the funeral home. As we entered the building, I had the urge to turn and run, but as if they had a mind of their own, my feet kept moving up the aisle where Mumma lay. Daddy and Jimmy saw her first. Jim was crying. Daddy fell apart. He had been crying off and on since we got the call, but this was worse. He finally came face to face with the truth. His sobbing wrenched my heart. I stopped, not wanting to go further. The mortician took me by the hand and led me to the casket. George, beside me, was crying. As I stared at Mumma, in shock, I couldn't believe that nine months ago she didn't know anything was wrong, and now she was dead. Here was my mother lying here dead, her make-up on and her hair styled as it had never been in life. The lipstick was too red, the hair too teased. No, this wasn't her at all. "Where are you Mumma?" I whispered. I wanted to believe she was somewhere free of pain. Despite my denial, I had known she was going to die. But the knowing didn't make it any less shocking. What I thought would happen in the future was quite different from the actual event, for now there was no going back. This was it for Mumma and for us, forever. That was the only time I approached the casket during the two days of viewing.

The next day I got up early and washed three floors in the house. Family and friends were coming from everywhere for the funeral the next day, and Mumma would have been upset if the house was dirty. After cleaning, we went downtown to get nylons, and when I got home, my final UMO semester bill had come in the mail detailing how it would be paid with the scholarships and loans. The worry over paying for college was gone, but what would I do now? Go to college? Stay at home? None of it seemed real.

My friends came to sit with me at the funeral home and promised they would be there for the funeral. Except for Sully. He was spending the summer in Florida with his Aunt Mary Ellen and her family. Before we left for the funeral home, I received a telegram from him expressing his condolences and his family sent flowers. That night after the parlor closed, the four of us went to Uncle Spike's house where we stayed for an hour and then left for Yiayia's. Yiayia wasn't feeling well, and Grampie was worried because she hadn't eaten anything all day.

The sickening smell of hothouse flowers covering the casket was overwhelming as we sat in the front row waiting for the funeral service to begin. Windows and doors were open to catch the August breeze, but the room was sweltering, with standing room only in the back. It seemed all of Waterville was there. Daddy sobbed. After the service, Uncle Tommy drove us to the cemetery where we said our last good-byes.

Back at home, the house was so overflowing it was difficult to walk from room to room. Some people brought food, but no one was eating. I don't think Daddy and Mumma's families were ever in the same room together. The Greek side sat in the living room and the north woods family was in the kitchen. I went from room to room, not really talking to anyone. A few friends came over and we just sat. Daddy cried and then laughed when someone told a funny story about Mumma. Then he cried again. I don't know where Georgeanna and Jim were. I don't remember what they were doing.

Then Mumma's sister, Aunt Doris, took matters into her own hands. She started looking for Mumma's diary to see if she had left her anything. How did she even know Mumma had a diary? When Aunt Doris couldn't find it, she insisted we bring it to her. George retrieved the book where Mumma had hidden it. She gave it to Aunt Doris who handed it to me to read. It was short and to the point. Mumma left all her things to Georgeanna, and anything George didn't want I could have. She said she loved us all.

I wasn't surprised that Mumma had left all her things to Georgeanna. She was always the good daughter. In our entire lives together, I never once heard George sass her or argue with her like I did. I wasn't the easiest teenager to live with. Still, I was hurt. And now there was no way to make it right. Mumma didn't have many possessions, some jewelry, dishes, household things. Nothing of real value. In the end, all she really had were her words, and she had the last word.

And then it was over. By 3 p.m. everyone was gone, and the house held a new emptiness. I went into my room, closed the door, and fell into an exhausted sleep.

Waking up at three in the morning, I grabbed my journal, sat up in bed, and did what I often did when life became unbearable: I began writing. Often my writing was in the form of complaints against someone I thought had done me an injustice, but this time I wrote a poem, a poem that was overly dramatic, and obviously influenced by Gerard Manly Hopkins, a poet I had discovered that year.

> From diagnosis to death, nine months
> Death's gestation, premature,
> Leaving three children shrinking in
>   shock.
> Startled by the speed of extinction, a new
>   reality is birthed.
> A first-born longs to search the firma-
>   ment, to grasp once again the life force
> Of mother gone.
> To make right all the wrongs that went
>   before,
> To hustle Hades, and grasp again the life
>   lost.
> Three left to suffer, motherless, so young
>   and unformed.
> Oh Fate! Too soon to cut the threads of

life, leaving us lost in the world.

Fire!

A few nights later I awoke surrounded by smoke and the odor of charred meat. Covering my mouth with my pj's, I raced into the living room.

Daddy was passed out on the couch.

"Dad, wake up! The house is on fire!" I shook him out of his lethargy until he bounded up off the couch as I woke up George and Jim.

Flames were devouring the kitchen curtains and while Daddy threw water around the window, I raced upstairs to warn our neighbors.

I repeatedly knocked on the door, but no one answered. Now I really panicked and pounded louder. Still no answer. Oh God, I prayed. Please don't let them be dead. "Fire! Fire! Fire!" Finally, the door opened and there was the father of the family looking at me groggily. "You need to leave!" I screamed. "Our apartment is on fire!" The smoke had not infiltrated the upstairs yet, and he was more irritated with me than anything else, but he and his wife and little girl left to spend the night with his mother-in-law.

Daddy put out the fire, but the apartment was still filled with smoke, so we grabbed blankets, and spent the rest of the night in Daddy's car. Mumma's cat climbed in the car with us, along with the caged bird Joyce Ann had left with us when she moved to New Hampshire. Both the cat and bird disappeared the next day. I don't know where. The damage to the apartment was minimal. Curtains in shreds, and black around the window, but after that night, I didn't go to bed without first checking that Daddy was done in the kitchen. He didn't cook much after that.

When Mumma died, it had seemed like the end of the world, like life would stop in its tracks, but I learned that nothing stops, even for death. It was weird to get up every morning without her in the world, but we did and went about our day, mostly in a daze at first as life took on a new normal without her. In the days following Mumma's death, I went on with my plans to attend UMO, mostly because I didn't know what else to do, and the plans were already in place. Life was in limbo and getting ready for college gave meaning to the lackluster days. Sully and my other friends were also getting ready for school, and we got together to talk about college, what classes we were taking and what we wanted to do in the future. Sully was in pre-med at UMO. I was majoring in English education. I didn't want to teach elementary school; I loved literature and couldn't imagine teaching math to anyone, even little kids.

Two weeks after Mumma died, I left for college.

Don't Worry About A Thing

Chapter Thirty-two
The Lie

The blue metal trunk held my wardrobe of bell-bottom jeans, tops, and winter sweaters. My pillow, sheets and towels, and typewriter, along with sundry necessities took up most of the space across the backseat of Daddy's old Plymouth. I wished I had brought my record player and records, but changed my mind at the last minute, leaving them home. I would regret that later. We had been sent a questionnaire about ourselves, and all I could remember about the paperwork was that I wrote that I'd like to have a roommate from out of state. I wanted to meet people from away. I wondered who she would be and where she was from.

The hour-long ride to Orono was unusually silent, sometimes with small talk between Daddy and me, but mostly with me staring out of the window at the monotonous pines along I-95. We pulled onto the campus, both in our own separate, silent worlds. I had no idea what Daddy was thinking. Driving to the University of Maine on that crisp September morning in 1968, I sensed I was entering another world, a surreal world in which I didn't belong. Maybe I was making a big mistake. We had left George, fourteen, and twelve-year-old Jimmy behind, back at home, alone.

I barely registered the stately brick buildings on either side of the mall as we drove toward my dormitory, Hart Hall, with 1912 emblazoned over the front door. We both stared as a girl with blond frizzy hair strolled along the sidewalk with her family, mother, father, sister, and brother. Coming out of his reverie, Dad said, "I bet that girl is your roommate." I smiled at the absurdity of his remark.

Arriving in Hart Hall, UMO

We parked in front of the dorm and hesitantly walked inside where students were introducing themselves to the housemother and picking up their keys and a list of all the dorm rules. Our hall monitor informed us we had a meeting scheduled that evening to go over all the rules, not the least of which outlined our curfews: 10 p.m. on weekdays, and midnight on weekends. Getting my key to room 112 on the first floor, we made our way down the hall only to find, already there, the girl we had seen earlier with her mother, father, sister, and brother, helping her move in. Dad and I glanced at each other, our eyes registering disbelief.

Daddy didn't stay long. After depositing my belongings in my new room, I walked him to the car, half-hoping he would tell me to come back home. He didn't. Going to college was all I had talked about for four years, and I knew he was proud of me. I think maybe he was betting on me becoming somebody. In any case, there was no question of turning back now.

Forgotten were all the hours of study, making honor roll, the small scholarship, and the accolades from my teachers. As his car pulled away from the curb, I wanted to run after him and yell, "Wait! Come back! It's all a mistake. I don't belong here." What made me think I should go to college? But I didn't run. Instead, I stood rooted to the spot on the steps of the dorm watching the car disappear.

I went through the expected motions, unpacking my few belongings, purchasing books from the campus bookstore, pretending to take part in this new world. Sitting in classes with my fingers putting pen to paper, taking notes, gave me a slight reprieve from my obsessive thoughts of death. I tried to wrap my mind around the pen forming words on the page, on the neatly written notes, straight margins, perfectly formed letters, and a meditation of words. Back in the dorm, I pretended to be interested in girl gossip. Everything seemed so trivial, talk about boys and sororities and parties, a life so removed from mine I could have been living on another planet. While these girls were on the cusp of a new life, one filled with endless possibilities, I could only see the shadows, the limited promises of an uncertain future.

I did try though. I tried to shake off the inner turmoil. I tried to hope that everything would turn out fine. If life was a play, as Shakespeare said, and we had our hour on the stage, I hoped the curtain wouldn't fall too soon. With morbid thoughts like those, I kept to myself and let the other girls do all the gossiping. I knew how fleeting life was. Here one day, then gone the next. It was as if I lived in two worlds; my inner and outer lives struggled to make sense of it all.

Camryn

Camryn, my roommate, was open, friendly, and curious. I was aloof, closed, and introverted. She didn't give up trying to coax me out of my shell, but I didn't break, even though I liked her right away. I thought she was lucky, being from Massachusetts, and I enjoyed her stories of growing up in the suburbs of Boston. She smoked too, so that wasn't a problem. But maybe I already knew that from the roommate application.

She probed, trying to figure me out. "Why didn't your mom drop you off with your dad?"

"She had to stay with my sister and brother."

Another time: "What does your mom cook that's your favorite?"

"Roast chicken on Sunday."

And yet again, "Does your mom have a job?"

"No, she's a housewife."

"Are your parents coming for family weekend?"

"No, my dad has to work."

I lied every time she asked me questions about Mumma. Even after we had lived together in that room for six months and became friends, I lied to keep the truth from her, and in retrospect, from myself. I had never told Mark and Sully not to say anything about Mumma's death; somehow it was understood that we would not talk about it. The truth was, Mumma was still very much alive and with me. I could pretend she was still there, back at home with the kids, just like she always was when I went away. So, I hid the fact that starting on August 21, two weeks before Dad and I drove onto the campus for the first time, Mumma had died.

I became an expert at deception until one day Camryn questioned Mark. I don't know why she didn't ask Sully; maybe because we were still sort of dating. Mark let me know he told her. After the shock of finding out Mumma had died, she stopped asking me questions. I was glad she finally knew because it was hard to be friends when I had to hide behind my lie. But we never talked about her death. It was the end of all conversations about my mother.

Don't Worry About A Thing

Chapter Thirty-three
College Life in the Sixties

With the exception of English literature and freshman composition, my classes were large lecture-hall introductory courses: Sociology 101, Psychology 101, and geology. I took geology for no other reason than I had heard it was a gut science course, but I like rocks, and was glad I did. We went on a field trip to Mt. Desert Island in Maine, one of the most beautiful rocky coasts in the world. Growing up, I'd only been to the ocean a few times with my family, even though we lived less than two hours away. I remember going to Belfast with Yiayia and Grampie to have seafood. Yiayia sat on a beach chair with her feet in the water while we collected shells on the small beach. A few times we went to Old Orchard Beach, where we lay on the warm sand and swam in the waves, but we were just as excited by the arcades with the pinball machines.

Geology in the field

Arcadia National Park was different. This was the real rocky coast of Maine. None of my friends took geology; they all took "real" sciences like biology and chemistry. So, except for my lab partner, who was anti-social like me, I was by myself that day.

I sat on the cliff overlooking Thunder Hole, which at the time had no steel barriers to keep people from falling into the hole or committing suicide, which happened every once in a while. Thunder Hole, naturally carved into rock by the ocean over thousands of years, really did sound like thunder when the waves crashed against the rocks. Mesmerized, I spent most of the day watching the waves come in, awed by the authentic command of nature. I sensed my own insignificance in the face of the power before me, and at the same time, I could identify with being a part of it all. I was both frightened and lulled into an inner peace. Could this be "God's Grandeur" that Gerard Manly Hopkins had written about?

Sometime during the day, I learned about how millions of years ago volcanoes and glaciers formed the cliffs where I sat, forming layers of different types of rock, but what I really took back with me that day was a new-found love of the Maine coast. And rocks. I left with a beautiful sample of pink granite and have been collecting rocks from my travels ever since.

Sociology

Sociology was interesting. I learned about ethnocentrism, defined as "judging another culture solely by the values and standards of one's own culture." This class was one of those defining moments for me. I could now understand why people judged so harshly the differences between themselves and people from other cultures. Why people felt the way they lived was the only right way. I saw it all the time growing up in a provincial town where the people never left. As my cousin Dino liked to joke, "Those Mainahs think they need a passport to leave the state." Their lifestyle was the only one they knew. It put in perspective the differences between my immigrant family and the families of my friends. I learned how important it was to put myself in another person's shoes. Sometimes I didn't like those shoes, but at least I tried to understand where they were coming from. I remembered when I had been judged and how bad it had made me feel. I wanted to learn as much as I could about people and places all over the world. And one day, I told myself, I would travel all over the world.

Maslow's hierarchy of needs

In both sociology and psychology, we learned about Maslow's hierarchy of needs, which he described as a pyramid representing the following needs that must be met: at the base physiological needs; then safety needs; belonging and love needs; esteem, cognitive and aesthetic needs; and self-actualization at the very top. This was fascinating to me. And frightening. The theory suggested that people are motivated to grow in an upward pattern, completing the bottom stages, and working up. So basically, as humans we work our way up the pyramid from basic needs (food, shelter, etc.), to feeling safe and secure, to belonging in a social setting (family, friends), to feelings of self-esteem, and finally to self-actualization (becoming a fully functioning human being). Where was I in this pattern, I wanted to know? I spent a lot of my early years worrying about food and shelter, and I still did. There were times when I still didn't feel safe. There were still times when I was lonely and wanted to fit in. And now here I was. I knew my self-esteem was low because I really didn't believe I could make it through college. I felt like a fraud, and there it was in black and white on the pages of my textbook. I spent a lot of time telling myself that I had come this far, and the only thing to do was keep going.

Psychology was scary all around. After reading about psychological abnormalities, I was convinced I had all of them. Sully and I, studying together in my dorm lounge, laughed about all the ways we were crazy. His childhood was, like mine, in no way normal, with both of his parents alcoholics. What were the chances we'd turn out okay?

Because most of those classes were large lecture classes, the exams were always multiple choice. I wrote notes furiously in class and studied for every test, but to no avail; the bell curve always placed me at the top of the bell, a good solid C every single time. Camryn, a math major, who took a statistics class, told me that if I had to guess, pick C. More of the correct answers were C. So, I decided one night I wasn't going to kill myself pulling an all-nighter. After reading over my notes before the exam, I answered the multiple-choice questions, circling the C when I had to guess. There were a lot of C's. I couldn't believe it when I checked my grade before the next class. C+! Lots of studying got me a C and a last-minute reading over notes got me a C+. Life became easier once I discovered the secret. I was a solid C student no matter what, at least in psychology.

Now I could focus more on my literature classes. I wanted to do well in my literature classes, and when I got positive comments on my writing, I felt euphoric and wanted to do even better. I equated grades with self-worth. No one else cared about grades like I did. No one except Sully knew how important those grades were to me, because if I did well, I was happy, but if I didn't, I got depressed, sure I would flunk out of college. We didn't have very many classes together because his major was pre-med, but in English, if he got a better grade than I did, I would get ticked off, which made me work harder. Unlike me, nothing seemed to bother Sully, even though he had been through so much at home. Maybe just being at school away from the craziness was a relief.

Friends and parties

Camryn and I did become good friends. She decided she wasn't going to pledge a sorority like her best friend from high school who also lived in our dorm. That gave her more time to hang out with Sully and me and a group of new friends. We spent a lot of time partying on weekends, drinking and smoking pot. Some of our friends were older and had apartments, and it wasn't long before I discovered that alcohol was a magic elixir. While many of my friends experimented with LSD and psychedelic mushrooms, I was too afraid to try any of that after spending one long night with a friend who had a bad trip. I had a hard enough time controlling my mind when I was sober, I wasn't going to make it worse. Pot was fun, but unless we all got silly laughing, I could take it or leave it.

Wine was different. It was easy to purchase, and two cheap wines, Lancer's Vin Rose and Mateus, were our favorites. And high on wine, we had great conversations where we solved all the problems of the world. Unlike some on alcohol, I never became morbid or depressed. I was essentially a happy drunk. Drinking was a band-aid on a wound that really needed stitches, but that's all I had, so I used those band-aids. With alcohol I could pretend I belonged and forget what I needed to forget.

The next day I always felt guilty. Even smoking cigarettes made me feel guilty. No matter how much I tried to convince myself otherwise, I knew smoking was unhealthy, and even though I couldn't imagine giving it up, I knew that if I was going to survive—which meant not get cancer—I should quit. I was convinced my life would be cut short like Mumma's. I smoked less than I did when I was sitting in the hospital with Daddy, but I didn't want to quit altogether. I loved that first cigarette in the morning with coffee and I wasn't ready to give it up.

I went home for Thanksgiving break. Nothing had changed. A week or so later, I got a letter from George telling me they had been evicted and had moved again, to Winslow this time, and she and Jim were now going to Winslow schools. She didn't talk about the new place except to say it was a trailer and gave me the new address. I didn't know what I'd find the next time I went home.

Inner turmoil

My inner turmoil was paralleled by the outer explosions going on in the country and in particular on college campuses. The world was changing before our eyes, and who knew? Maybe it would all go up in smoke, and did it really matter if I smoked or drank too much? Some of our new friends were invested in the resistance, protesting against the war in Vietnam and for equal rights. My generation was sick and tired of the way adults were destroying our world; we rebelled against the establishment. It was "going to hell in a handbasket" as Grammie liked to say, but she was on the other side. Someone in the movement said, "Don't trust anyone over thirty," and it made sense to me. Most of the adults I knew and knew of in the world were crazy. They'd rather go to war on the other side of the world, killing our young men and thwarting equality of the races in our country, than make the world a better place. If someone came along who tried to change things, like John F. Kennedy and Robert Kennedy and Martin Luther King, Jr., they ended up dead. Closer to home, students who were speaking out were being attacked. Like many of my college friends, I was angry.

Some of my anger had to do with Mumma's death, but it was easy to transfer that anger to society as a whole. Not so much, though, that I became political. I wasn't about to burn the only bra I owned. I wore my favorite bell-bottoms and tie-dyed tops, and even attended one meeting of the SDS (Students for a Democratic Society) with Sully, but they were so serious. Both of us had always been rule followers, and although we now hated the rules, we didn't want to jeopardize our education. We marched in the protests along with the others and believed in a liberal ideology, but neither of us could really commit to fighting. I rationalized my actions by thinking that, unlike some of the kids, I had too much to lose. Sully felt the same. There was no one we could count on to bail us out if we got arrested in a protest—no family to come to our aid and no money. No safe place to fall. But we still had hope we'd make it through and come out on the other side still intact. We burned the candle at both ends, but not enough to burn it out completely.

Chapter Thirty-four
A Piece of My Heart

Sully and I were becoming closer. We had a lot in common; both our families were falling apart because of addiction and death, and this created the perfect recipe for a co-dependent relationship. We settled into a routine of studying together in the student lounge on weekdays, and partying on weekends. Sometimes Camryn or other friends studied with us, but usually it was just the two of us. We walked to the library when we needed to do research and ate burgers in the Bears' Den at the student union. And we found the perfect place to make out.

One freezing night, the ground covered with snow, we left the library and we ambled behind the dormitories to a grove of trees. Even though we were shivering, we were in no hurry to go back to the dormitory. As we approached an ancient oak, we noticed that on one side there was a hole as tall as we were. Peering inside the tree, we discovered it was hollow, with just enough room so that we both could fit inside. Snuggling inside the hollow tree, we lit a match and laughed as we realized we weren't the only ones to have found the tree. Initials inside hearts were carved all up and down inside the trunk. We added ours, K + S inside another heart. I'd be willing to bet I wasn't the only college freshman who lost her virginity inside a hollow tree. After that night, unless it was snowing too hard or below zero, the hollow tree became our place to escape from the world. Neither of us knew where the relationship would take us, but we were in too deep now. We made each other laugh, and that was enough.

The challenge of a nor'easter

When it was time to leave campus for Christmas break, everyone was in a rush to get home because a nor'easter was predicted. Sully and I had placed an ad on the board in the student union for a ride to Waterville. Someone from the biology department offered to drive us for the price of gas, but the guy couldn't leave early because he had some research to finish. That evening we worried that he had forgotten about us as the wind picked up and snow started falling. By the time he finally arrived in his VW Bug at 8 p.m., the snow was coming down full force. We made it to I-95, the main road home, with the increasingly strong wind making it difficult for our driver to stay on the road. After driving for a half-hour or so, we heard on the radio that I-95 was closed. Too late for us as we were already on it. At that point the little VW was the only car on the road, and all we could see in front of us was a wall of white beyond the headlights. Inching along for the next two hours, praying we wouldn't go sliding into the ditch, we finally made it to Sully's house in Waterville around midnight.

Sully took out his father's car to drive me home. I wasn't sure where home was since my family had moved again, but driving to Winslow, with visibility near zero and the headlights bouncing off the snow, we made it to the address Georgeanne had sent. My heart sank when I saw the sad tin trailer, looking like it would topple over if the wind got any worse. I knew this had to be it. Saying goodnight to Sully, I entered the trailer with only a dim light over the stove to guide me. Without noticing my surroundings, I fell into a strange bed in George's room and spent the night listening to the storm lashing against the thin windows. How many times would home change over the next few years, I wondered, before falling into a fitful sleep.

I woke up in that trailer for the first and last time. Daddy was already up, sitting at the table in the kitchen drinking coffee. He looked beaten. Then I realized all of our old furniture was gone. Before moving, he had sold everything we owned. Everything I had left in our old apartment was gone: my bed, my bureau that still had clothes in the drawers, my desk, and everything else I couldn't bring to college, including my record player and records. My albums! I wanted my albums back. But I didn't ask what he had done with the money. Maybe he had to pay off a loan, maybe he needed the money to rent this place, or maybe he gambled it away. It didn't matter. I have no memory of Christmas that year.

Losing Yiayia

Back at school, we fell back into our routine: study and party. And by the beginning of March, an air of hope infiltrated the air with the promise of spring. But then, one afternoon Daddy called to tell me Yiayia had fallen and broken her hip, and I had better come to visit her before it was too late. He picked me up later that day.

I had never seen Yiayia without her gray hair in a bun covered with a hair net, so I hardly recognized her lying in the hospital bed. Her gray hair had changed to white overnight and was splayed across the pillow. She didn't speak but recognized us as we kissed her goodbye. I knew then it would be forever. I returned to school.

On March 18, 1969, I returned to the dorm after my morning classes to find a message in my mailbox: Yiayia had died. Once again I was shocked by the swiftness and finality of death. I felt guilty that I had not gone to visit her more often during high school, as I often did when we lived downtown. She was close to my younger cousin Dino, but Uncle Tommy and Auntie Dee had moved to New Bedford, Massachusetts, so she might have been lonely. I should have visited her. I remembered the "facts of life" talk she had tried to have with me in her broken English when I was younger, and how she hated it when I did cartwheels across the lawn, convinced a nail would crack my head open, and I smiled inwardly. I left school to go to her funeral service, held at our old church, St. Mark's. Grampie looked like he had aged overnight too, shrunken and thinner. Now he and Maria would have to take care of Tony by themselves. I wondered if Tony knew what was going on.

Yiayia was buried next to Mumma. And when she died, her past went with her. Who really knew what her life was like growing up in the small village in Greece? All we have today are a few pictures, but her smile and high-pitched laugh remains with me. "Hoo, hoo, hoo," she would cackle when something struck her as hilarious, usually the antics of one of her grandchildren, all of whom she loved.

Spring at last

Back at school, spring semester was in full swing and as the snow melted a little more each day, we looked forward to being outside, craving the warm sun on our faces. I don't remember much about my classes, only that I managed to maintain my GPA so that I wouldn't lose my scholarships and loans. We met more people, and weekends began on Thursdays, when we caravanned out to farms and open meadows on land owned by someone who knew someone and houses owned by older students where we could party all weekend.

We were heading out to our friend Anne Marie's birthday party when Sully informed me that the guy who was going to jump out of her birthday cake couldn't make it, so he was going to do it. "Why?" I wanted to know.

"Just for fun. And by the way, I'm doing it naked."

"And what else are you going to do naked?" I was not amused.

"It's no big deal. It's just a party thing."

"Well, I think I'll pass. You can make a fool of yourself if you want." I refused to go, so I missed a drunk Sully jumping out of a cardboard birthday cake. I heard he was a hit.

But I wasn't so innocent either. When I drank too much, I tried to channel Janis Joplin. Dressing in a long Indian print hippie dress, my long hair flowing, a bottle of Southern Comfort in my hand, I would belt out "Ball and Chain" and "Piece of My Heart" and did a pretty good impersonation, at least for everyone in the room who were all so messed up they probably thought they were seeing the real thing.

A black guy from Washington D.C. showed up at one of the parties and opened up the trunk of his Mercedes. Inside was a complete bar, with more liquor than a store, along with mixers and even glasses. He became a regular at our parties. We had music, alcohol, drugs of choice, and friends, like us, who just wanted to live it up a little, aware it wouldn't last. We knew the world was disintegrating faster than we could keep up, a fact that punctured our lives with an undercurrent of desperation. The volume kept getting louder, with music, marches, and sit-ins on campuses all across the country, even in our corner of the world in Maine. For the guys, especially, it was a time of being in limbo, of not knowing whether they were going to have to go to Vietnam when their student deferments were over. We all had to live it up while we could.

Changes for Sully

By the end of that first (freshman) year, Sully had decided to change his major to English. His father wrote him a letter telling him that he'd been fired from his job and could no longer help him with school. Sully was angry because he knew his father's drinking was the cause. He went from vice president of a bank to no income at all. Medical school was out of the question, but he took it all in stride. He had been thinking of switching his major, realizing he didn't have the dedication to stay in school for as along as medical school would take. But now he had to figure out how to pay for school.

I made it through the first year, but I didn't feel good about myself. My grades were only average, and I knew it was because of all the partying. School, along with everything else, just didn't seem important. I couldn't get out of my slump.

Don't Worry About A Thing

Chapter Thirty-five
Tukey's Whip

Before the spring semester of freshman year ended, Daddy surprised me by showing up at my dorm one day. We went for coffee. Georgeanna and Jim were in school, and I had to cut class to see him, but I didn't tell him because it was so unusual for him to pop by like that. I didn't know what was up now. "Is everything ok at home?" I asked. I didn't know what was coming, but realized he probably left the house on the spur of the moment the way he had always done before.

"Just the usual. What are you doing this summer?" He got right to the point.

"I don't know. I don't have a job yet, and I'm not going back to New Hampshire again."

"There's an old snack bar near Camp Bomazeen. You can run it for the summer and stay at camp with us. If you want the place, I'll let them know."

"I...I guess so." I was less than thrilled, but without a car, could think of no alternative. He would be giving up the trailer, so there would be no place for me to live in the city.

I found myself alternately panicking about what I would do that summer to not caring what life would bring. Recently I had finished *Catcher in the Rye*, which didn't help my own sense of alienation. Like Holden Caulfield, I was asking the same question: what was the point of it all anyway? It had been nine months since Mumma's death. And death was still my constant inner companion. So I agreed to the snack bar even though I had no idea what I was getting into. Right then, it didn't really seem to matter all that much.

For the past two summers while I was working in New Hampshire, the family had had a real camp on the point close to the water, a quaint cottage with a huge stone fireplace. But Dad couldn't bear to stay there now without Mumma, so that left us sleeping in a storage shed on camp cots next to the mess hall. George, Jimmy, and I, despite the hot summer nights and heat from the kitchen, sweated under heavy blankets to hide from mice scurrying over our bodies in the middle of the night. Dad had a cot in the mess hall, and I don't know if mice bothered him as well, or if it even bothered him that we had to share living quarters with rodents. What we could see though, was that he was just going through the motions, passing the days in a grief-stricken haze. We survived the best we could.

Bringing Tukey's Whip back to life

In his happier days, Dad had loved to come up with money-making schemes. The ideas were plenty, the money not so much. When he approached me with his next idea, I think I agreed in part because he was showing an interest in something.

The ramshackle snack bar on the road to camp

looked like it had not seen customers since World War II. The old sign atop the building said, "Tukey's Whip." It was the previous owner's name. The plan to open the snack bar, sell pizza, Italian sandwiches, and soft-serve ice cream might have worked. I might have made enough money to at least pay for books during sophomore year.

The owner was only too willing to let someone else clean up the place, so he gave us a discount to rent his snack bar. I couldn't believe we actually had to pay to rent the place. As Dad handed me the keys on that first day in June, the heavy front door fell open, disturbing layers of dust. We coughed our way to the windows, trying to rid the place of stale, musty air. Something scurried across the floor. I looked at Dad as if to say, "Are we really going through with this?" He just shrugged.

I got to work, sweeping the cobwebs out of the windows and corners, and scrubbing the floors, the counter, the round stools, eight of them in all. There were no booths. The fridge and stove took lots of elbow grease, but finally they were done, and the pizza oven was turned on to 400 degrees. Everything seemed to work. Dad ordered food from the vendors who came out to camp, and it wasn't long before I was set up with all the makings for pizza and Italian sandwiches. The soft- serve machine was an enigma though. How did it work? I asked the owner if they had a manual. They didn't but gave me a cursory lesson on how to make the ice cream. It seemed simple enough. I scrubbed the machine until it shone and ordered vanilla soft-serve mix.

The morning before opening day, Sully, who had

gotten a job working at the Keyes Fiber paper mill, arrived to help.

"How was work yesterday?" I asked even though I knew the answer.

"Brutal. It's 110 degrees in those damn box cars. They're supposed to relieve me every fifteen minutes so I can re-hydrate, but the assholes stay out there smoking and fooling around while I sweat to death. I'd quit, but Uncle Bob got me the job, so I guess I'll stick it out for a while. Shoveling sawdust out of box-cars is not my idea of a fun summer!"

"I know," I said. "Guess I can't complain about this place." We made a sign with menu and prices, and then I was ready to open. "Here goes nothing. Let's see what happens. I'm actually a little excited for tomorrow."

"Good luck. Hope you make lots of money."

Early the next morning, after Dad had driven me from camp, I turned on the gas in the pizza oven, made the ice cream, and chopped onions, green peppers, and tomatoes for the Italians. At 11 a.m., I put the OPEN sign on the door and waited. Tukey's was off the main road, but since it was an area with many summer camps and a number of beaches, I was optimistic that people would stop in on their way to the beach or on their way home.

With the radio turned on to WBZ, a Boston rock station, I grabbed a cigarette and a Pepsi and sang along to the Rolling Stones, the Beatles, the Doors, and Hendrix, and waited for customers. Two hours and many cigarettes and sodas later, I was still waiting. The DJ kept talking about a concert that would take place in Woodstock, New York, later that summer. Janis Joplin would be there along with almost every famous rock star. They expected 50,000 people to show up. "Three days of peace and music," he said. Unreal, wouldn't it be cool to be there!

Finally, I heard the crunch of wheels in the gravel parking lot. My first customer! The owner of the building and his daughter appeared, checking on how things were going. I offered them ice cream on the house. Then after dinner, Dad and the kids showed up. They had ice cream, sat around for a while and left for camp. I was about to give up when a group of teens going home after a day of swimming stopped in for pizza. Then a family arrived for ice cream. I made them cones and almost forgot the take their money. After sitting alone for two hours, around 11 p.m., Dad arrived to help close. Not much to do. I cleaned out the ice cream cooler, and we left. I made four dollars on the first day.

The weekend changes everything

The rest of the week was more of the same. A few stragglers came in during lunch. Some friends showed up in the evening for pizza, and a few families came for ice cream. But on the weekend everything changed. It got busier with families stopping on their way to Bangs Beach. I realized I had forgotten to order potato chips and made a note to add that to the next order.

Business picked up on Saturday. That evening, a camp counselor visited from one of the boys' camps nearby with a proposition. I knew the guy, who was a friend of my old boyfriend Henry.

"Hey Kathy, how's it going? You in charge of this place?"

"Yeah, we just opened this week. What's up, Paul?"

"I'm a counselor at Camp Matoaka. We take the kids for ice cream once a week. Usually we go into Belgrade, but you are closer. Can you handle a bus-load of boys?"

"Of course, bring them in!"

True to his word, the next evening, Tukey's Whip was filled with campers who wanted chips, cokes, and ice cream. Everything was going smoothly at first. The first in line got beautiful vanilla cones before things started to deteriorate. After the tenth or so soft-serve, the ice cream began getting softer and softer, becoming more like soup.

"Bummer," I said to Paul. "It seems to be over-heating. I'll have to stop serving for a while and wait for it to cool down."

"Sorry," Paul said. "We'll have to go into Belgrade; they only have thirty more minutes before they have to be back at camp."

I watched glumly as my textbook money walked out the door, and that's the last we saw of the campers that summer.

I settled into a routine of slow weekdays and only slightly busier weekends. The money wasn't coming in, though, because I had to replace food that went bad. This was becoming an expensive proposition, and if things kept on like this I'd have no books in September. As August rolled around, Sully and I both became increasingly fed up. He was exhausted shoveling out boxcars, and I was bored sitting in the snack bar all day, mostly by myself, smoking and listening to the radio.

On the morning of August 16th, we sat outside on the stoop (the snack bar was empty), having a cigarette, and listening to the DJ talk about Woodstock. The festival had begun the day before, and it would last for two more days. It cost twenty-four dollars for the weekend, thirteen for two days, and seven for one day. Thousands of kids from all over America were descending on this farm in upstate New York. Music was playing day and night.

"Wow, wouldn't it be cool to be there?" I commented.

"It would be far out! Carmen is going with a group of friends."

Then we heard something we couldn't ignore. So many kids were pouring in from all over the country, they stopped taking tickets. They were getting in for free!

"How long would it take to get to Woodstock from here?" I asked.

"About six hours, I think."

"Are you thinking what I'm thinking?"

"Let's go!"

I shut off the pizza oven, locked the doors, and grabbed a couple of pre-made Italian sandwiches, chips, and Pepsi, my contribution. "I have a little bit of money at camp that I managed to save. It's not enough to buy books anyway."

When I brought the keys to Dad, I stopped at our shed to retrieve the box where I kept the little bit I had managed to put away. When I opened the empty box, I wasn't surprised, only pissed off.

"What the hell happened to my money?" I

shouted. What always happened to any money that came into the house? Dad had taken it to the races, where he spent his day off. It was gone. I know he planned to replace it when he won big, but of course that would never happen. Without any pangs of guilt for leaving, we got in the car and left for Woodstock.

Chapter Thirty-six
By the Time We
Got to Woodstock!

Sully had his paycheck from sawdust shoveling, so we hopefully had enough money for gas and food. "Ok, Carla, I know you can do it," Sully muttered under his breath to his car as we headed out.

I laughed with the sheer joy of our impending adventure. We were free! "Carla will make it. I know she will. She might have a few orgasms along the way, but she'll get us there," Sully assured me. He had bought an old Comet, which we called Carla the Coming Comet because she was known to shudder every time we shut her off, hence the name. Filled with the optimism of the young and foolish, we turned up the radio and sped south toward the Massachusetts Turnpike. When we stopped to gas up, we picked up maps of Massachusetts and New York because we only had a vague idea where we were going. Only a six-hour drive stood between us and the festival, which was actually in the town of Bethel, New York. With plenty of cigarettes, singing along with Country Joe and the Fish's "Fixin' to Die Rag," we began our pilgrimage to the Mecca of

Music, the Woodstock Festival, without a backward glance.

Our excitement increased as we left Maine and drove across Massachusetts. We knew our friend Carmen was already there and hoped to meet up with her and her friends when we got there. Carla was cooperating so far. The continuous radio announcements spurred us on. The day before, the crowds were getting so large that the musicians couldn't get in, so they helicoptered them in. Richie Havens was the first to play, and a guru from India had been there talking about peace and love. Far out! We couldn't wait. First the announcers on the radio said there were twice as many people as expected. Then it went up to 200,000 and more were arriving despite the rain that turned the huge field into mud. Then they re-played what someone announced that morning, "What we have in mind is breakfast in bed for four hundred thousand."

We were nearing the end of the Mass turnpike when Carla began to complain. Suspicious engine lights kept flashing on the dash. Bummer! Was she going to have her last orgasm now, right before we made it to New York? Holding our breath, we kept going, afraid if we stopped, she would die. What a relief to see "Welcome to New York." We were almost there!

As we drove into the town of Kingston, the road toward Bethel, which the map said was about sixty miles away, was teeming with hippies—young people like us anxious to be at the concert.

Then it happened. "Oh damn, there she goes," Sully moaned, as Carla came to a stop in the middle of the road. Before she died completely, we were able to roll into the parking lot of a Dairy Queen. "Stay put. I'll go see if we can use the phone to call a tow. Then maybe we can hitch a ride into the concert." But the DQ manager wasn't having it. "Go home, hippies! Damn hippies! And get that car out of my lot before I call the police!"

"We passed a convenience store a half-mile or so down the road; let's walk back and use a phone there. They can't all be jerks like that guy," Sully suggested.

Soon after we left the car, from out of nowhere, we heard the vroom-vroom-vroom of motorcycles blaring as a horde of what must have been a hundred Devil's Disciples surrounded us as we jumped over the ditch alongside the road, but they passed us, stopping at the same store we were headed.

When we reached the store, we found groups of hippies along with the bikers. We asked if they were headed to the concert, hoping we could get a ride. "No man, we're leaving," said one. "The traffic has stopped, no one can move. If you haven't made it there by now, it's not happening."

But we decided not to give up. Inside, the manager, although not rude to us, informed us we could not use the phone. What do we do now? Leave the car and go on? The road outside was becoming increasingly jammed with traffic. As we stood outside in the crowd, I noticed a middle-aged man staring at us. He seemed out of place among the hippies and bikers.

We decided to head back to the car. Maybe those guys were wrong and kids were still trying to make it to Bethel. As we strode back toward the DQ and our car, we sensed a car sidling up behind us. The man we'd seen earlier rolled down the passenger window. "Can I help you kids?"

"We're ok. But thanks," Sully answered.

"I heard you say your car broke down. Would you like me to call a tow truck?"

We looked at each other and nodded. "Ok, yeah, thanks, that would be cool."

He drove off as we continued on.

"Do you think he's going to do it?" I asked, getting discouraged.

"Who knows, but we'll stay here and see. Doesn't look like we're going to get a ride anywhere."

We waited. The DQ closed, and the owner warned us again to move the car. With more conviction than we felt, we told him a tow was on the way. He left, and we accepted the fact that we'd be sleeping in the car.

Just when we'd given up, along came a tow truck with the man driving his car behind him. We wanted to ride in the truck back to the garage, but the driver refused, something about it being against the law. So now it looked like we'd be walking all the way back into town if we couldn't get a ride.

"C'mon," the man said. "I'll take you to the garage." What choice did we have? We both got in the back seat. "Where are you from?" he asked. We told him and rode the rest of the way in silence. It wasn't long before we arrived at the garage.

"Thank you very much for the ride. We appreciate it."

"I'll hang around in case you need a ride someplace else."

We sat around waiting to find the verdict on Carla. In the meantime, the man went to McDonald's and brought us back burgers. Then we found out

Carla needed some kind of belt that they could not get until the next morning. Just our luck.

"Look, my house is not far from here," the man offered. "You are welcome to spend the night there. I have plenty of room." And although the man didn't look like a serial killer or anything, we were still suspect.

"No we couldn't do that, but do you know if there's a hotel close by? We'll stay there and come back in the morning."

"Come on then. We'll see." Of course, with the population of the town tripled because of the concert, there were no vacancies. "There's one last place we can check." We drove through the run-down section of Kingston and stopped in front of a dilapidated building with a green neon sign over the door that flashed "*Hotel*" on and off. Well, it was this or the man's house.

As luck would have it, or not, after stepping over the derelict on the front steps, we got a room. We thanked the man for his help. "I'll be back in the morning to take you back to the garage," he said. We thanked him again, expecting that was the last we would see of him.

After a sleepless night in the neon hotel, which could have been the setting for a story in the *Twilight Zone*, or a Stephen King novel, we hurriedly left, glad to get out in the sun and away from the strange cries and loud noises coming from other rooms. We decided to find a taxi to take us back to our car, but the man from yesterday was waiting for us.

The first thing Sully said when we got in the back seat was, "We appreciate your help, but why are you doing this?"

"When I was in the service, I was driving home from Louisiana when my car broke down in the deep South. I waited by the side of the road for hours, but no one stopped to help me. I vowed if ever I could help someone in trouble like I was, I would do it."

We thanked him again and wondered why we hadn't asked that question the day before. We could have avoided our roach hotel!

"Let's get some breakfast. The garage doesn't open until eight," he said, offering to take us to the local diner. That was fine with us as we were starving. The crowded diner buzzed with kids covered in dried mud. Still excited about how the concert blew them away, they shared concert stories. Janis was a hit, playing all night long. When the rain started, at first it was fine because everyone was hot and sweaty, but there were so many people and not enough shelters, so they had to sit in the mud. The local newspaper on the counter blared with the headline, "*Hippies Mired in a Sea of Mud.*" I took the paper, folded it, and wrapped it under my arm. If we couldn't make it, at least I'd have a souvenir.

Back at the garage, the car was soon fixed, and we were ready to leave. Once again, we thanked the stranger who had helped us for the two days, flashed the peace sign, and headed back to Maine. The biggest disappointment for me was missing out on seeing Janis Joplin. Our friend Carmen did make it, and her sign, "Sully we made it!" is in the movie that was made about that historic concert we missed.

Chapter Thirty-seven
Good-bye to the North Woods

That fall—my sophomore year—Daddy and the kids moved to another apartment in Winslow, and I went back to college. Sully moved out of the dorm and into an apartment on North Main Street in Bangor with our friend Peter; the apartment was a thirty-minute drive from campus. Camryn still wanted to room with me even though I told her I would probably be spending most of my time at Sully's, so technically my address was Androscoggin Hall, but I was rarely there. Sully and I were in love, and Mumma was right. I didn't have to question whether I was in love; I knew.

We went to class during the week, worked our work-study jobs, and went "home" at night. Sully's work- study job was in the art department where he made friends that invited us to parties on the week-end. Like the previous year, we managed to keep up our grades while partying too much.

More loss

In October I received a message from my cousin Roberta up north telling me Grammie had died. I hadn't seen Grammie since she had spent part of the winter with us a few years earlier, but I knew she had been battling breast cancer. I called Mumma's brother, Uncle Bernard, to ask if I could ride with them to North Lincoln for the funeral. Funerals were becoming a habit, like a re-occurring bad dream.

All Grammie's living children were there, along with Joyce Ann, who came from New Hampshire. Standing in front of her casket, what struck me was that in death she looked so much like Mumma. I never really thought they looked alike. I was transported back to Mumma's funeral, staring at her in the casket. Were they together somewhere in the afterlife, sitting at a kitchen table, drinking coffee and smoking cigarettes? That's how I would always remember them. I don't think it was a secret that Mumma was Grammie's favorite child, and more than one person there that day mentioned how hard she took Mumma's death.

Back at Grammie's house after the funeral, my uncle asked if I wanted some of her books, then being stored in the attic. I chose one that seemed like an odd tome in the midst of old worn novels. It was a hard-bound illustrated Paul Gustave Doré book called *The Doré Bible Gallery*. The illustrations were beautiful, and I thought maybe it would give me some insight into God. I couldn't help wondering how Grammie came to own a copy of a book by a French artist and illustrator in her small attic in the North Woods of Maine.

Before we left, I visited Aunt Ruby at her house on the hill. I sensed it would probably be the last time I would see her. With Mumma and Grammie gone, I didn't think I'd ever come back. That era of my childhood had ended.

Back at school, I worried about what was going on at home. I knew nothing there had changed, and life was getting worse for George and Jim. Daddy was drinking and gambling more and was constantly out of work. He had given up. As always, the kids didn't know whether they were going to eat or where they were going to live if they were evicted again.

We thought things would change when Daddy got into an accident. While drinking, he ran off the road and crashed into the woods. He wasn't injured, and it didn't scare him into stopping. He just didn't care anymore. His life was on a course of self-destruct, and George and Jim had a first-row seat to the disaster.

Then Daddy started bringing the kids to Bangor on weekends to stay with us. There was room, and Sully and Peter never complained that my family was now part of our lives. We spent more time at the apartment and less time partying. Slowly but surely, we were growing up.

On my twentieth birthday in February, 1970, Sully and I went to dinner at Pilot's Grill in Bangor. We talked about getting married after we graduated. He never really proposed; we both took it for granted that we would continue our lives together. He gave me a watch for my birthday, and we made plans. We'd both get teaching jobs upon graduation. We were both hopeful for the future while at the same time, fearful about the fate of our families.

Don't Worry About A Thing

Chapter Thirty-eight
A Wedding

By mid-June in the summer of 1970, I was working in Bangor as a clerk in the Soil Conservation Service of Maine, a summer job I got through the university. I had to cut up maps and glue different sections of them back together to create new maps of the soil topography of different parts of the state. The glue made me dizzy and nauseous. Or at least that's what I thought. One afternoon at work, while trying to fight waves of dizziness, I went into the bathroom and threw up. The nagging suspicion became impossible to ignore. I might be pregnant. My periods were never regular, but I could sense there was something different about my body and knew I had to find out.

Searching through the Yellow Pages, I found an obstetrician, made an appointment, and what I had been suspecting but mostly ignoring for a few weeks was confirmed. I couldn't pretend or deny my way out of this one. For some reason, I stupidly thought I could never get pregnant. Me, with my Twiggy figure, weighing all of ninety pounds, it was not possible that my body could nurture life. How wrong I was. I think the shock made us both numb, because at first, we just went along as if nothing had changed;

but soon enough, reality set in. Sully, to his credit, also took responsibility even though he must have been as frightened as I was. Our wedding, which we had planned for after graduation, was pushed up to September, just before the fall semester of my junior year. I would stay in school until the baby was born in February. Sully would get his teaching degree, and then I would go back and graduate with my teaching degree later on. That was the plan.

And then there were three

All of our energy went into establishing a life for us and the baby. With our work-study paychecks and student loans, we paid the bills, saved for the wedding, and bought food for all of us, which included my family when they came on weekends. Smoking made me nauseous, so I gradually smoked less and less until it was easy for me to stop altogether. Not forever—and I do wish it had been for good. I started up again after the birth. It wouldn't be until I was thirty-three that I finally quit for good.

My pregnancy became real as I was sitting in the waiting room at my first doctor's appointment. Surrounded by pregnant women with protruding bellies, I could hardly even imagine that that would be me in a few short months. After I was given a clean bill of health, a schedule of future appointments was set. I was clueless about childbirth but too embarrassed to ask questions. I also knew very little about infant care. All those years of babysitting and I had never cared for a newborn. The doctor recommended a pediatrician that I would meet when the baby was born.

Probably noticing my naivete, he also suggested I buy a copy of Dr. Spock's baby book. Since I had no one else to turn to, Dr. Spock became my teacher.

Meanwhile, plans were made for our shotgun wedding, which would take place on September 5. It would have made more sense to get married at the courthouse, but I hoped we could get married at St. Mark's, my childhood church in Waterville. Sully had grown up Catholic. He was forced to be an altar boy when he was young, but he left the church and had no desire to go back or be married in the Catholic church. We had to find a place for a reception, so we decided on the Holiday Inn in Waterville.

While making plans, when Daddy came to pick up the kids after a weekend with us, we made him give us a list of his family and Greek friends to invite. With a list from Sully's family, which was a bit shorter than mine, we ordered invitations, sending out around eighty. Camryn, who knew how to sew, volunteered to make my wedding dress. She lived outside of Boston, so we stayed at her house one weekend in order to shop for the material in Filene's basement, the same bargain basement where my friends and I had gone shopping a few years before in high school. This time I had a mission, rifling through the bins of yard goods until I found the material I liked. The wedding pattern was a simple dress with a small train. Camryn went to work on my off-white gown made of ribbed silk and a few yards of lace around the sleeve and neck.

The wedding came together quickly. Father Glendenning, the new priest at St. Mark's, officiated. George was my maid of honor and I had two bridesmaids, Camryn and Chrissie. Brian, Sully's brother, was his best man, and his two groomsmen were Pete and Will.

The day before, we went to Winslow, and Sully dropped me off at Grampie's house where I would stay for the night to get ready for my wedding day. It was a strange night. I slept in the upstairs empty bedroom with the window open, a mild autumn breeze floated the curtains into the room, swishing them back and forth, sounding like someone breathing every time the curtains moved. I didn't sleep all night as I lay there wondering about my future with a husband and the new life arriving in February. I felt Yiayia's presence in the room. I thought of Mumma. Did they know what was happening? Did they approve? Mumma always said, "You make your bed, you have to lie in it," so here I was, and there was no going back.

Tying the knot!

My hippie friends mixed with my Greek relatives made for a strange combination of people, but everything went fairly well, except for Lee-Ann, who came dressed in her best red dress. We didn't see her when she came into the church, but certainly everyone else did. Underneath her sheer red dress, she seemed to be missing a few essentials, namely her underwear! Auntie Dee didn't stand for it, telling her in no uncertain terms that she had to leave. I don't know what she said, but our nearly-naked guest disappeared. We didn't know her well—she had come as a plus one—but when we found out later, we were embarrassed. I hoped Daddy didn't see her.

When the time came for Daddy to walk me down the aisle in his tux that Sully had gotten for him, we were both shaky and nervous. I didn't notice at the time, but later, in the pictures, I saw that he looked proud and scared and very thin. Although I felt the empty places where Mumma and Yiayia should have been, I was grateful Daddy was beside me.

I loved the Episcopal wedding ceremony, especially near the end of it when Father Glendenning wrapped our hands tightly together with a binding cloth and intoned, "Those whom God hath joined together, let no man put asunder." We literally had tied the knot.

At the reception we did all the things one does at weddings, the buffet, the toast, the first dance, the father-daughter dance, the cake-cutting, and throwing of the small bouquet of stephanotis. And because my Greek relatives were there, we did the Greek dance, circling around the dance floor. We left amid a rain of confetti. On the surface, everything about the day was perfect. But despite the celebration, I couldn't shake the free-floating anxiety that gripped me, like soft whispers in the back of my mind, just loud enough for me to hear, just enough to make me worry about the unknown future.

After the reception, Sully and I returned to our apartment in Bangor. It was then that Sully told me his Uncle Bob hadn't come to the wedding because we had not married in the Catholic Church. In his uncle's mind, we were not married. This uncle had helped Sully and his brothers when their parents were not capable of taking care of them. Now, evidently, he had disowned his nephew over religion.

On the other hand, Sully's uncle's sister, Aunt Mary Ellen—the aunt he had spent the summer with after graduation—had had a wedding shower for us in Florida with her friends. She had three little girls under three and couldn't come to the wedding, but took the time to have a shower for us and sent us a large box of kitchen gadgets and utensils. Mary Ellen was also a devout Catholic who followed all the rules of the church, but she didn't judge us for not marrying in the Catholic church. I think she embodied the real Christian spirit. Along with Camryn making my wedding dress, getting that box was one of the nicest things anyone had ever done for me.

Daddy found a job in Bangor that fall, and he left Georgeanne and Jimmy with Grampie in Winslow so they could go to school while he worked in Bangor. The arrangement didn't last long. After Yiayia had died, Grampie had to take over Tony's care, so although they stayed at his house, the kids were on their own. But it wasn't long before Daddy returned home, got another place in Winslow, and they continued to struggle while Daddy's health deteriorated. He'd been feeling sick for a while, but we thought it was because he was drinking too much. There was more to it than that as we were soon to discover.

Daddy struggles

One day, in what must have been extreme stomach pain, Daddy took himself to the emergency room. After a series of tests, we learned the prognosis was not good when we heard that word "cancer" again. The same doctor who had treated Mumma informed me that Daddy had bladder cancer. Later on that same week, as I walked down the hall to his room, Dr. A waylaid me and asked me to come into his office. Feeling a sense of déjà vu, I listened as the doctor told me there was nothing more they could do for Daddy there, so they were sending him to Togus, the veteran's hospital. It seemed that nothing could shock me anymore, and yet, here I was sitting in shock, hearing the C word again.

Then, unlike when he had told me about Mumma a few years earlier, I broke down in his office, crying, begging the doctor not to move him. I was pregnant, Daddy was dying, and I wasn't going to let the doctor send him away to die. I believed that going to the veteran's hospital would be an instant death sentence. I don't know why I felt that way. I must have heard some stories about the hospital that made me think the care would not be good. The doctor was patient, letting me cry it out until, embarrassed that I had made a fool of myself, I stopped. Then he assured me there were excellent doctors at the VA, and besides that, they had equipment there that Daddy needed that the Osteopathic Hospital lacked. In short, there was nothing else they could do for him, but if he went to Togus, he might have a chance. We had no choice, so as the ambulance took him to the hospital in Augusta, we followed behind.

I met his new doctor, Dr. Emmanuel, a short kindly man who assured me they would do everything they could for Daddy. And they did. He had surgery, but eventually he had to have a urinary catheter, a difficult adjustment that he had to live with, but one he never really accepted He returned home, and we were hopeful he would settle down with the kids. Maybe this scare would make him want to stay alive.

Moving back to campus

Just before classes began, Sully and I moved back to Orono, within walking distance of UMO; Carla the Comet had finally died and we had no car. Our new place was a second floor one-bedroom apartment in a large Victorian house that had been converted into apartments. The kitchen and bathroom were small, but the living room, once a parlor, was a large room with built-in bookcases and windows from floor to ceiling that looked out onto a park across the street. I loved our first home as a family.

Three months pregnant and without a car, we walked or got rides to classes each day. It was fine in the autumn, and the long walk was pleasant as we were surrounded by shades of orange, red, and yellow, reminding me of Silver Street when I was child. Sully and I had some of the same English classes, and after class we ate in the Student Union or came home and experimented with cooking. Neither one of us was very good at it. Sully made his mother's Campbell Soup meatloaf, and I perfected a pretty good spaghetti sauce. We joined a food coop, volunteering our time setting up and working the cash box in exchange for discounts on fresh fruit and vegetables, cheeses, and other dairy products.

Sometimes George came for the weekend, but

she now had a boyfriend, and Jimmy was becoming increasingly difficult to handle, often running off with his friends, no one knew where.

In the midst of everything, we had a bit of good news. When Sully was eighteen, like all young men at the time, he had to register for the draft. When he started college, he applied and received a college deferment. The war in Vietnam was winding down, and there was a chance he would not have to go. They were drafting younger men first, and a lottery had been instituted by the government based on date of birth. We paced the floor awaiting our fate as the draft lottery numbers were announced. What would we do if his number came up early? Would he have to go half-way around the world to kill people for no reason, for a war to stroke the egos of a power-hungry government? We even talked about moving to Canada, but it was just talk that made us feel we had options when we knew we didn't. We couldn't afford to do anything except stay in school, live on our student loans, and see what happened. As the numbers were picked and his birthday, June 10, was not called, we began to hope. More and more numbers were called and we began to exhale with relief. When his number finally came up over 300, we were ecstatic! We knew he wouldn't be called up. He dropped his college deferment. We had won the lottery!

Don't Worry About A Thing

Chapter Thirty-nine
The Baby Arrives

The last semester before I gave birth, school life revolved around poetry and English literature classes while Dr. Spock's *Baby and Child Care* dominated life in the apartment. On the days when I didn't have class, I read Dr. Spock over and over, afraid I might miss something important. When I wasn't spending hours with Dr. Spock, I studied and watched *The Brady Bunch* on the old black and white TV we had purchased at a second-hand store. In the evening we read Shakespeare together as we gorged on my one craving: oranges. I lost track of how many bags of oranges we consumed. I couldn't get enough of them. When we finished with class work, once again it was back to Dr. Spock.

Even though my belly swelled more every day, the reality hadn't sunk in. It seemed as though we were playacting, pretending to be adults. Outside in the real world, we had family issues to deal with, but during that fall and winter, inside the apartment, we were hibernating in our own world.

By the end of January, with snow drifting all over campus, it became increasingly difficult to maneuver my pregnant belly over the snow and ice, but

I refused to miss class. After one all night snowstorm, I made my way across the recently plowed mall and entered Steven's Hall to see my poetry professor, Dr. Richards, staring down at me from the top of the stairs, a worried look on his face. "You shouldn't have tried to come in today after the blizzard," he lectured. "The walks are still too slippery."

His concern made me feel guilty. In 1971, despite the nascent feminist movement, it was an odd sight to see a nine-months-pregnant student waddling across the snow-covered quad, mingling in the milieu of campus life while attempting to keep the pregnant belly from bouncing off a snowdrift.

"What? And miss a day with Gerard Manly Hopkins?" I asked sliding sideways onto the desk chair preparing to drop into the world of "God's Grandeur."

The semester ended the second week in February, and after the short break, Sully went back to school without me. My due date was February 14. I worried I'd go into labor while I was at home alone; we got a phone so that Sully could call me between classes. Our neighbor, an art professor at UMO, offered to take us, anytime, day or night, to the Eastern Maine Medical Center in Bangor when the time came. We had planned to call a cab, but it was a relief knowing someone close by had a car and could take us.

Like the Dr. Spock book, our baby-name book became dog-eared as we poured over every page time and again searching for the perfect name. Nothing sounded right. We laughed at all the outlandish names but couldn't imagine calling our baby any of the common names.

And finally, labor and the arrival of Sophia!

The night I went into labor, two weeks after my due date, it wasn't snowing. Sully was reading from our now well-worn copy of *Baby and Child Care*, the only information at our disposal on what to actually do when the baby arrived. The famous doctor had the answers.

"Stop!" I interrupted as he read.

"Do you want me to repeat it?"

"No, I think this is it!" I was trying not to panic as I felt the first contractions. A few hours later, when the pains were three minutes apart, I called the doctor.

True to his word, our neighbor came through, and we arrived at the hospital just before midnight on February 25. In a few minutes it would be my twenty-first birthday.

Labor continued through the night, labor pains for birthday breakfast, and stronger labor pains for birthday lunch. The doctor gave me something to slow down the labor so he could go to lunch. When he returned, he gave me something to speed up the labor, then injected me with scopolamine, which would make me forget the pain. It worked because even though I had probably screamed bloody murder all through the process, I had no memory of the entire birth. The drug doesn't relieve the pain, just gives you amnesia. Promptly (from the doc's perspective) at 1:16 p.m., our baby girl was born, six pounds three ounces, on February 26, my twenty-first birthday. Even though they placed her in my arms after she was born, I have no memory of it. It wasn't until later that afternoon when I awoke and groggily asked Sully that I found out we had a daughter! Sully saw her before I did.

They brought her to me, swaddled tightly in receiving blankets. I uncovered her and stared in awe at this amazing little creature. Her skin was so delicate, a perfect peachy pink tint. And the top of her head was covered in a downy fuzz. Touching her tiny fingers, her arms, and miniature toes, I couldn't believe this perfect tiny baby came from me. With eyes wide open, we stared at each other. I was both awed and petrified.

Now more than ever, I wished Mumma were here. At that moment I missed her more than ever. How could I do this by myself? I needed someone who would know what to do. Maybe it was the lingering effect of the drugs, or just my wishful thinking, but as I held my baby in my arms, I sensed that I wasn't alone. Just like the night before the wedding, I felt Mumma's presence there with us, and although the responsibility was overwhelming, I knew she watched over us.

I had zero confidence I could breastfeed my child, so the next day when my milk started to come in, I cried as the binder covering my breasts to dry up my milk squeezed tighter and tighter, causing excruciating pain. This was the price I had to pay for not breastfeeding. I believed, wrongly, that my baby would be healthier with cow's milk.

On day two, the nurse came into my room with paperwork. We had to decide on a name. We couldn't decide. She left saying she'd be back tomorrow, and we absolutely had to have a name. Daddy came to visit while Sully was at work, and the first thing he asked was her name.

"We don't have one yet," I said. "I'd like to give her a Greek name, but we can't decide." The Greek first names sounded funny with an Irish last name. At this point we were overthinking this.

Then Daddy said, "I've always liked the name Sophia. Sophia Sullivan sounds good. It sounds like a movie star. Maybe she'll be famous."

I chuckled. But I remembered from the name book that Sophia meant wisdom. We had highlighted it. I liked it, and I also liked the fact that Daddy had named her. Later when Sully arrived, I was already calling her Sophia in my mind and was relieved when he had no objections. But then we couldn't decide on a middle name. Finally, Sully said she could use Sullivan for a middle name when she got married. When the nurse arrived on the third day with the forms, we put Sophia Sullivan down and left the middle name blank. She gave us a judgmental look but didn't say anything. After my doctor checked me, and the pediatrician examined the baby, we left the hospital with our Sophia, a bag of free hospital samples, and instructions on how to make her formula.

At home with Sophia

At home, we placed Sophia in Sully's old baby crib and stood staring down at her, speechless, as she slept. I think that up until this moment in my pregnancy and childbirth experience, I had been tiptoeing past or navigating around the edge of life, living in a bubble. Not anymore. Life got real. There was no observing from the sidelines or escaping into books; the responsibility was overwhelming, and it was mine. For the first time in my life, I understood that it would be my actions that determined not only my life, but that of my child. I was afraid but at the same time determined to do the right thing; and by the way he looked at our daughter, I knew Sully felt the same even though our feelings fluctuated from besotted to panic.

As we stood watching her in the crib that first day, neither of us wanted to ask the question, "What do we do now?"

"Formula, we have to make her formula," I commanded with more confidence than I felt. Soon the tongs, the glass bottles, the Pyrex cup, and nipples were boiling as we mixed the Carnation milk with water and a teaspoon of Karo syrup. Every few minutes one of us would escape from the kitchen to check on the baby to see if she was still breathing. Cloth diapers were piled on the dresser/changing table, waiting for the first diaper change. The formula finished, six bottles for the next twelve hours, once again we stood staring as she began to squirm. "Do we pick her up or let her cry?" Sully asked uncertainly.

"Pick her up," I said, trying to sound like I knew what to do. "We need to change her, though." Wrapped in a nightgown with strings pulled tight around her feet, she looked like a little parcel as I loosened the gown and pulled it up around the belly-band that was wrapped over her belly button. Off came the rubber pants, the safety pins, and the white diaper. "Nothing. She's not even wet." On went a new diaper, pinned on both sides, and rubber pants.

I held her gingerly, careful to support her head and settled into the old rocking chair we had bought at a second- hand shop, while Sully heated the bottle, checking a few drops on the inside of his wrist to make sure it wasn't too hot, per Dr. Spock. "Well, what do you know? She seems to know what to do! She's sucking like a pro!" I said, my relief palpable as I settled more comfortably into the chair watching her attached to the nipple.

"Should we burp her?" Sully asked, "before she eats too much?"

"Sure," I answered, not sure of anything. I lifted her onto my shoulder and patted gently, waiting for I was not sure what. Suddenly a strange noise erupted from the bottom of Sophia's tummy, a rumbling, a roiling, a gurgling that moved up her trunk like a mini volcano about to explode. We stared at each other, but before we could say anything, vomit spewed from her tiny body—loud, fast, whirlwind vomit that flew across the room and splattered the far wall. For a second we were silent with shock. Before I could think what to do, I cried, "Get Dr. Spock! We read something about baby vomit. Find out what he says. Hurry!"

"Here it is. It's called 'projectile vomiting.'"

"Well, what does it say?" I cried in alarm.

"Call the doctor," he mumbled.

"What? Is she sick? Is she going to die? Are we killing her before she even has a chance to live?" I was in full-fledged panic mode.

"Wait, wait, it says, call the doctor if it continues. I guess if it happens once or twice it's okay. Look, she's falling back to sleep. She looks fine."

"But she threw up all her food! She has to eat. She lost it all!"

"Ok, let's let her sleep for a while and try again a little later," Sully suggested as he wiped down the walls.

"God, I wish we had someone to call, anyone," I moaned. "I wish we knew someone with a baby, or had a parent or grandparent or even a stranger at this point. I don't think we can do this."

"What do you want me to do, walk into town and ask strangers if they have a baby and can answer some questions?" Sully asked. We both laughed, and the tension released for the moment.

"Don't laugh," I answered. "It may come to that."

The next twenty-four hours were a blur of exhaustion as diapers were changed and vomit was cleaned from the walls, floor, and whichever parent happened to be holding the baby. The doctor was called. "Is she having bowel movements?" the nurse asked. When told she was, the nurse seemed unconcerned. "She's adjusting to the formula. Give her a little at a time, then stop." That worked a little better, and we eventually got the feeding under control.

During that first month we endured a variety of what we thought were life threatening crises, like diaper rash, days without sleep (us), sleeping too much (Sophia—was she still breathing?) Somehow, with Dr. Spock by our side, miraculously, we all survived. As winter turned into spring, another couple with a small child moved into the apartment building. We made friends, and life took on a new routine.

Sophia continued to grow in front of our eyes, learning new things every day, and the summer before Sully's senior year became an idyllic time, with no major catastrophes occurring in the family. We got together with three other couples in the building on the weekends, two of whom had children. While the kids played together with their toys, we played cards. Sully worked at school and when he came home, we walked around the neighborhood, Sully proudly pushing the carriage as if he were the only daddy in the universe.

That same year Sully's great-aunt Bessie died unexpectedly. She and her sister, Aunt Sarah, having no children of their own, had often taken over the responsibility of caring for Sully and his two brothers. Sully was given her car, an old 1960 Pontiac Firebird that she rarely drove—it looked brand new. Now we had a car and could drive to Waterville on weekends when we needed to.

Sully nears the school finish line at last

Sophia was seven months old when Sully began senior year. Our plan was still in place. He'd get a teaching job when he graduated, and I'd go back to school. In the meantime, I stayed home with Sophia, amazed at how quickly she was learning and growing. When she awoke in the morning, we pretended to be asleep as we listened to her cheerful baby-babbling as she played with her stuffed animals. When she got older and could pull herself up in the crib, she looked over at us and gave her breakfast orders. "Mummy, Dadda, bwekfass, egg, tose, juus." We opened our eyes laughing as one of us changed her and the other made breakfast. What a wonderful beginning to our days. And, according to Dr. Spock, she did everything early! Every new milestone, every new word, we celebrated while continuing to make stupid new parenting flubs. Like the time Sully ran out of the kitchen with her on his shoulders, while they both laughed, not accounting for the fact she was so high up. I heard a scream from the next room as she banged her head on the doorframe. Or on her first birthday when she grabbed her candle before I could stop her, burning her fingers. But miracle of miracles, she survived our stupidity, and we settled into family life.

Chapter Forty
A Wedding and a Funeral

We tried to make it to Waterville as frequently as we could on weekends because Daddy's health was deteriorating. Each time we came home, I could see the change. Daddy and the kids moved into the duplex upstairs apartment in Grampie's house. On moving day, Sully and Georgeanna's boyfriend, Ken, moved them in, but Daddy couldn't be there because he was in the hospital. I talked to Dr. Emmanuel on the phone. Daddy would be coming home for the weekend, but the doctor told me to watch out for him; he was worried. Daddy was depressed because they told him there was nothing else they could do. We took Sophia to Winslow, hoping we could raise his spirits, but I was on pins and needles with fear that something would happen before he had to be back in the hospital on Sunday afternoon. After that weekend, he was in and out of the hospital at various times until April, when we finally knew he'd not be coming home again.

George had met and fallen in love with Ken, her high school boyfriend. They were planning to marry in June after she graduated, but when she talked to the doctor, he told her Daddy wouldn't make it that long, so they decided to get married in the hospital chapel on April 29.

On the day of the wedding, a nurse wheeled Daddy down the aisle in his wheelchair with an IV drip, George walking beside him. My memories are blurry about that day. I vaguely remember the chapel with a sanctuary and altar that would serve any denomination, a place more fitting for one or two people to pray for their sick loved ones than to attend a wedding. But I do remember that despite his pain and the difficulty of staying awake due to the drugs, Daddy rallied and smiled. He smiled that big full-face smile of his that seemed to say how proud he was to give George away and be there at the very end. Tears welled in his eyes, but his smile remained firm, determined as he was to do this one last thing.

After the short ceremony, we hugged Daddy goodbye and left for a luncheon at George's new mother-in-law's house. Mrs. Carey prepared a big buffet as friends of George and Ken arrived. It was impossible to forget that Daddy was left behind in the hospital, and I had a perpetual lump in my throat as I forced myself to swallow tears that surfaced periodically. On that day we were celebrating a new beginning for George and Ken, while grieving an ending that would come any day. I prayed we wouldn't get a phone call before the day was over, and maybe He listened this time because everything went as planned. For George, the day was not only the beginning of her marriage, but the beginning of a loving relationship with her new mother-in-law.

On Saturday, May 6, we went to the hospital where I saw Daddy for the last time. Unlike Mumma, who was in a morphine-induced sleep the last time I saw her, Daddy was thrashing about, crying out. I don't know if he knew we were there or not. Even though I knew it was cowardly, I couldn't stay in his room. Leaning on the concrete wall in the hallway, I broke down. Something unlocked inside of me. He always told us not to worry about a thing. He was wrong, though. There was so much to worry about. Life. Surviving. Somehow we had to find a way to get through this crazy life. Mumma was forty-three when she died; Daddy was in his late fifties or early sixties depending on which documents we believed. Time was short. What if I lived only until forty-three?

Daddy passes away

On Monday, May 8, 1972, I received the call. Another funeral. Once again, we went through the motions, doing what had to be done. After the funeral service, our family, along with the Honor Guard from the US Army, followed the hearse to the graveyard. Before the casket was lowered into the ground, a bugler played Taps and the Honor Guard took the flag off his casket, folded it, and presented it to me, the eldest.

I didn't cry. But this time, unlike with Mumma, there was no denial, no pretending that he was still alive; instead, my feelings went straight to rage, and it took all I had to control it. Rage that life had made us orphans too soon. Rage that my parents would never know their grandchildren. Rage that there was nothing I could do about it. Rage at life in general. Rage at God. Why couldn't He let Daddy win big just once?

In spite of the anger boiling inside, a prayer entered my mind that day that I repeated to myself throughout the years, "Please, God, let me stay on this earth until Sophia and any other children I might have are grown up and settled." With trembling hands, I picked up a handful of dirt, dropped it on top of Daddy's casket, and turned away as he was lowered into the ground at Pine Grove Cemetery, next to Mumma and Yiayia. And that was that.

Chapter Forty-one
The Winter at Admiral Dot Farm

The winter of 1972 would be our last winter in Maine. It would turn out to be a time of introspection, a time of learning to be both mother and wife, a time of questioning my life, and a time of grieving,

Jimmy and Georgeanna and her husband Ken continued to live in Grampie's upstairs apartment, but it was a difficult arrangement; by now Jim was used to his independence and George and Ken had a hard time keeping him at home. At sixteen, he had a girlfriend and spent a lot of time with her. I think he was becoming a lot like Daddy, always on the go. Or maybe like us, he was looking for a place where he belonged.

A few weeks after Daddy died, Sully graduated from UMO. He had already begun to search for a teaching position, although his search did not go well. We were in the midst of a recession and teaching jobs in Maine were scarce. Our future was up in the air. Ken joined the National Guard and had to go to boot camp that fall, so the six of us, George, Ken, Jim, Sully, Sophia, and I moved to an old farmhouse in Cornville, Maine that we found to rent. The sprawling white house with a sign on the mailbox that read, "Admiral Dot Farm," stood on a hill at the end of a mile-long dirt road. We later discovered the farm had been named after the owners' father who was named after a circus midget. The farm was the summer home for an extended family that came from various parts of the country every year. So our rent would be paid from September 1972 to June of 1973, and it was cheap.

On moving day as we drove up the long drive, a cool breeze flowed across the meadows, heightening the smell of recently mowed hay, cut short like the head of a newly enlisted GI. I had reservations about moving with a small child so far away from a town. What would winter be like out here? The six of us settled into the large old farmhouse and shortly thereafter, Ken left for boot camp. We knew that moving into the country would be a temporary arrangement before we figured out where to go next and what we would do, but for now, we all needed that time to be together.

The large two-story farmhouse had a big kitchen, a dining room, a summer kitchen in the back, and plenty of spare bedrooms, nine rooms in all. In September before it got too chilly, it was ideal. Sophia had fields and meadows to run and play in and lots of barn kittens everywhere. But we were quite isolated from the outside world. Still, unlike the time Daddy moved us out to the country, I enjoyed being alone with just my family this time. I think we all needed time to heal.

Right after we moved, Sophia had a bout of roseola, with a high fever and rash, and when she felt bad, I felt sick too, from fear. I panicked, thinking the worst would happen. But as soon as she felt better, she wanted to play in the sandbox and on the large tree swing in the dooryard. As the month wore on and the days became colder, the nagging worry stayed with me about being way out there at the end of a long dirt driveway in the middle of winter.

Welcoming visitors

Although we were far from the city, we had many visitors that fall. Our friends from college, our neighbors who had lived in our apartment building in Orono, and friends of Ken who became our friends as well, all made the trip out to Cornville. Sophia had a cousin to play with now in Waterville when Sully's brother Brian and his wife Linda had a baby girl, Erinn, so we'd sometimes go into Waterville so the girls could play. I kept in touch with many of our college friends, writing letters back and forth. George's cat had six kittens, and we gave a small black kitten to Sophia.

Autumn came and went with the swiftness of a college weekend away from studying. With winter approaching, George and I spent our days learning to cook. We qualified for food stamps because Sully was the only one of us working and his job as a substitute teacher was sporadic. Even in our poorest days growing up, we had never had help from the government; we went hungry instead. Now, when I went to the grocery store, I learned to keep my face averted from the judgmental eyes watching when I paid in food stamps. But was this shame any different from the shame of being hungry and having nothing in the cupboard? One thing I knew for sure: my child would not go hungry. And if I had to use food stamps for a while, so be it. In June when we moved again, I would get a job and we'd find a babysitter for Sophia. But for now, with only one car, I had to stay home.

We got $29 in food stamps every month and were able to buy enough food for a month with that. We made large pots of beef stew, bean soup, lentil soup, and chowders. Sometimes we made pumpkin pies and cakes for dessert. I got Adele Davis's book, *Let's Eat Right to Keep Fit*, but it was discouraging because the recipes called for so many ingredients we couldn't buy. I bought some basics: wheat germ, yogurt, whole wheat flour, and lots of fruit and vegetables. I also got a small paperback cookbook, *Cooking with Whole Grains*, and learned to make biscuits and bread. We didn't eat a lot of meat because it was too expensive, but sometimes we splurged and bought a steak. Living frugally on a limited food budget forced us to learn how to make nutritious meals that fed the lot of us, including friends. A friend of ours opened a health food store in Bangor where we bought brown rice in bulk, and with carrots and peas and tamari sauce, we put together large concoctions that tasted surprisingly good. Sophia loved the rice dishes more than the soups. George and I wished we had paid more attention to Mumma and Daddy's cooking when we had had the chance. But after a while, we became expert soup makers, mastering a delicious lentil soup and beef stew although we were never able to replicate the simplest recipe of all: Daddy's famous bean soup. Something was always off.

The temporary pioneer

I enjoyed being home with Sophia. Knowing it was temporary, I was grateful for the time we had together. The day would come when I would have to get a babysitter while I went back to school and to work. I hated the thought of leaving Sophia with someone else, but my student loans were due so we had no choice.

I felt like a pioneer that winter, hibernating in the wild until spring would arrive and we'd once again return to civilization. Besides cooking, I came up with a to-do list to keep busy. Reading topped the list. I must have been in full-fledged homemaking mode because I thought I could make a quilt. In spite of my past experience with sewing, I spent many afternoons cutting up old coats and flannel shirts into squares that I would then piece together, although I wasn't sure how. I never actually made the quilt, and those squares came along with me in our subsequent moves until I finally threw them out.

I also wanted to work on a family tree before I lost more family members. And finally, I wanted to study both the science of astrology and yoga. Mumma and I always read our horoscopes, along with Dear Abby in the newspaper. Mumma was a Gemini and I'm a Pisces, the sign most interested in the occult. I was looking anywhere and everywhere to find answers about life and death.

A friend gave me a copy of *The Autobiography of a Yogi*, about the life of Paramahansa Yogananda. Ever since Swami Satchidananda opened the Woodstock Festival, many young people our age had become interested in yoga. Yogananda was a pre-curser to Swami Satchidananda and reading his book was the beginning of my life-long study of yoga and Eastern religion. The yogic philosophy made sense to me. It was based on the belief that all religions adhered to the same truth, the belief that God was love and all paths led to the same God. Paths may be many, but there was just one truth. I learned that yoga and meditation helped with stress, and with worry being my constant companion, I desperately needed the help. There were no yoga classes out in the country, and I could not have afforded to go if there had been anyway, so when Sophia napped, I took out the yoga books that I had begun to collect and wrote down and memorized how to do the asanas (postures) and pranayama (breathing exercises). I also started reading *The Tibetan Book of the Dead* because, well, death was always on my mind. This book teaches the art of dying, that the moment before death is very important because whatever one's frame of mind and thoughts are at the time of death will determine the future of the spirit in the next life. "We are what we think," it said. I wondered what Mumma and Daddy and our grandparents had been thinking when they died. I began writing in my journal again, the journal I had started when I was sixteen, and decided then and there that one day I would write a book.

Winter in the country

With winter not far ahead, we bought Sophia a snowsuit in October to get ready, and with the weather getting colder by the day, it wasn't long before we were bundling up to play outside. Sophia caught a cold and the only thing I could get into her was orange juice. Every time she got sick, I thought for sure she would die. I had panic attacks, blaming myself. What was I doing wrong? We stayed inside most days, napping, reading, and eating hot soup until she finally felt better and I could breathe again.

My yoga practice, self-taught, was coming along. I was learning pranayama, the breathing practices, and doing Hatha yoga, the postures, early in the morning. Following the directions in *Yoga, Youth, and Reincarnation*, I tried to meditate but was too fidgety, so that wasn't working very well.

Jimmy struggles

Jimmy refused to go to school, and the bus driver, tired of driving down the long driveway for nothing, stopped coming. Sully tried to take him in when he left for his subbing jobs, but Jimmy refused to go. We did everything we could to keep him in school, including doing lots of yelling every morning, but there was nothing we could do to convince him he had to go. He got in the habit of leaving to stay with friends for a few days and coming back when he felt like it. We never knew where he was unless he called to let us know, but we couldn't talk about personal things on the phone because we had a party line and someone might be listening in. Nevertheless, we were always relieved when we heard from him.

On one of those calls he let us know he was having girl problems and would be breaking up with his girlfriend. Although only sixteen, he was taking it hard. He didn't feel good. His stomach had been bothering him off and on the past weeks, and one day, in a lot of pain, he went to the hospital. After undergoing some tests, they said he had ulcers. The doctor gave him some medicine to take for a few months to help with the pain. If it got worse, he would have to go back.

Sully's Job hunt

Sully's substitute teaching jobs were too sporadic to make much money, so he decided to look for other work. His stint with subbing made him realize he didn't want to teach. He got a job working at the Dexter Shoe Factory, removing nail tacks from shoes, and then at McDonald's, making more money. He had to shave his mustache and cut his hair, which we both hated. He had already cut his long hair to teach, and now he had to get rid of his mustache and cut his hair even shorter. His job at McDonald's was set-up man, which meant he had the early shift and had to be at work by 5 a.m. to open. He hated it, but the paychecks were regular. No more weekends off, as he worked six days a week. We knew these jobs were temporary because Sully had decided he was going back to school to get his master's degree. By June 1, when we had to leave the farmhouse, we'd have another plan: either grad school or better jobs for both of us.

On Halloween we took Sophia to Waterville and visited family. We visited Grampie and Jimmie who was staying there at the time. Then we visited George's mother-in-law who was happy to see us. George and Mrs. Carey had taken to each other right away, and since Ken was at boot camp, she was especially glad to see us. I was glad George had Mrs. Carey in her life now, and it was obvious Mrs. Carey was glad too. She offered us lunch and some of her homemade wine, and we had a great time talking about the days when she was raising her two boys. With the wine flowing, it wasn't long before I realized I had had too much and became horribly sick before we left. I don't know how strong her homemade wine was, but I vowed not to repeat that incident again, although she gave us a bottle to take home when we left.

We later dropped in on Sully's parents who were living in a trailer, but we didn't stay long. We ended the day at 13 Broadway, Sully's old house, now owned by Brian and Linda. Sophia played with her cousin Erinn who was eight months younger than Sophia. Heading back to Cornville after a full day, Sophia was asleep before we left the driveway.

Then it was November 27 and Thanksgiving came and went uneventfully. Jimmy stayed in Winslow and Ken was still at boot camp, so it was just Sully, George, Sophia and me. One of Ken's best friends visited over the weekend, and we spent an entire day playing a new card game called Whist. We got hooked on the game, playing it endlessly throughout the winter.

Finally, winter hit in full force with a blizzard at the beginning of December and we knew why the family that owned the place only lived there in summer and why the rent was so cheap. The furnace blasted all day long. With oil prices skyrocketing that year, we were paying a fortune for heat. As the snow drifted higher and higher around the house, we felt like we were being held prisoner behind the wall of white. Just as Sully and I had finished shoveling the driveway, we'd awaken the next morning to more drifts. We shoveled just enough to get the car out so Sully could get to work. George, Sophia, and I were stuck inside. I washed sweaters, sheets, towels, and diapers, cooked, and made a Christmas toy list for Sophia.

Dreams of lost loved ones

I repeatedly dreamed of my family members now gone. Having Sophia made me realize more than anything what a loss we had endured. I hated that she would never know her grandparents.

In my dreams I trudge along a country road, much like the one outside our window in Cornville, staring at my feet as dust clouds cover my sneakers. I cough to clear my parched throat. In the distance, the trees that line the meadows blend together and with the tall grasses, create a watercolor.

Suddenly a long black hearse passes beside me, its tires sending more dust into my face as it slows to a snail's pace just ahead of me. Inside the hearse, I catch sight of Mumma and Daddy, next to each other, their faces alight with joy upon seeing me. As I approach, I also make out the faces of Yiayia and Grammie. They all wave, glowing with smiles as if on a typical Sunday outing.

I race toward the car, relieved they are alive! The pain of their leaving is temporarily suspended as their love envelopes me like the dust on the country road. As I near the driver's side, Daddy rolls down the window. "Wait for me!" I yell frantically. He shakes his head. "It's not time for you," he says kindly as the car accelerates. "Mumma, Daddy, come back!" I yell desperately. As the car disappears in a cloud of dust, they all turn and wave, still smiling lovingly. All too quickly, they vanish, leaving me desolate as I awaken.

Over just four years, four of my family had gone. I think I grieved in my dreams because in my waking life, I had no time for grief. I made sure I didn't have time, sweeping my feelings away, focusing on other things, like figuring out how we were going to survive the winter and what we were going to do with our lives.

Winter at Admiral Dot's

It was too cold to take Sophia outside to play, so I stood by the window one winter Sunday with her on my hip. Blinded by the sun's glare on the snowdrifts piled deep against the house, we watched as icicles formed on the sills, and Jack Frost's artwork sparkled through the glass. Sophia's tiny hand played on the cold window, touch, hand off, touch, giggles. I smiled, glad she didn't feel how overwhelmed I was, made worse by that oppressive slant of light as only Emily Dickinson could have articulated:

There's a certain Slant of light, (320)

> There's a certain slant of light.
> Winter Afternoons—
> That oppresses, like the Heft

Of Cathedral tunes—
Heavenly Hurt it gives us—
We can find no scar.
But internal difference—
Where the meanings are—
None may teach it-Any—
'Tis the seal Despair—
An imperial affliction
Sent us of the Air—

I could envision Emily sitting at her desk in her room in Amherst, Massachusetts, looking out the window as I was doing now. I thought, it's only here, in a New England winter, that one can experience the weight of the sun piercing the whiteness, creating long afternoon shadows over the carpet of snow, a weight so heavy:

When it comes, the landscape listens,
Shadows-hold their breath—
When it goes, 'tis like the Distance
On the look of Death.

I couldn't shake off the feeling that Death stalked me. Too many family members had died in so short a time. Who would be next? How could I keep disaster at bay? Death had taught me life was fragile. And there was nothing to be done but watchful waiting.

But in spite of my fears, life went on anyway. Our days were filled when friends visited and when Ken came back from boot camp. We spent our evenings playing cards, an escape from the frozen world outside our windows. But no matter how busy

I tried to be, there was no escape from my inner world that was sure of impending disaster.

And then, Christmas

With Christmas approaching, Sully and I went into the woods in knee-deep snow to find a Christmas tree, but all the trees were either too tall or too wide, so we came back discouraged, deciding to go into town the following day to buy one. It was Sully's day off, so we went into town to buy Christmas presents for Sophia and groceries for the holidays. With our first Christmas tree decorated, we welcomed college friends who stopped by to visit throughout the week. The flu was going around and a few days after Christmas, we all got sick and spent the rest of the month recovering.

In January we were inundated with one storm after another. We spent most of our time inside as the furnace blasted all day long, but the house never seemed to get warm enough. During that time I found a measure of peace in my study of yoga philosophy. I learned about the *yamas* and *niyamas*, or ethical principles of yoga, which constitute the Eastern version of the Ten Commandments. The path to enlightenment consisted not only of Hatha yoga, the physical exercises, but also *pranayama* (breathing practices) and meditation. The more I read, the more interested I became, but it wasn't easy, especially since I was teaching myself. There's a saying, "When the student is ready, the teacher will appear." I knew I needed a teacher, but no one was appearing.

Finally, the weather broke at the end of the

month and the snow melted enough during the short January thaw to reveal the dirt driveway, making everything look dirty brown. Friends ventured out and we had a stream of visitors. After Sophia went to bed, we played cards, listened to music, smoked cigarettes, and drank too much beer and wine.

When I got up the next morning, guilt would kick in. I wanted meditation and yoga to be the healthy alternative, but I wasn't ready to give up drinking and smoking, especially. Although we always had a good time when friends came over, I couldn't get the nagging worry out of my head about our future. I tried the yogic practice of non-attachment, which is to step back and observe without becoming involved in my own thoughts, to observe without judgment, but it was difficult. Was meditation the answer? If I could quiet my mind, I could control the constant worrying. I wrote a short poem one morning after an unsuccessful attempt at meditation.

> No simple task it is,
> This job of sitting with the infinite,
> Aches, pains, physical joints blot out
> all calls to the
> Unknown and striven goal.
> The mind wanders outside the circle,
> time and again,
> Until forced back within.
> Uncooperative organism of mind,
> will you ever be still?
>   Winter 1973

The thaw didn't last long, and winter returned

with a vengeance. Sully got stuck in a snowbank about half-mile up the road and had to plod up the driveway to get a shovel and dig the car out. He managed to get the car back home, but the plow wouldn't come all the way up the driveway in the morning, so we had to get up before dawn to shovel out so he could get to work. He bought a heater for the car so that the engine wouldn't freeze overnight. In the below-zero temperatures, just getting into the car made the frozen seats crack. Outside on those cold mornings helping to shovel, I vowed we'd never spend another winter out in the country.

Welcomed by the neighbor ladies

One morning after the roads had been cleared, we had a visit from one of our neighbors from a nearby farm inviting George and me to their weekly Thursday morning coffee. All the neighbors took turns hosting, making donuts, coffee cake, or muffins to serve. I was glad to meet other women in the neighborhood. At the time I didn't realize how much I needed the wisdom of other women in my life. They were farmers' wives, most of whom had lived in the country their entire lives. Two were younger mothers like me, and the others were middle-aged or older. They were very welcoming and inclusive. They were also great cooks who loved to share their recipes with us. When it was our turn to be the hosts, we made a coffee cake from a recipe on the back of a Bisquick box. It wasn't a scratch cake, but we didn't want to take a chance it would flop. When we left in June, they had a special get-together for us and gave me a copy of *Maine's Jubilee Cookbook* that has become tattered and dog-eared from so much use over the years.

The miscellany of mid-winter

Mid-February. I spent the morning playing with Sophia as I did most mornings after I cleaned the house, put a soup on to simmer, or did the laundry. Washing clothes was the worst, with our old wringer washer that took forever to work: putting clothes through the wringer, rinsing them, and putting them through the wringer again. Sometimes we just went to the laundromat on Sully's day off where we could wash and dry everything in a couple of hours. On a sunny day, we hung the clothes outside on the line where they promptly froze, stiff as corpses hanging in mid-air, even in the sun. Sometimes we hung them in the shed, where they took even longer to dry. Diapers took forever. I started potty training Sophia, hoping it would take so that I wouldn't have to wash diapers.

Sophia and I drew pictures, Sophia illustrating my journal with her scribbles. She said she was drawing a puppy dog. I asked her if she needed to go potty. Yes, she was excited to go. I couldn't have been more excited myself. I sat her on the antique potty chair that belonged to Sully's mother, and she looked at her books as she pooped. Potty training was going well ... until it wasn't. Sophia had a mind of her own, telling me more often than not she didn't want to go on the potty. I asked her if she wanted to go on the big potty, but that was a definite no. We kept trying, but she wasn't two yet, so I knew she wasn't quite ready according to Dr. Spock. But she was growing up so fast.

Continuing yoga and meditation

During Sophia's nap time I continued my meditation practice. After a meditation session I wrote in my journal. This was one session.

My concentration was on a tree outside my window. According to the meditation books, I was supposed to focus on a mantra (a saying), a word ("peace" or "om"), or a visualization (the tree) or anything else. I was to focus on the tree and every time my mind wandered, I was supposed to bring it back to the tree. My mind wandered off, back to the tree, wandered some more, back to the tree, someone laughed downstairs, irritated, Sully riding to work in a storm, worried, another blizzard today. This was one long winter. Sigh. Meditation not going well. After much trial and error, I closed my eyes and focused on the word "peace," shanti in Sanskrit, and that worked a little better.

Birthdays!

On February 26, Sophia and I celebrated our birthdays with cake and a party with friends. I turned twenty-three and Sophia was two. Carmen brought us a chocolate birthday cake that her mother had made. The dining room was decorated with balloons, and we all wore party hats. We bought Sophia a Fisher Price Little People doll house. My friends gave me books. It was a perfect day. I knew Sophia was tired when she started sucking her thumb, so we settled in a chair and watched *My Backyard* until she fell asleep.

The next morning, we watched *The Dinah Shore Show*, with Dinah doing yoga with an expert. Sophia and I did the yoga poses along with her, but when the yoga expert did a shoulder stand, we put our feet up in the air and laughed. We didn't know what we were doing. The expert taught me a new breathing exercise and said yoga should be done for twenty minutes per day.

One of the reasons yoga philosophy had attracted me was its belief in reincarnation. Supposedly, every soul has millions of lifetimes, even encountering the same souls over again until all of one's karma has been eliminated and enlightenment occurs. I wasn't sure I actually believed that, but it made me feel good to know I might be in another life with my family again. It seemed just as believable as the stories in other religions. Hell, according to Catholics, was all I had to look forward to anyway. Reincarnation sounded so much better.

The last time we had attended church was on our wedding day, and I was still too angry with God to think about going back to St. Mark's. I didn't really blame God for everything, but I wasn't ready to allow him off the hook either. Sully didn't really care about religion, so we put off going to church until we were settled somewhere. In spite of my anger, I wanted Sophia to be exposed to church, to learn about the possibility that He existed. If He existed as Love, then all the better.

Spring was not far off and it would not be long before our lives would change again. With the end of winter, spring always brought a feeling of hope. Hope that life would change for the better.

Chapter Forty-two
A New Life

Carol, a friend from our old apartment building in Orono, called one afternoon to tell us she and her husband were moving to Virginia. Another couple in the building had already moved to Richmond where the husband would be working at Virginia Commonwealth University. Evidently, the recession had not hit quite as hard there and jobs were plentiful. I wondered whether we should consider doing this too? Virginia was 700 miles away—a long way to go without knowing whether we could get work. But then, what was here in Maine? Plenty of black flies in the spring, mosquitos in the summer, and snow all winter, lots of snow. Only jobs were scarce in Maine. I wished them luck and told Carol to keep in touch.

The beginning of March came with a hint of spring, and it wasn't a minute too soon. We were all suffering from cabin fever, rarely having gone outside for most of the winter. Even on sunny days, the winds blew across the fields taking our breath away, burning our cheeks and chapping our lips. But now with melting snow, mud time had arrived. Sophia was thrilled to squish around in the muddy driveway, but once again, she developed a cold. By now I was used to our getting sick, but that meant staying inside again. Blaming myself for taking her outside, I held my breath until she recovered when I could exhale with relief.

Visiting a nursery school

Nancy, one of the women at our weekly coffee, who was pregnant, asked me to go with her to visit a nursery school that had recently opened in a nearby village. Maine had become a destination for young hippies who wanted to go back to the land, many of them combining funds to form communes. This was one of those places where a group of like-minded people from away—or as we Mainers called them, "flatlanders"—had settled. While we were thinking of moving out of Maine to survive, they were moving in.

The nursery school was in a small shed-like building that smelled of fresh cut wood. Creative wooden toys lined one wall, and the center floor was covered with blue gym mats for the kids to jump and play and nap on, but on that day, there were two strikes against it in my mind. One, the bathroom consisted of a bucket in one corner where the little boys peed, and like little boys, often missed as we noticed streaks of wet on the walls. Sophia stared wide-eyed as the little boys gave her an unintended lesson in male anatomy. Secondly, there were no little girls that day for Sophia to play with. The lack of toilet facilities was a deal breaker for Nancy, so we left knowing our kids wouldn't be going back. And anyway, people with money who moved to Maine to buy land and build their own utopias made me a bit resentful. They had visions of a wonderful life working the land while having plenty of money to make that life easy. Good luck to them, I thought; they would still have to deal with the long winters.

Spring at last?

Finally by the end of March, it looked like spring was here for good. Sophia and I spent our days outside. I raked and cleaned around the garden area. Even though we wouldn't be here to enjoy them, I planted some herbs along the sunny side of the house while Sophia played in the sand box and on the tree swing. We looked forward to our income tax return so that we could pay off the overdue oil bill, the phone, and everything else we owed. I hoped we'd have enough to buy Sophia some new spring clothes; she was growing out of everything.

But as always, winter wasn't ready to give up yet. The middle of April brought more snow. And Sophia regressed in her potty training. She was rebelling, telling me vehemently, "No potty, Mummy, no potty!" If I had to wash one more diaper, I was going to lose my mind! I think she probably reflected the stress we were all feeling.

What were we going to do in June? Sully and I lay in bed many a night trying to figure out what we were going to do with our lives. As Sophia quietly snored in the crib. I whispered, "Maybe we should just go back to Waterville."

"I don't think there's going to be anything there. At least we should go to a bigger city where the chances of finding work are better," Sully mused.

"Should we take Carmen up on her offer to stay

with her in Westbrook?" I wondered aloud. "That's just a few miles from Portland. We can try that and see what happens."

"That's probably our best bet."

I thought about mentioning Virginia, but the idea of traveling all that way seemed crazy in that moment as I lay in the chilly darkness, so far away from anything. Getting up to make sure Sophia was warmly covered, I stared at her sleeping form in her thick pink footy pjs and said a prayer that we'd land in a place that was right for our family.

And then, later that week, we got a call from Carol in Virginia. She invited us to come to Virginia, stay with them for the month of June, and look for jobs. She was optimistic about job prospects, positive we'd find work just as they had done. She even offered to give us gas money for the trip. So that became the question: Go to Virginia, or stay in Maine? Sully and I spent the month of May waffling back and forth. Should we travel 700 miles into the unknown? What if we didn't find jobs? Did we even have a choice? What was here for us?

Deciding on Virginia

Ultimately we decided to go. Sully's Aunt Sarah agreed to store our furniture in her basement. After Sully got a job and we were able to rent an apartment, he would fly back to Maine, rent a UHaul and drive our furniture back to Virginia. We were both nervous, but at some level we convinced ourselves we had no choice. What was the big deal anyway? I thought of Yiayia and Grampie and Daddy emigrating from Greece to a new country, and it gave me courage. And after all, we weren't leaving the country.

Those last few weeks before our departure date on June 1, I fluctuated between excitement and fear, but kept busy with all the packing and spending as much time as we could with friends that we wouldn't see for a long time. Sully, Sophia, and I went to say goodbye to Grampie, who had not been feeling well—his blood pressure was out of control. Every day he took a shot of Metaxa that he was convinced kept his heart going. We sat at the kitchen table, Sully taking a drink with him, as we talked about Daddy. He would switch from English to Greek. He cried. When we said goodbye, I knew I might never see him again.

Carol flew up to Maine to attend to some business and came to visit with maps and written directions. She loaned us $50 for gas. We planned on staying with Carmen in Westbrook on Friday, June 1, and leave from there for Virginia the next day.

Departing Admiral Dot

In the middle of our preparations, things were happening at Admiral Dot. A farmer up the road who rented the land for his cows to graze on appeared early one morning with a truckload of cows. They had been in the barn all winter and this was their first time outside. One of the last visions I had of the farm was of Sophia and me staring in surprise and laughing as the cows cavorted all over the pasture, kicking up their heels, ecstatic to be free! As we watched their joy, I couldn't help feeling that would be us. Out in the world, a new beginning.

Don't Worry About A Thing

We said our goodbyes to George, Jim, and Ken, who were moving to Winslow shortly after we left. And with $60 in our pocket, we left Admiral Dot Farm. Piled into Aunt Bessie's Firebird were: three suitcases, a box of blankets, bags of sheets and towels, a box of food, a few boxes of books, two boxes of toys (along with Sophia's doll house, a toy boat, and her favorite books), a laundry bag of clothes, the diaper pail and diapers, and pillows and Sophia's potty chair. With Sophia in the backseat in her metal car seat surrounded by her toys, we were on our way. Filled with uncertainty and not a little apprehension, we drove into the unknown, toward a new life.

Epilogue

Early one gray Saturday morning in early spring—I think I was sixteen at the time—I was lazing around the house, bored, when Daddy popped out of his chair and barked, "Kathy, let's take a ride!"

"Where are you going now?" Mumma wanted to know. Daddy was between jobs and couldn't sit still. She knew he wouldn't hang around the house all day.

"I think we'll take a little ride, to Massachusetts," he said.

Mumma eyed him skeptically, "Jesus Christ, George! Four or five hours in that old car? It won't make it. What do you want to go all that way for? Running off to Massachusetts on a wild goose chase? Did you check the paper for jobs today?"

"Don't worry about a thing. We can visit my uncle, and I can check out the job prospects."

"That's foolishness. We're not moving to Massachusetts."

But he had made up his mind. We were going.

Mumma looked worried as we heard him yelling into the phone, ordering Aunt Maria to be ready in five minutes. Always ready for a change of scenery, she needed no convincing.

Ignoring Mumma's protests, we were out the door before I had time to grab anything but my winter coat. Most of the snow was gone, but the March winds were still biting and it was cold enough to see our breath as Daddy defrosted the windshield. As soon as we picked up Aunt Maria we were on Interstate 95 headed south.

Four hours later we arrived on the doorstep of Grampie's brother John. After the initial surprise at seeing us, Uncle John and Auntie welcomed us in. Immediately, Auntie got on the phone to let the cousins know we were there. Cupboards were opened, pots and pans placed on the stove, and before long the smells of Greek lamb stew permeated the house, making our stomachs grumble.

While the women cooked, Daddy and his uncle talked, in both Greek and English. Uncle John was sure Daddy could find work if he wanted to leave Maine. Worcester was a large city filled with factories and restaurants, good prospects for Daddy.

Truth be told, I was beginning to get worried. Did I really want to leave Waterville and my school to start over somewhere else? But it wasn't long before I knew my worries were unfounded. Daddy was nodding, but he seemed distracted. I could tell he had no intention of leaving Waterville. He probably regretted coming all this way and was thinking about going back home. Maria was oddly silent. I don't think she liked the idea of us moving to Massachusetts either. I was relieved. By the time dinner was over, it was late; I half expected Daddy to say we were leaving, but he didn't, so we planned to stay the night.

The dishes cleared, I watched as Auntie brewed Greek coffee in a small copper pot, called a *briki*, on

top of the gas stove. She poured the coffee in a demi-
tasse cup and ordered me to drink it all. I hesitated
as I stared at the brown sludge-like substance before
forcing it down. It was so strong I felt a caffeine jolt
in my body. Next, she instructed me to turn it upside
down and place it on the clean white cloth on the
table. We waited for a few minutes. Then she lifted
the cup and peered inside at the grounds that made
a pattern on the inside of the cup. She began reading
my future.

Expressionless, she started speaking to Daddy
in Greek. As he listened, he nodded back and forth.
What was she saying? Then in her broken English,
just like Yiayia, she tried to explain my fortune, but
switched to Greek again, and I could only make out
bits and pieces. My life was going to be long. I would
marry and have three children. She could see troubles in the future, in mid-life, but I would make it
through and eventually have a happy life. I would
move far away, and I would travel. She said a lot
more than that, but I didn't get all of it.

Early the next morning, it was still dark when
Daddy woke us to leave. After saying our thank-yous
and goodbyes we piled into the cold car. Daddy drove;
we all sat in the front seat with me in the middle. At
first because we were still groggy from our early start,
we rode silently, absorbed in our own thoughts.
Eventually I broke the silence and tried to get Daddy
to tell me more about my future, but he didn't remember all of it, and Maria wasn't any help either,
which made me even more curious. I wasn't happy
about the fortune telling. Troubles in mid-life? Hadn't
we had enough struggles to get by already? Anyway,
she was definitely wrong about one thing; I was never

going to have kids. Daddy didn't think it was a bad fortune. For me, the best part of the whole thing was when she said I would travel.

I was beginning to doze off as we passed the signs for Peabody, when, without any warning, one of the wheels popped off the car and went rolling down the highway. Maria was shoved against me by the impact, causing her cigarette to burn a hole in my coat. Luckily we were not hurt. Maria and I waited while Daddy ran to retrieve the tire, and thankfully, someone stopped and offered to get help. Three hours later, after sitting around the garage, (the only one we found that was open on Sunday), and only eating chips from the vending machines, we were back on the road. By then, we were all in a bad mood, riding the rest of the way home in silence.

Mumma could tell by the look on Daddy's face not to say anything when we got home that afternoon. I escaped to my room, not caring that I hadn't eaten anything but potato chips. If Auntie was so good at fortune telling, why didn't she let us know the tire was going to go flying off? Anyway, I hoped she was wrong about my fortune. I didn't want to wait until I was an old lady to have a happy life.

***

Remembering that evening years later, I realized Auntie was right about some things, traveling for example (if you counted moving 700 miles to Richmond to find jobs as "traveling"). And later in life, we did get to travel the world.

The move turned out to be the best decision for us, one we've never regretted. We both found jobs right away and slowly settled into our new life. Sully went back to school to get his MBA and began his climb up the corporate ladder in the banking world. I got a clerical office job, paying stocks and debentures in an employee-owned company.

A few months later, we were excited when I became pregnant again. The second pregnancy was easier; I knew what to expect, and my doctor assured me that with an epidural, I'd not have the same labor experience I had the first time. I also decided to breastfeed, and this time I had met new friends who were pregnant at the same time, which was helpful.

On September 6, 1974, our new baby girl, Tara Katherine, came into the world. Our family was complete. She was another brown-eyed baby who adored her big sister, following her around the house as soon as she could crawl and walk, calling her "Dobia."

Although the move was the right decision for us, we suffered from culture shock that first year in the South. The heat and humidity were sweltering even first thing in the morning. Leaving our air-conditioned apartment felt like walking into an oven. And the whole concept of southern hospitality was new to us Yankees who grew up in an atmosphere of polite but not demonstrative society. While people were kind and friendly, sometimes they seemed too friendly, making us a little suspect when strangers wished us a, "good day, honey." Everywhere we went, we were subject to honeys, and dears, and sweeties. Young children said, "Yes, ma'am," and "No, ma'am" when speaking to adults. But my reserved Maine roots ran deep, and I could not help but find it odd. Some probably thought us rude that I didn't make my girls address adults in this way.

I discovered an oddly-named store called Ukrop's Grocery. When I was checking out one day, I offhandedly mentioned that a product I had purchased the previous week was damaged when I got home. The manager, who was bagging my groceries, overheard me and told me to come with him. Leading me to the aisle with the product, he handed me not one, but two of the same item, no charge. I became a Ukrop's customer for life right there. It didn't take long to adjust to this new way of treating people.

It wasn't long before we settled into our new life, made new friends, and even got used to the heat. And in winter there was only the occasional snowstorm. That was worth the move all by itself.

It's never easy starting from scratch, but we were young and willing to work hard. We became bona fide members of the "Rat Race." While Sully climbed the corporate ladder, I changed jobs. So that we wouldn't have to pay a sitter, I watched children before and after school and cleaned apartments during the day in the complex where we lived. When Sophia started school, and once she was on her bus with the others, I would take Tara with me, and sit her on a blanket with her toys while I raced around cleaning before the bus dropped the kids off in the afternoon.

When we could afford to get a second car, I added another job, working two evenings a week and Saturdays at Ukrop's Grocery, the same grocery I had discovered when we first moved to Virginia. They were a wonderful family to work for because they were willing to work around my schedule.

Then it was my turn to go back to school. I started taking classes, one at a time. Virginia Commonwealth University accepted almost all my credits from UMO, so I had two years to finish, but it took me longer going part-time. I worked at Ukrop's for ten years, both in the grocery and the main office, quitting only when I had to do my student teaching. After graduating from VCU, my life-long goal to become a teacher became a reality.

As the girls got older and were involved in extra activities outside of school, our lives revolved around work and the girls. We made sure they had everything they needed, but saving for us always came first. Every time Sully got a raise, the money went into savings. The food budget was not negotiable; our weekly meals were predictable and cheap. The girls laugh now about fish sticks, spaghetti, and pizza night, along with other regulars every week. But they never went hungry. McDonald's was a treat. We were so caught up with working and putting away as much as we could that we forgot to enjoy our life in the present. We were spending less time with friends. Our social life consisted of Sophia and Tara's extra activities. I co-lead Sophia's girl scout troop, sat in Tara's dance studio waiting room while she went to class, and despite not liking football, we were in the bleachers every Friday night while the girls cheered. On Sunday we attended the Episcopal Church where I served on the vestry and taught Sunday school.

Still, I always felt something was missing. I just didn't know what or how to find it.

In his little spare time, Sully started running early in the morning, a great stress reliever for him, and he eventually completed two full marathons. In my spare time, usually at night before falling asleep, I wrote in my journal. I had started journaling at sixteen and continued throughout the years. Something happened when I took the time to put my thoughts on paper: I was calmer, better able to face what the next day would bring, and better yet, in letting it all out on the page, I was better able to understand myself. That was my therapy.

But we rarely had time for ourselves or for our friends because we were always focused on the future, working to make our lives better, doing what we thought was right. I remember hiring a babysitter once so that we could go to the movies. But when we came home earlier than expected, we caught the sitter's boyfriend running out the back door. That ended our date nights until the girls were old enough to stay by themselves.

Even though our lives were much improved—neither one of us could imagine going backward—life took its toll. Caught up in the rat race, with life out of balance due to work, work, and work, there were days when I felt like I was becoming invisible, as if I were slowly being erased. Looking through the photo albums of those years, I was struck by the realization that there were very few pictures of me. Where was I all those years? I had no idea who I was outside of motherhood and work. There were days when, working on my degree, I would drive to the end of our driveway, and then sit for a minute and think: do I go left, to school, or right, to work?

We worked hard so that the girls would never have to worry like we had growing up. We wanted to pay for their college educations and their weddings so they could begin life debt-free. Neither of us ever regretted that. We would do it all over again, but the universe, as it often does, sent me a message that life had to change when I started having thyroid issues. First it was hyperthyroidism, which created a thyroid storm that essentially destroyed my thyroid, and I then had hypothyroidism; my system went from working overtime to barely working at all. It was a major wake-up call, and I was forced off the work treadmill.

Then one day, when I was in my early forties, a friend from school asked if I would be interested in attending a yoga class with her at the YMCA. Remembering my early interest and attempts to practice yoga, I quickly accepted. That first yoga class was a turning point in my life. Early in life, when I had read, "when the student is ready, the teacher will appear" came true. The teacher said to us, "Come to a comfortable sitting position, close the eyes, and look within." Look within? I thought. What does that even *mean*? Where is within? Do I have a within?

I went back to class and back again. I took more classes and discovered there was a self within me. And even a higher Self that was connected to every other Self. Slowly I began to re-draw the lines of my being. I realized I had spent my life up to that point always living in the future and running the race to get somewhere else, all the while sacrificing the present, time I could have spent enjoying my girls instead of always striving, working, yearning for something else.

Today yoga has become so mainstream that one can take a goat yoga class, or yoga and beer at a brewery, which might make for an entertaining afternoon but misses the point entirely. When I first started taking classes twenty-five years ago, yoga had a reputation for being an esoteric practice, something that was "out there." This couldn't have been further from the truth. My teacher, Swami Satchidananda, the founder of Integral Yoga, used the metaphor of a tool belt. Like a carpenter using the tools on his belt, the yoga practitioner uses all the tools of yoga to have an "easeful, peaceful and useful" life. You have physical issues? There's an asana (physical posture) for that. Are you feeling anxiety? There's *pranayama* (breathing exercise) for that. Are you stressed on a daily basis? There's meditation for that. Each physical posture is a seat for meditation, each deep breath centers us into our true self, and each pause in stillness between two thoughts carries us to the realization that we are sparks of the divine. Finally, and one of the best lessons of all, yoga taught me not to take life so seriously. Using the tools of yoga brings one into balance, grounded in the here and now. It works.

When both Sully and Sophia were diagnosed with different cancers just a few years apart, yoga helped all of us get through the crises. After they both recovered, we all continued with our yoga practice. And in 2005, at age fifty-five, I became a yoga teacher. My daughter Tara and I went to classes together for years until she became pregnant and then she went to prenatal classes. To this day, Sully and I have made our yoga practice an integral part of our lives.

When we graduate from yoga teacher training we are given the option to receive a Sanskrit name. I wrote a poem that I read at graduation, filled with gratitude for my yoga journey. The Sanskrit name I was given at graduation is Kavita, which means "poetry."

Who knew all those years ago when I attempted to do yoga and meditate at Admiral Dot Farm that those studies would manifest so many years later? Auntie was right about having a great life when I got older. After I retired from teaching middle school English, my focus changed from teacher to Yiayia. In homage to my Greek roots, I wanted my grandchildren to call me Yiayia. I have learned not to ever take anything for granted, and I am grateful to still be here enjoying my later years and the greatest blessings of all, my five grandchildren.

As far as religion goes, I'll always be a seeker, searching for answers that I may or may not find. But that's okay. Sometimes the only answer is what life gives us in any given moment, and in this moment, I think religion is too divisive. I do believe there is a God. Call it what you will: He, She, Source of all, Mother Earth, but there are many different paths that lead to the Creator. As humans, if we just allow all paths to co-exist and not force our way onto others, we may create a world without wars fought in the name of religion. We are all part of one human family. Ultimately, all religions, if practiced in their truest forms arrive at the one Truth – God is Love. Sadly, we have not evolved enough to realize that. Maybe one day.

As of this writing, Sully and I have been married for fifty-two-years. Like most marriages, our has been fraught with highs and lows. Now in our third act, unlike in the movies, I know there's no such thing as "happily ever after." There's always in some way feast or famine. You just have to get through the famine times and wait for the feast days to return. The great zen master, Thich Nhat Hanh said, "without mud, no lotus." We have to get through a lot of mud in our lives, but I'd like to think it made me a better person. Through it all, our life together has been based largely on three principles: our children always come first, work hard and never give up, and education was and is of paramount importance. We never stop learning. Life is ever evolving. The key is to evolve with it.

Maybe Daddy was right all along: Don't worry about a thing, he said often. Maybe what he meant was we ultimately have very little control over life, so don't worry about it. Enjoy the good times. I'll always have my favorite memory of him dancing the Greek dance with unbounded joy.

When I think of Mumma and Daddy leaving us so young, I know to never take my life for granted. Over the years, the anger, resentment, and shame I felt growing up poor, diminished as I understood my parents were products of their environments, like we all are. The only way to get beyond the pain of growing up in a family with addiction issues is to forgive. So, I focused on the happy memories, the feast times instead of the famine. Sometimes though, those feelings are replaced with sadness. Sadness that they would never know their children as adults, and they never knew their grandchildren.

Or maybe they did.

It was a moonless December night about two years after Daddy died. Sully was working nights at the Federal Reserve Bank, and Sophia and I were sleeping in our bedroom, upstairs in the townhouse apartment we rented. I was dreaming. Mumma was in the kitchen in our Silver Street apartment, smoking and watching TV as music from *Twilight Zone* woke me up. The eerie music intensified, so I covered my head with my sheet.

Coming out of my dream, I hear the door downstairs open in our townhouse. I sit up in bed, heart pounding out of my chest. Then I hear Daddy's footsteps on the stairs. His flat-footed steps in his worn black leather shoes create a familiar pattern of sound on the creaking stairs. My heart nearly stops as I wonder if I'm dreaming or if this is really happening. Finally, his last foot thuds on the top step, and he stands framed in the doorway. He looks as he did in my childhood. Black wavy hair, large brown eyes twinkling. I want to run to him but I can't move. He sighs long and deep with relief. In a soft whisper, he says, "I've finally found you." Then he's gone.

And that is that.

Don't Worry About A Thing

Acknowledgments

First I would like to express my profound gratitude to my grandparents, James and Olga Yotides, who had the courage to leave their homeland and travel thousands of miles over land and sea so their children could live in freedom.

I will also be forever grateful to my parents, George and Betty. Despite an age difference of twelve years and with vastly different backgrounds, they came together to create our family. Thank you for giving me this precious life and all it entails.

Thanks to the many family and friends who have encouraged me to write over the years. Especially to all the teachers who said, "keep writing," when I had very little self-confidence that anything would come of my writing. I wrote because I had no choice, not thinking I would ever get published, and the fact that this is out in the world is due in no small measure to the encouragement I've received over the years from wonderful teachers.

Thank-you also to the groups of writers I've had the privilege to call friends over the years, people who have been kind and supportive about my writing. Special thanks to Pat Sullivan, my writing partner for many years now. We have shared our lives on the page, and probably know more about each other's lives than anyone.

Thanks also to The Memoir Network for the editing help and book production.

Thank you to my loving sister and best friend George, who kept asking when I would finally finish this work. You kept me going during my many writing blocks.

Finally, thanks to my husband Richard who chose to embark on this life's journey with me. Miracles never cease!